H.P. TWYFORD

revis

CHRIS R

IT CAME TO OUR DOOR

British Library Cataloguing in Publication Data
H.P. Twyford 1892 - 1964
It Came To Our Door
Plymouth in World War II – A Journalist's Eye Witness Account
A catalogue record for this book is available from the British Library

ISBN 0-9543480-3-6

Revised and illustrated by Chris Robinson
Design Ewan McKnight
© Chris Robinson 2005

First published 1945
Reprinted (3 times) 1946
Revised 1949
Sixth Impression (revised) 1975

Seventh Impression (revised) 2005

Published by
Pen & Ink Publishing
34 New Street, Barbican
Plymouth PL1 2NA
Tel; 01752 705337/228120
Fax; 01752 770001
www.chrisrobinson.co.uk

Printed and bound in Great Britain by
Latimer Trend & Company Ltd
Estover Close
Plymouth PL6 7PL

Devon

CONTENTS

Plymouth in the twenty-first century; St Andrew's and the Guildhall have been rebuilt and Royal Parade today truly stands as the 'great and worthy heritage' that Twyford hoped for.

PREFACE TO THE SEVENTH EDITION

There has been much written about Plymouth during the war years, most of it at a distance with the benefit, or otherwise, of hindsight, but Pat Twyford's account stands head and shoulders above the rest as it was written at the time.

First published in 1945, just a few months after the end of hostilities, it is a fascinating first-hand insight into exactly what happened when, for the first time in over 500 years, Plymouth came under fire from a foreign power.

When I first bought a copy - a 1946 edition - over 25 years ago, I was struck by the straightforward narrative which dealt honestly and yet not too sentimentally with those troubled times. But then Pat Twyford was a very capable journalist, a fearless war correspondent and a veteran of an equally horrific World War fought out a generation earlier. He understood the soldier, the politician and the man in the street, and it is that grasp that gives this book its potency.

As a text-based book (when first published it included four, eight-page picture sections) it has already been reprinted five times. However the last print run was thirty years ago and the world has moved on, and most so-called text-books are now full of photographs as an increasingly visually-aware world raised on a staple diet of cinema, television, video and DVD now expect images as a matter of course. Hence this latest revision which now features some four hundred images of Plymouth during those years.

The process of collecting together the images that you see in this book has itself taken many years, however so well do we believe that they complement the text that we felt it would be a great shame to miss the opportunity of introducing a new perspective into the greatest book written on the greatest chapter of Plymouth's recent history.

With local studies now firmly on the National School Curriculum perhaps this will help re-establish *It Came To Our Door* as the standard Plymouth World War II text-book that it has always deserved to be.

The hope then will be that the current generation of Plymothians, and indeed their children and their children's children, will come to appreciate what their ancestors did for them during those dark times.

As he wrote in a chapter produced especially for the 1949 edition of the book; "When after the awful ordeal of 1941 it was obvious that vast reconstruction would be necessary, Plymouth was told, I think it was by Lord Reith, to 'plan boldly'. It did so, and at the end of 1949 we can say that is has implemented that plan as boldly as the conditions of the time have permitted. The picture of the new Plymouth is now there for all to see. Bit by bit, the pieces of the gigantic jig-saw are being fitted. It may, indeed, it will, take a long time for the picture to be finished. Many of us may not see it, but let us hope that the verdict of posterity to all who took part in the reconstruction will be: 'You have left us a great and worthy heritage'."

Happily, whatever your feelings maybe about the 'modern' Plymouth City Centre, I believe it is impossible to deny that what has been achieved is truly remarkable. Charles Church stands a fitting memorial to the civilian casualties, while the City Centre itself is a beautifully open and accessible area without a direct parallel anywhere in the world. Nowhere else will you find such a vast site - over seventy acres - that sits within a city as record of achievement over just two decades. Royal Parade itself was laid out in less than ten years and is today attracting architectural students from around the globe who come here to see what no other city can offer them - a stunning series of buildings, each one designed by a leading European architectural practice of the time. Dingles, Derry's, Debenhams, the Pearl Assurance Building, the erstwhile Pophams and the National Westminster Bank, these are all quality buildings and it's all too easy to allow our familiarity with them to lead us to undervalue them. But value them we should, both as wonderful buildings and as the 'great and worthy heritage' our forebears have conferred upon us.

Taste is often a cyclical thing and history books are full of how one generation after another will be critical of its parents and yet respectful of its grand parents. I remember when Victorian architecture was dismissed for being overly fussy, ornate and ostentatious, now it is seen for what it was - a product of its time. So too is Plymouth's modern city centre. However as this book hopefully will make many generations yet to come, aware, it is also much much more than that - it is, rather like the Royal Citadel on the Hoe (which was an indirect product of the last war that had come to our door - the Civil War), a memorial to one of the most significant chapters ever recorded in Plymouth's history. Long may it be preserved.

Chris Robinson
Plymouth, November 2005

ACKNOWLEDGEMENTS

In the absence of any acknowledgements from the author to the forties editions of this work I should like to thank Pat Twyford's daughter, Monica, for sanctioning this current revision and providing a brief pen-portrait of her father.

In the interests of authenticity I have endeavoured to avoid making any comments written with the benefits of hindsight when it comes to captioning over 350 photographs which are new to this version of It Came To Our Door. Indeed in some instances Pat Twyford's text has been used for captions and in others contemporary captions from the Western Evening Herald and Morning News have been used.

As a journalist/historian for the Herald for over twenty years myself I should also like to thank successive editors, notably Alan Qualtrough and Bill Martin, for their encouragement and support, and the girls, Nicky, Nic and Joan, in the picture library at the newspaper offices. Many of the photographs here have come via readers of my regular Looking Back column and to them too my very grateful thanks.

Other contributors include Barbara Hampshire, Robin Hoskin, Daryl Jago, Peter Waterhouse, the irrepressible Steve Johnson and the late Arthur Clamp.

Over the years I have built up a reasonable library of images of the City and it was this collection that first prompted the idea of illustrating Pat Twyford's book, so to anyone who has made any contribution to that collection, great or small, over the last twenty-five years, thank you most sincerely.

If I have left anyone out, or have failed to acknowledge the provider of any of the images may I offer my apologies now, the accessions register is not nearly as detailed as it ought to be! I know how frustrating it is to find your work being used with no thanks, but the publishers would be happy to hear from anyone who has information concerning the copyright of any of the material contained herein.

From a practical angle, thanks to Terry Guswell who first re-typed Pat Twyford's script onto disc some years ago and to Doreen Mole, Patricia and Laurie Greathead, Rob Warren and my darling wife, Clare (my publisher), who together have all done stirling work; proof reading, typing and archiving. Thanks too to Chloe Robinson for many of the scans, and to Ewan McKnight for his scans, his suggestions and his first class design skills. And finally thanks to Bob Mills and his wonderful team at Latimer Trend & Co, printers of note at Estover. It will interest many older readers to know that Latimer Trend actually bought out the Underhill concern (original publishers of the first six impressions of this book) some years ago.

HP (Pat) TWYFORD
(1892-1964)

H. P. Twyford

My father was born at Dartington Hall in 1892, where his father, Charles, was head gardener and personal assistant to Mrs Champernowne, the original owner of the estate. They later moved to Staverton, and then to Totnes, where my father started work on the Totnes Times.

In 1910, at the age of eighteen, he left home and became a cub reporter on the Western Morning News in Plymouth. Throughout the First World War he served with the Royal Artillery and in 1917 he was gassed and wounded. He returned to Plymouth and the newspaper offices the following year.

During the Second World War he was the accredited War Correspondent for the Western Morning News and Evening Herald, covering a number of operations with the forces. These included the Normandy landings, the liberation of Caen, the breakout from Normandy, the liberations of Paris and Brussels and other centres, and the German surrender of the Channel Islands.

He was eventually forced to return home after his car was struck by a 27-ton tank - by then they were at the border of Holland and Germany.

My father also flew with the Australian Air Force on anti-submarine patrols over the Atlantic and was in Plymouth's Special Constabulary (he eventually retired as Divisional Commander).

As a jounalist he covered Lady Astor's election campaigns for many years and was also the agriculture and sports specialist.

He regularly reported on Plymouth Albion's rugby matches and when Plymouth Argyle won promotion to the old Second Division back in 1929-30 he took over as 'Pilgrim', as well as writing under two other pseudonyms - 'Tamar' and 'Flagstaff'.

He was also chairman of the Institute of Journalists for Devon and Cornwall and the honorary secretary of the Bristol and West of England Newspaper Fund for the counties.

Under the pen name 'Frankfort' he started the Evening Herald's regular Citizen's Diary column and in 1946 covered the first meteorological flight out over the Atlantic for the paper. He also made regular radio appearances.

It was just after the end of the Second World War that he wrote 'It Came To Our Door' and the book was an instant success. First published at the end of 1945 it was reprinted three times the following year and in 1949 he added another chapter - Reconstruction.

It is now thirty years since the last revision and I feel sure that he would welcome this latest version and be delighted to think that there is still interest in his work and that it may yet help to commemorate the work of a generation of Plymothians who toiled so hard on our behalf when the war 'Came To Our Door'.

Monica Twyford.

Moncia Twyford
Helston, October 2005

Monica Twyford, WAAF 1941-46, clerk special duties

This book is dedicated to
the ordinary Men and Women of Plymouth
as a tribute to
their
indomitable courage
and
unconquerable spirit

"This is their world: this portion of the earth
Means much to them - nay, do not mock or jeer;
This spot has held the things to them most dear:
Their earliest dreams, their sorrows and their mirth."
MARGARET E BINNER

INTRODUCTION
by LORD ASTOR
LORD MAYOR of PLYMOUTH
(November, 1939 to November, 1944)

"The balloons glowed and glimmered in the last rays of the setting sun."

Few day-to-day diaries can stand immediate publication. Too often the need for discretion blunts the edge of the commentary. We know well that the best diaries are the most indiscreet, those set down at night when the author, fearless of censor or critic, is alone with book and pen, and — like Petruchio — can "tell you flatly what his mind is".

It is not enough to be discreetly factual. The diary must bear the impress of the writer's personality: he must not speak from behind a mask. "Inside" knowledge, the day's gossip — whether inspired or casual — sharp comment, the fixing of the passing moment, the rapid impressionist sketch: all these belong to the diary proper. It cannot afford to be a mere official bulletin.

Mr. Twyford kept a diary during the past years. As a journalist he had special opportunities for obtaining facts and information which could not be made available to the public at the time.

As Lord Mayor of the City during the five years of its ordeal, I can speak for the vividness and veracity of his story of Plymouth at war.

We welcome the chronological account of the raids in Chapter 16 — a passage which recalls for us in their proper order events which had become a confused memory. Once more we hear the doleful wail of the siren in the night, and remember again the moments of indecision. Shall we turn over, cover our heads and try to sleep? Shall we, however raw and cold the night, follow official advice and seek a shelter? Or is it best to go out, to see the searchlights probing the sky, the glow of the tracers, the sudden blaze of the flares, and — with raiders overhead and the guns cannonading — do all we can to help?

The book restores these nights and days of anxiety. After five years of total blackout, of searchlights in the darkness, and of aircraft droning overhead, I still feel startled when a stray beam escapes from a curtained window. I still look for the steel cables of a blimp before my house in Elliot Terrace, and I miss the wonderful sight when, long after twilight veiled Plymouth Hoe, the balloons far overhead glowed and glimmered in the last rays of the setting sun.

Mr. Twyford writes of the Women's Services. I shall never forget our last big parade just before D-Day, the discipline of the ATS, the WRNS, the WAAF, of the women of the National Fire Service and the Police Service as they swung by, marching in perfect rhythm. But I get an even greater thrill when I remember the first march past, on Plymouth Hoe, of our original Civil Defence units, women middle-aged and imperfectly trained, not marching here as a Brigade of Guards, but stepping out with a determination which showed what they would do in the days ahead. Later, when Plymouth was in travail, its houses blasted and the perilous rescue work in progress, we saw how gloriously the Civil Defence workers could answer their supreme challenge.

No history, official or unofficial, can record the meaning of the raids in terms of individual human endurance. Once a single bomb was dropped. It hit a small house, killing the occupants, a woman and her children. The place was blown into fragments, into utter ruin. Nothing human could be collected for burial. When the woman's husband arrived from the Fleet he could find nothing, not the smallest souvenir, to remind him of his married life.

On another occasion a rescue squad began to dig in the remains of a collapsed house. Six dead bodies were recovered, and the workers wondered whether or not to continue. Had there been six people in the building or seven? They were on the point of going away, agreeing that no one could remain alive, when they heard a faint sound. Beneath the collapsed building a woman lay pinned. She had heard them digging, heard their argument, and had just strength enough to moan. Not many weeks later she was again cheerfully at work.

During the first small raids we learned much of the human side. Many people, it seemed, had hidden their savings in "stockings", behind cupboards, and in all manner of secret crannies. I had to broadcast an appeal urging them to safeguard themselves by banking their money. Often, too, a man or a couple would be killed, and we found that though for years they had been known to their neighbours, none had the remotest idea of their past, whence they came, or whether they had relatives who should be notified. Here, too, another difficulty arose. What was their religion? What burial service should be used?

Far the grimmest task was that of assembling human remains. After a serious raid it was intensely trying. Once, when casualties were high, we had to call in some young men to help; overcome by the horror of the mangled bits of flesh, they found it impossible to proceed. It was doubly harrowing when relatives were summoned to identify the remains. (There was an especially sad occasion when human fragments, cleaned and arranged, were placed in one building and clothing and belongings, identified by numbers, in the next. On the following night a bomb fell on the clothing store, and every vestige disappeared.)

Mr. Twyford recalls our last serious raid on the night of August 13, 1943. On the previous day we had conferred with London officials in an effort to get more labour to repair our houses. It was agreed that, with all the skilled and unskilled labour they could send from London, and with all that we could scrape together in the City at least eighteen months work lay ahead. That night Plymouth was raided sharply for thirty-five minutes. After reports had been sorted at the A.R.P. headquarters, we learned that we must add three thousand houses to those already listed as being in need of some repair. It seemed impossible to catch up with our task.

Forty-one people were killed that night. Yet, on that same afternoon, I was able to stand on the Hoe and thank our people for coming as usual in their thousands to listen to a military band and dance to its music. I thanked them then for showing the same calm spirit that, long before on Plymouth Hoe, had enabled Drake and his comrades to defy Philip of Spain and finish their bowls before sailing out to finish the Armada.

What is the spirit of Drake which still persists in Plymouth, and the spirit of the Navy — which is also the spirit of the Services, of our pilots and gunners, and of all our fighting men and women? It is a strange thing, invisible, intangible, imponderable, and, as we know now, of an audacity well-nigh incredible. It can hardly be analysed. It is neither guns nor armour nor Fleet Orders. It is something which is nursed, nourished, and found where men live close together in daily, hourly, peril of their lives.

As Kipling wrote, "The life of which this spirit is born has always been a life more lonely than any life there is". In years of peace many forget this spirit of the Navy, but when war comes we turn to it and expect to find it there on guard day and night. In time of danger we know that eyes will be watching and brave hearts beating; skilled hands will be swift and firm. When the burning hour has struck and guns are roaring across the water we are filled with gratitude and exaltation at the news of victory.

Who, then, can wonder that we revere this spirit? The war has proved again that, although ships are built of steel instead of wood, though they are moved by coal and oil instead of the winds of heaven, the spirit of the Services is still the same spirit of the British Navy, is still that which for centuries past has secured for our homes and our country the continuance of its high tradition and of the British way of life. There is only one word more. During the raids I faced, like others, the possibility of death. So close was my union with the people of Plymouth that I left instructions — in the event of disaster — for communal burial with my fellow-citizens.

I could think of no more honourable ending than this.

Lord Astor

The communal burial ground at Efford.

THE GATHERING STORM

When first I started pulling out the threads from the tangled skein of the war years for the purpose of this book, I grew a bit frightened, not so much over the things I had noted or remembered, but the countless other incidents which might be overlooked and so go unrecorded. Even now when I have read through the manuscript, I am fully conscious of the acts of omission rather than those of commission.

But if this book reflects something of the spirit of unshakeable courage which animated what, for want of a better phrase, I would call the ordinary men and women, yes and children, of Plymouth during the terrible ordeals of blast and fire which they experienced, then I shall have achieved my aim.

I write this book with a sense of pride in being a Plymothian, if only by long adoption, during the great overflowing days of the world war. For more than thirty years I have been actively chronicling the everyday life of Plymouth in my capacity as a journalist. This book is an attempt at my greatest assignment.

It may be that the reporter, by virtue of his training and experience observes a bit more than the ordinary person. My work in reporting local events brought me into close personal contact with men and women in every walk of life, the seamy side and the bright side, the joys and the sorrows, and above all that imperishable and indomitable "something" which enabled Plymouth in the hour of trial to be faithful to great traditions.

It was an unconquerable spirit which defied the worst that a ruthless enemy could vent on a civil population; not something which was pulled out for a special occasion, but something which we regard as inherent in the true British character. I saw how the people awaited those awful onslaughts the heroism which they showed during the worst attacks, when all that was precious to them was crumbling about their heads. I saw them in the great clearing-up aftermath and in the tense hours of reaction. I saw their character reflected in a new comradeship and good-neighbourliness, and, above all, in the grim determination to carry on.

As I write I recall the words which the Prime Minister himself said to me when I was introduced to him at Lord Astor's residence on the occasion of his visit to Plymouth after the particularly heavy raids in 1941. I asked him for a message of encouragement to the citizens.

Pat Twyford makes notes behind a young Lady Astor, in 1920 Above, neighbours make light of their troubles in the rubble. Below, Winston and Lady Churchill outside Eliott Terrace.

"What can I say?" he asked, adding, "Your homes are low, but your heads are high." What a happy choice of words!

I remember, too, the tears that were in that great man's eyes when he stood in the Guildhall Square, with the ruins of the once imposing buildings all around him, and the wonderful spirit of the cheering people as they pressed in on him from every side, and a girl slipped a rose into his hand for a buttonhole.

There was another occasion when a very apt phrase was used. It was during the visit of two distinguished Canadians. They had toured the city's devastated areas and had been shown how the people were carrying on, how the city's public and private life still flowed with a full pulse, they had talked with men and women in their homes and at their work. At the end of the tour one of them turned to a leading city official and said, with what sounded almost like emotion, "I think you are a very brave people."

The official turned for a moment and regarded him, and then very quietly replied, "No, not brave, just British."

The Union Jack goes up amid the rubble that was the Guildhall.

In my work as an accredited war correspondent I travelled far and saw much. Frequently when I met people far from Plymouth they would say, "Oh, you're from Plymouth. You've had it pretty bad, haven't you?" And there was a great respect in their voices.

On one occasion I met an old journalist colleague who left some years before for London, but who had retained a great affection for the city. He said, "I was down there the other day. I knew you had had a bad time, but I hadn't realised it was so bad. You have to see it to understand. When I looked around I felt sick. Yet the people are wonderful. They seem to have taken it almost as they used to take a bad Argyle defeat in the old days always ready to come up for the next round."

When the war clouds were gathering over Europe in the months of smouldering fire I well recall reading a sentence by a famous American reporter. He said, "The lights are going out one by one all over Europe." How true that was.

But there was one light that never went out. It burned very low, even flickered. But it was never extinguished. It was the light of the British spirit. And Plymouth helped to keep that flickering flame alive!

Those who read the signs aright in those faraway days, saw the approaching storm, but the extent of its violence and how it would come to every door, and like an ever growing avalanche envelop the whole world in its awful grip, could not be seen by the ordinary man and woman. In their imagination they could only measure by past standards. But the madmen of Europe had put a spark to start a conflagration beyond human comprehension. Perhaps it was as well that we did not know.

In those long and anxious months which preceded September 3, 1939, there were many in this country who never dreamt that the war would come to their door. They hid behind the far-away barriers of "1066, and all that". They said to themselves that not for nearly a thousand years had a Continental invader set foot on these shores. They were content to sit behind their barrier. There was still, they said, "that strip of water", and whatever we might have to do on the Continent, England's "green and pleasant land" would be inviolate. So they were content to think, and complacently go their way.

Some months before war broke out I was assigned by The Western Morning News to visit every town, large and small, in the Westcountry and report on their preparedness to meet enemy air attack. There was no censorship in those days, and one could write freely. I found an amazing divergence of opinion and readiness. In some places there were public men who flatly pooh-poohed the idea of air-raid precautions being necessary.

"We are too far away."

"A sheer waste of public money."

Those were some of the remarks I heard. In most places, however, there was some measure of doubt and fear in the minds. "Better be prepared" they said. So it was that while some set about their preparations wholeheartedly, others did so with half enthusiasm, and in a few places there was a contented policy of drift.

Plymouth, on the whole, was one of the places where possible danger was taken seriously, so that when war did come there were already in existence certain civil defence services such as wardens, auxiliary firemen, special constabulary, casualty services, and others, trained in their duties.

Plymouth men and women volunteered for these duties in considerable number, and many will recall the lectures, demonstrations, and training which gave them a certain measure of proficiency in anticipation of events. Looking back, we can see how it was all leading to the great upheaval. The grim pictures of modern warfare were painted in all their lurid colours by the instructors. Perhaps some were a bit credulous. But how we later had to thank those instructors. They built well on good foundations.

But even in the early months of the war, when we blissfully sang about "Hanging out the washing on the Siegfried Line", when our Expeditionary Force was still in France and armies were just sparring from behind their defences, when the shape of things to come was still hidden in the thick mists of conjecture, there was, admittedly, a shamefully complacent outlook as far as danger to this country was concerned – especially as regards the remote Westcountry.

It was not until Dunkirk, the capitulation of France, and those never-to-be-forgotten evacuation scenes, that we were really shaken to the realisation of the peril to our country. Yet, even then, there were those who were content to sit back, change the record from "Hanging out the washing on the Siegfried Line" to "There'll always be an England" and do nothing.

Up to that shaking out of our complacency we had accepted the blackout, the national registration of individuals, the scares of fifth

17th Battalion Devonport Home Guard

columnists, the steadily increasing regulations and restrictions, the rationing, and the general imposition of war conditions, in a sort of self-satisfied conviction that war was not likely to engulf us in its stark grim realities such as we read about in Poland and other places. It was some distance from our doors.

What an illusion those early days were!

We had, in some measure, tasted both the glories and the tragedies of the war in a general way. There was that first awful shock when the aircraft-carrier Courageous a ship we knew so well at Devonport was sunk by German submarine on a Sunday evening within the waters of the Western Approaches. Hundreds of Plymouth homes were bereaved by that sinking, the first grim incident of the war. I well remember interviewing many of the survivors at the Royal Naval Barracks, and the anxious scenes as relatives scanned the lists of rescued as they were posted outside the main gate.

The triumphant return of HMS Exeter to Devonport Dockyard

Then there was the tremendous thrill when crowds lined the historic foreshore, on the separate occasions, to welcome home the battle-scarred cruisers Ajax and Exeter - the latter a Devonport ship - after their memorable victory in the River Plate battle, which led to the destruction of the German pocket-battleship Graf Spee. Those were occasions when Plymouth turned back the pages of her history book for nearly four hundred years, and as the people then "manned" the foreshore to welcome Sir Francis Drake back from his great adventures, so the twentieth-century citizens did so for the modern "Drakes".

There were other events, too, for it was impossible that a great garrison, air station, and naval port like Plymouth - even though in the remote Westcountry - could be entirely disassociated with the events in different parts of the world, which, in those early months, were marking the comparatively steady flow of the war.

Plymouth bore these events with characteristic spirit. In sorrow she was courageous; in the victories she found inspiration. Even then, however, the city's great agony was not to be foreshadowed.

With the direct threat to this country there came a steady awakening of the public conscience to individual and collective responsibilities. We were slowly beginning to realise that this war was something very different from what we had known in the past.

We began to hear the phrase "total war", but still not quite realising what it meant. We heard about Warsaw and Rotterdam and other places devastated by the new war weapon fashioned by Germany; we read of the ferocity of Nazi bombing of our troops as they fought their historic rearguard action through Belgium and France and the miracle of Dunkirk which followed.

Then, following Dunkirk, came the Battle of Britain - and a nation really awakened to its danger. It had needed a Dunkirk and a Battle of Britain to arouse us from our complacency.

But were we too late? Anxiety grew, and we began to look around. We saw the sandbags with which we had barricaded public and other buildings at the start of the war - what feeble protection they would have been - had begun to rot and were spewing their contents around sodden bases; the trenches which had been dug were crumbling in. These things which seemed sufficient when the war was far away were no longer adequate. Something more concrete had to be done, and done quickly.

In the face of the direct and real threat of invasion Britain began to seriously throw itself into the war. From the early complacency we passed to anxiety, as we realised how ill-prepared we were from the material point of view to meet the challenge.

Out of anxiety there grew the new determination, the spirit of Britain was awake. As the Nazi armies swept through France and took full command of the French Channel and Atlantic coasts, we knew that our danger was very real.

The Battle of Britain, remember Churchill's historic words, "never in the history of human conflict was so much owed by so many to so few" stirred us. But was that glorious victory and the stirring it caused enough?

Surely Hitler would still try invasion. Well, this is not a history of the war, but rather the story of Plymouth's repercussions. Yet you cannot entirely dissociate the two.

We know that for some amazing reason Hitler held his hand. Did he hope to get us on his side against Russia? Did his massive military machine overrun itself? Did Hitler have at least one sensible "intuition", that invasion of this country would fail? Was that air victory in the Battle of Britain a sign-post? Did Hitler think he would beat this nation to its knees by the unrestricted air bombing to which he later subjected so many cities and towns, to say nothing of villages? Did he think he would starve us with the U-boat sinkings on our sea trade routes?

The man in the street just asked the questions. He still asks them. It will be for the military historians in the welter of post-war analysis to tell us - that is, if the man in the street will then still be caring.

All we know is that the danger awakened a new spirit of grim determination that any attempted invasion should fail. Do you remember how Churchill's clarion call went forth, how hastily-erected defences were prepared all along the beaches, which not so long before were our summer playgrounds, how all road sign-posts were removed and place-names obliterated, how road blocks and anti-tank gun and machine-gun emplacements were erected at strategic points, how bridges were mined, how barrage balloons sprouted like mushrooms over all protected areas, how men – youngsters in their teens and veterans of two wars – rallied to the call for Local Defence Volunteers, later to be the magnificent Home Guard, how Civil Defence organisations were increased and trained, how the factories intensified their war output, how the rich pasture lands were ploughed and planted to "grow more food" in order to save shipping space, how every householder stood by night after night with sandbag and stirrup pump, long-handled shovel and scoop?

Yes, Hitler's threat aroused us. I saw all this, and much more, for I travelled near and far in those anxious days, seeing how Britain was preparing to meet invasion.

I saw, and I still marvel that he did not come. Materially we were very ill-prepared to meet the threat for many a long day. But in the midst of it all there was one heartening feature which never faltered. The spirit of the people. In spirit we were grandly equipped. It was the spirit which was to carry us through the dark days ahead.

There would have been unpleasant surprises for the invader even though many of them were crude. Behind that spirit of resistance there was a lively ingenuity. Improvisation played a big part. The magnificent spirit expressed itself in a thousand ways.

Sometimes in my travels I would come across a country Home Guardsman at a lonely road junction, armed only with a sporting rifle or a double-barrelled shot-gun. I wondered what he would be able to do if a German armoured car or tank came lumbering around the corner? All I was certain of was that he would "have a go", even if it was with his bare fists. You see, his home was being threatened.

Above a barrage balloon at Mount Batten. Below the sea defences at Devil's Point.

That was the spirit awakening in England even before the big raids became general.

I can now reveal that my War Office appointment as an Accredited War Correspondent was in its first instance specially to report the invasion. The particular area for which I would be responsible would be that country within a line drawn from Weymouth across to Weston-Super-Mare and down as far as the Isles of Scilly in the extreme south-west. My instructions were such that I was, in a sense, "on my toes" waiting for the emergency call – first a code word indicating that invasion was imminent, and then a second code word calling me to my "battle station" – for months.

For the purpose of reporting the invasion the country was divided into regions, and I was one of a number of accredited war correspondents allocated to the task. But, of course, as we know, that call never came.

Periodically I went off on various missions with the Navy, Army, and Air Force to see how things were developing, and to describe operational jobs. Many secrets were unfolded to us as to how the invasion would be met, the strength with which it would be challenged. Defences were examined, strategy was explained. There were unceasing invasion practice battles in the danger areas, and with it all there was a relentless watch. Britain was waiting and watching, ill-prepared for a long time, but with stout heart. I don't ever remember hearing anyone say that they were afraid; the official mind was skilfully masked.

Thus the war clouds hung heavily over Britain, with the enemy in "full force" just across the water. At one time there was strong reason to believe that the enemy plan would include a determined effort to secure control of the Western Approaches. To do that he would need to possess the airfields in the South West and possibly Ireland. Then the question arose as to whether he would invade Ireland and make it the jumping-off ground for an attack on the south-west. I do not think I shall be breaking any confidences at this distance of time if I say that such was the concern over this threat that for a period very special attention was given to the defence of airfields in this part of the country. There was always a powerful mobile force within call to meet such emergencies.

Hitler kept us guessing. How, when, and where the possible – probable would be the better word – blow would fall, we knew not. But Britain was aroused and was prepared to meet it, whether airborne or seaborne, with whatever tools were available. At the same time it must have been a pretty anxious job for the Services' staffs. I remember attending a conference of the Combined Services after one important anti-invasion exercise in this part of the country at a time when the invasion threat was at its height. The Navy frankly said it would be able to help very little in the way of stopping a seaborne force crossing the Channel, for the very simple reason that the available ships were otherwise engaged. The Air Force did not anticipate being very helpful. That was the frank position.

"Well, it means that we shall have to stop the invasion ourselves," calmly said the military commander. And that was what at that time – 1941-42 – it amounted to. "But you can take it from me that the beaches will be a bloody shambles," grimly said another military staff officer.

It was a grim picture; a rather bleak outlook, save for the unquenchable spirit which had now crept into the life of the country. Steadily and surely the outlook had changed. I must, however, confess to being a thorough optimist over this invasion business. I always had a feeling that it would never come off. Month by month Hitler's chances receded. But even war correspondents had to keep many anxious secrets "under their hat" and much that we saw and much that we were told was, in official parlance, "off the record".

Churchill's great cry to America went echoing across the broad, barren wastes of the Atlantic – "Give us the tools, and we will finish the job!" And it was not in vain. Tools came with every ship.

The Americans respond to an appeal from overseas.

Men and materials flowed to the motherland from the Colonies and the Dominions – the vast army from Canada, airmen from Australia, sturdy sailors and lumbermen from Newfoundland, farmers from New Zealand, and later the Americans themselves. Britain became an armed camp, an island fortress.

And woven into the growing force being marshalled against the enemy were the Poles, the Czechs, the Belgians, the Norwegians, the Dutch, and the Free French. We came to know them all in Plymouth, and they on their part seemed to realise that this was the final hope for the liberation of their own overrun countries. They sailed our seas, they flew in our skies, they marched in our streets and country lanes in great singleness of purpose.

This, then, was the awakening, the steady change-over from defence to attack, until the day came when it was Germany and Italy themselves who became fearful of invasion. There came the changed step in the marching of men who prized freedom above all else.

Britain began punching harder and harder, and on the other hand every threat to this country was entailing a growing price for the enemy. So it came about that no German soldier ever set foot on these shores, no German airman came down in our country, save those who were shot down, no German sailor ever sailed into our harbours, save as a prisoner.

The air was Hitler's last card in direct vengeance against this country. He played it with hideous hate, but slowly, too, that card lost its value. The unquenchable spirit of the people of this country triumphed against the storm of physical and material destruction. Then we watched the pendulum swing in the opposite direction.

But through these months and years Britain was called on to endure. It was in that endurance that the nation's spirit rose to such supreme heights. Hitler brought "total warfare" to this country; he aroused a previously complacent nation's "total spirit". The debts were being repaid with terrible interest.

At that period my mind went back once again to Mr. Winston Churchill, as he stood amid the crowd in the ruins of Plymouth.

"Give it them back" was the cry of vengeance from the people as they swarmed around him.

And he answered, "We will."

Churchill outside the ruins of Plymouth Guildhall May 1941

PLYMOUTH BECOMES THE FRONT LINE

Periodically from September, 1939, Plymouth practised emergency measures to meet attack from the air. As far as the general population was concerned air-raid defence was expressed through the Civil Defence organisations. Later, Plymouth men in the Home Guard were also to form an integral part of the defences from a military point of view, and when they manned the anti-aircraft barrage they had the tremendous satisfaction of being among the first Home Guard to bring down an enemy aircraft.

But in the early days it was the civil defences which concerned us directly as a citizens' responsibility. Sirens were tested, and from individual control they were put under single remote control at the Greenbank police headquarters, where, by the simple process of turning down an electric switch, a synchronised air-raid warning could be sounded from sirens at Greenbank, the Guildhall tower, Milehouse, Ker Street, Camels Head, St. Budeaux, and Crownhill.

Left, An early bomb hits the Hoe. Above, women in uniform at Plymouth Police HQ.

How we got to know those warnings! The novelty was soon lost in familiarity. Plymouth was quickly made to realise her danger when the Germans got control of the coast on the French side of the Channel. Within five days of the "cease fire" in France the first air-raid "alert" was sounded in Plymouth. That was on June 30, 1940. In the next four years Plymouth was to hear that ominous wailing more than six hundred times!

The majority of the "alerts" produced no incidents; enemy planes were merely in the region and did not have Plymouth as their special objective. But there were a great many when death and destruction rained down on the city. Nevertheless, those attacks, large and small, were met with the same unflinching courage, and while hundreds of civilians, men, women, and children, were killed and many more were injured, while public buildings, many of them rich in association with Plymouth's history, churches and schools, and thousands of the homes of the people, were either totally destroyed or damaged, the courage remained unquenchable.

It was on Saturday July 6, 1940, that Plymouth experienced its first raid. Shortly before midday the sirens sounded the "alert". Wardens and police, and other Civil Defence organisations, sprang to action. The city was basking under a perfect summer sky. With the "alert" all Civil Defence stations were manned. Soon the sound of aircraft flying very high was heard.

Eyes searched the sky for the first glimpse of an enemy raider – the first over Plymouth. High up in the blue dome, making clever use of the sparse cloud cover, the intruder was just a small speck, occasionally catching the sunlight like some silver-winged bird.

The crack of anti-aircraft guns and the puffs of white smoke against the blue sky as the shells burst, helped in the direction-finding.

Suddenly there was an ominous whistle. It passed high over our heads where I was standing with a warden, and, "green like", we both plunged to the protection of the nearest wall. Fortunately, he was a small man, otherwise I might have been a casualty.

The first enemy bomb was falling on Plymouth. With a crumping thud that took my mind back to France in the 1914-18 war, it fell on the Swilly Corporation housing estate. Out of the blue had come the first agent of death and destruction on the city's civil population. In that blast three houses crumpled like a pack of cards, two more were badly damaged, many others in the area sustained minor damage.

Plymouth's first enemy bomb hits four houses in Furneaux Road.

One woman, one man, and a boy were Plymouth's first air-raid victims in this overture of Hitler's "total war". The woman was a housewife who had slipped back into the house from the garden shelter to look at the cooking dinner. Six other people were injured, four having to go to hospital.

Recovering from the dive to shelter as the bomb had passed over us, we saw the column of smoke and dust rising above the devastated houses. "That's the first taste", grimly said the warden, as he dusted down his clothes and set his "tin hat" at a new angle, adding, "But I'm afraid it's only a taste." How true were his words!

The raider could be seen speeding away over the sea back to its base on the other side of the Channel. A few desultory bursts spaced the trail, but there were no pursuing aircraft. The enemy had a clear run home, and I did not derive much comfort from the remark of an old gunner of the last war, "I'spect they'll be tillin' for 'ee outside." We had not got the fighter patrols in those days like we had later.

The next day was Sunday. Private motorists were still enjoying a ration of petrol for pleasure – just enough to have an occasional short run out to the moors. I spent the afternoon on Roborough Down. It was another perfect day.

In peacetime we should have been enjoying the break, but somehow that afternoon the memory of the previous day's first raid on Plymouth was very fresh in our minds. We felt sort of restless, wondering what was really in store for the city. If the enemy was not to attempt the invasion proper we expected these air raids would become persistent, bringing grim realities and the tragedies of war right into the homes of the people. Plymouth had, in effect, been "blooded" by that short previous day's experience. Not for centuries had an enemy's mark been left on the face of Plymouth. What next?

I wondered all this as I lay on that heath looking up into the clear afternoon sky listening to the larks as their songs of freedom filled the air and the summer life browsed all around.

In the distance I could see the barrage balloons – so few and far apart they seemed in those days - floating serenely over the port. I remember trying to calculate just what protection they would be able to give us, and I thought of the high "ceiling" from which the German bomber had released his first bomb on the city. And the guns had seemed so inadequate. Yet we knew that these things were all that could then be spared from the country's slender defence resources.

As I drove back through Crownhill about tea-time the sirens' wailing notes came again, rather frightening. Puffs of white again flecked the blue sky, a succession of heavy thuds came reverberating from the direction of the city. Ominous thuds they were.

We grimly realised that the second raid was in progress. This time it was the poor east end houses of Plymothians that provided the target. And this was tea-time on a Sunday afternoon!

South Milton Street, Cattedown takes a direct hit.

Cattedown, closely adjoining the gas works and other vital industries, was suddenly transformed from that pleasant Sunday tea-time to a scene of horrible death and devastation. The raiders had come in low over the coast to the east of the city and, flying down the valley of the Plym, released their bombs over this thickly-populated district. Six people were killed, including a policeman and a soldier. Many homes were destroyed. Again it was the ordinary homes and the ordinary civilian people who suffered.

I think that night we grimly realised that Plymouth was right in the war zone. War had come to our door with stark reality.

The next morning, almost before the city was awake, came the third attack. This time bombs were dropped in the vicinity of Morice Square, Devonport, close to the Royal Albert Hospital. A butcher's shop in the close-by Marlborough Street was destroyed by direct hit. The proprietor was killed and ten people were injured, three seriously. One bomb went straight down through that imposing building, the Royal Sailors' Club, from roof to basement. It exploded in the kitchen and destroyed the dining-room, which half an hour before had been crowded with sailors having breakfast before going aboard their ships. Yet, by amazing luck - how many times we were to know that strange luck in the coming months! – not a single person was killed or injured in the building.

Two days later came another early morning raid, and bombs were dropped in Exeter Street and the Hoe district. Five people were killed and seven injured, with many private houses and business premises destroyed or damaged.

Thus in five days Plymouth had been brought right into the war's front line. It was a grim prospect. But Plymouth did not flinch. The city went on with its work; "business as usual" was the motto.

I do not propose to give the full catalogue of the raids until later in the book. These first four I here recount to indicate how quickly the war had been brought right into the homes of the people. This was the beginning of "total war" as far as Plymouth was concerned.

It was an astonishing fact that even after these raids, with their roll of killed and injured and the heavy destruction of homes and properties, that the authorities in London would not consent to Plymouth being made an evacuation area as far as the children were concerned. The obvious pointer was that there was worse to come.

Above, Slee's butcher shop, Marlborough Street,
Right, the Dining Room of the Royal Sailors, Devonport.
Below, a bomb crater in Exeter Street. "This was the beginning of 'total war' as far as Plymouth was concerned.

Plymouth children would just have to go through it. There were those who were sent away by their parents, but they were private arrangements and not part of any official scheme. The official mind said the children had to stay.

The city was to experience the most fearful bombing, many more mothers and children were to be killed or maimed in night after night of nerve-shattering horror, before the official mind altered its decision. Let us be quite clear. This was not the fault of the local authorities. They pressed again and again for the children to be sent away through a properly organised evacuation scheme, but to no avail.

Lady Astor at North Road station with local evacuees.

The scheme for official organised evacuation did not come into operation until well into 1941, when the worst of the raids had been experienced. I do not think Plymouth ever quite forgot or forgave that disregard of their appeal to send the children away. I am quite well aware that when evacuation did come it was still to a very large extent voluntary, but the children who did go went in properly organised parties to properly, organised reception areas, where complete arrangements were made for their schooling and billeting. There were still thousands who did not go. Their parents were content to take the bold risk of keeping them with them in the city. As the raids lessened

Lord Astor greets an evacuee at North Road Station, Plymouth.

there were thousands of those who did go "into the country" who came home again. But, be all that as it may, the fact remained that Plymouth was about the worst blitzed place in the whole country before the official mind at Whitehall agreed that the children would be better out of it.

Realising what was likely to come with the development of the war, Plymouth, both officially and privately, began to ensure fuller precautions. The Civil Defence services were increased considerably in personnel and equipment. New and bigger underground and surface shelters were rapidly constructed. But even in this we had much to learn. In the first winter of heavy raids many of the shelters lacked proper organisation and in wet weather became flooded.

I remember doing a tour of the underground shelters because there was so much complaint about their condition in wet weather. I found many of them leaking badly, with walls dripping wet, and the floors in some places where there was lack of proper drainage with anything from six inches to a foot of water. There were at least two where it was utterly impossible to get through the entrance without waders. But these were some of the lessons we had to learn, and remedies were applied as speedily as possible.

Gardens and back yards were, in the majority of cases, equipped with the sturdy Anderson or private shelters. The Anderson shelter was free to households with an income of less than £250 a year, and assistance was given in the construction. Others were able to purchase an Anderson shelter at a reasonable figure commensurate with their income. In many parts of the city basements in private houses were strengthened to a degree which was considered capable of taking the weight of a collapsed building. Most of the big business houses arranged shelters in their basements, where staffs and customers could be accommodated in the event of raids during business hours. A very curious psychological fact was that after the first few "alerts" comparatively few people went to the shelters either private or public, in the daytime. The fact of being able to see something of what was happening in the sky seemed to make all the difference. I was in the streets and on the Hoe on several occasions when the "alert" sounded during the day. In the main people just glanced up into the sky and carried on. If there was anything to arrest their attention they would stand and follow its course, and even to remind them that "what went up had to come down" did not seriously change their attitude.

It was, however, very different at night. The darkness masked all ac-

Above, the outdoor Anderson. Right the Morrison shelter is deomnstrated by Scouts.

tion, save that of the searchlights, the flash of the guns, and the "star-spangled" dark sky, as shells burst and tracers sent chains of orange lights racing through darkness. Darkness intensified everything, and so it was that shelters generally were much more in use during the night "alerts" than in the day.

On the other hand, there were many people who did not like shelters. I must count myself among them. But in my instance I think possibly it was largely the reporter's natural habit of wanting to see what was happening; to have, as it were, the usual "ringside" seat. I am not going to say that a handy bit of cover was not acceptable when the air seemed alive with whistling fragments or a bomb was screaming perilously close. In those moments I could hold my own with the best in diving for protection.

It was my lot to be through some of the heaviest bombardments in France during the previous war. They were vivid, almost dazzling. But the spectacle of some of the big raids on Plymouth was something very different. It must have been a fearsome sight to have been a spectator from such a vantage point as, say, Kit Hill or Peeke Hill.

Later in the war came the indoor Morrison shelter, which could be erected in the dining-room or the kitchen, and when not being used for its real grim purpose was almost an article of furniture and used as a table. They were very strong.

Yet again there were those who pinned their confidence in the strength of the cupboard under the stairs.

Thus it was that people were not regularised or regimented into what they should do in the seeking of protection during a raid. There were all these expedients, and as long as they gave confidence to the users, that was what most mattered.

This, however, was a war in which, from the civil defence point of view, most things had to be learnt from experience. Civil populations had not been very materially concerned with realities of war before this. "Total warfare" was a very different thing to what had been experienced before.

Thank goodness we never reached the stage of gas attacks. But the attacks by blast and fire followed the lines of scientific research in the most intensive fashion. Every month and every year brought their developments for the promotion of mass destruction and mass killing.

In the early raids Plymouth experienced attacks with only the high explosives, and the bombs were of small calibre compared with the later inventions. But they soon grew in size, and quite a number which fell in the city subsequently were over a ton in weight. We also had fairly early experience of the devastation which could be caused by land mines.

30 November 1940 - a parachute mine lands at Prince Rock.

I well remember what I think must have been about the first of these land mines which fell in the city It was late one evening, and I was standing outside the Mount Gold First Aid Post in Edith Avenue when the raid took place. We actually saw the mine dropping by parachute. It fell in open ground adjoining some allotments at Prince Rock – the best part of a mile away. The blast came to us like the lash of a whip. There were no serious casualties, but the blast ripped the roofs and blew out the windows and doors of hundreds of houses in the vicinity. The scene next day gave us a full picture of the effect of blast from one of these mines.

All too soon came the other form of air attack – by incendiaries. First they were of the small type which could be tackled with water and sand immediately, and without any great personal danger. Remember how the men, women and children tackled these when thousands fell in various parts of Plymouth during those early raids? Then, however, the range of incendiaries increased, and with that came a growing personal danger for anyone handling them without due care. To cause delayed action in dealing with the incendiaries the enemy mixed explosive types with non-explosive types. Thus it was that the utmost care had to be shown. As it was, many people became casualties from the premature tackling of the incendiary fitted with explosive.

The gasmask is modelled in Mutley.

Later still the enemy dropped a number of anti-personnel bombs which the least vibration within considerable range made active. Fortunately, however, Plymouth did not experience this type of bomb.

It was obvious as the war advanced that the enemy was more and more mixing the types of bombs. There was the even more deadly incendiary bomb which could not be tackled under seven minutes, and even then the method of approach had to be very carefully calculated and applied. These bombs were no longer the simple types that in the earlier days were boldly tackled by children.

Then there was also the oil bomb and the phosphorous bomb. The latter splashed its contents over a considerable area, and every "splash" was a potential fire when the liquid dried. With these the chief method of attack was to keep the phosphorous wet until it could be removed.

Incendiaries were, of course, dropped by aircraft in large containers, and in the course of the war quite a number of these containers failed to open in mid-air after release from the aircraft, and they were picked up intact with their contents to make interesting "exhibits" for the bomb experts.

I do not know the number of incendiaries which were dropped on Plymouth in the course of the war, but I do not think the estimate of a quarter of a million would be erring on the wrong side.

I do not think anyone who went through those raids will ever forget the very distinctive sound they made as they fell in their thousands. The nearest description was to that of dried leaves being rustled along the pavements and gutters by a high wind in the darkness.

From the point of view of incendiaries alone Hitler certainly gave Plymouth the benefit of a mixture which we can aptly describe as "all sorts".

At first bomb craters were very much a novelty.

WAR'S EARLY TOUCHES

In their everyday lives, habits, and customs the citizens met the full violent force of the dramatic upheavals and changes which the war brought in its train. Looking back over those years one can only stand amazed at the manner in which these were accepted in the place of the carefree "come day, go day" life of the pre-war years.

The life of the city, so dramatically changed in every phase, flowed through the deep and turbulent waters of the world tragedy with a spirit which was at times criticised as complacency, but which, in its real sincere depth, was just the spirit of a nation grimly determined to take on the chin whatever came for as long as was necessary, in the sure and certain knowledge that the difficult road was the only way to winning the war.

And so it was that the people, without any apparent sudden disturbance, adapted themselves to changes, many of them violent, in a manner which made one proud.

One of the privileges for which Britain was fighting was freedom to criticise. There was often criticism, some justified and some not, but Plymouth's leadership was on the whole sound, and if the imposition of severe war conditions did no more, it certainly awakened a new sense of citizenship and a greater appreciation of good fellowship.

The proud housewife of Mannamead went on her hands and knees to clean her own doorstep without any loss of dignity or prestige, and learnt with a new appreciation and understanding that Mrs. Jones, the daily help, was something of a jewel, certainly a fellow-creature in days when good companionship was necessary at every turn.

There were no privileges in the queue, whether it was waiting at the fish shop or for the crowded buses. War, in which we fight for a common cause, is always a great leveller - never more so than in these last years.

Naturally, nerves were sometimes frayed. How could it be otherwise? Life had been badly jolted from its ordinary easy course. It had become violent, exacting, tiring, and the strain was bound to find some outlet.

Spooner's Corner in those carefree 'come day, go day' pre-war times. Left, the war is still a few years away as HMS Exeter steams past Plymouth Pier.

But, taking all in all, Plymouth worked hard, loaned its money for the conduct of the war generously, gave with characteristic Westcountry freedom to welfare and comforts schemes, shared the extra burdens without complaint, and at the end of the heavy daily round took what limited pleasures life could give with a grateful heart. Most people still found welcome pleasure and diversion against the sinister background of war. They argued, quite rightly, that long faces and dismal conversation were dangerous rather than helpful. So it could well be said that while citizens worked with goodwill in their "go to it" working hours, they also lived for the day in their well-earned off-duty time.

Plymouth had its full share of the joys and sorrows of war right from the word "go" This was inevitable from the fact that it was one of the nation's greatest naval ports, garrisons, and coastal air stations. Thus it was bound to be hit tragically by events on the sea, on land, and in the air. Such heavy happenings as the sinking of the aircraft-carrier *Courageous* in the very early days of the war, the later sinkings of the *Prince of Wales, Repulse,* and the famous cruiser *Exeter* by the Japanese, the loss of other naval craft, large and small, dramatic events in Hong Kong, Singapore, Crete, and other notable happenings in the onward march of the aggressors, could not fail to strike sadly into many city homes. After all, Plymouth had for centuries been a Services town.

But there were brave hearts in those homes, and the tears of sorrow were mingled with the tears of a great pride. Plymouth indeed had a proud list of heroes and heroines to honour.

These losses were the inevitable price of war. Plymouth knew it could not escape that price – a price it had had to pay many times in history But those losses belonged to what might be called the honourable side of war.

Greater, however was the stark tragedy which marched through Plymouth in the wake of the heavy air raids, when the victims were denied the glory of battle, but were the ordinary men, women, and children of the civil population, and when street after street of once happy and contented homes were laid to a shambles by an enemy who thought he could win by the new technique of "total warfare".

Plymouth's physical wounds were terrible to witness. Its heart was torn out with a violence beyond imagination; its once fair face was mutilated with agonising fiendishness by an enemy which hypocritically called itself the champion of culture.

But Plymouth wiped away her tears, healed her wounds as best she could, and steeled her heart and will to "take it" and to "carry on". It became another epic in her stirring history. You cannot "kill" a people either physically or spiritually who "took it" night after night, who could see their homes and workshops devastated and still chalk on the battered walls "Business as usual" and "Hitler can't get us down"; who could sit through an entire cinema performance after the notice "The air raid alert has sounded", hearing the anti-aircraft guns punctuating the entertainment; who could dance on the Hoe or listen to the band in the evenings after heavy raids; and who, when the shadows lengthened and the sky turned to purple, would go to their homes knowing full well "Jerry will be over again tonight".

That was the spirit of Plymouth – a spirit which merits a high seat in the shrine of her great deeds.

It was in very truth the spirit of the city's great hero, Drake. All through those violent nights, when the whole city shook with the reverberations of intense bombardment, when public buildings and homes, containing all that people honoured and held precious, were crashing in piles of blasted and burnt-out masonry, when monstrous fires illuminated the scene like Dante's Inferno when innocent citizens were being killed and injured in their hundreds, when the smoke and dust were choking and the din nerve-shattering, Francis Drake stood calm and serene on his pedestal on the Hoe, a commanding figure facing the enemy. His monument came through unscathed while bombs burst all around and nearby houses and other buildings were devastated.

Left, the men of HMS Exeter parade through Union Street. Above, Drake's statue overlooks the dancing on the Hoe

Often I used to look at that famous and familiar memorial and feel that Drake was inspiring the people with his fearless spirit in the hours of her awful agony. I liked to think that the spirit of Drake *"quit the port of Heaven"* on those nights to help his old town. Whether it did, or whether it did not, I do know that there were many fearless "Drakes" fighting against the odds as he did in his day. It was the everyday courage of the ordinary men and women – yes, and children too – which stirred emotion and fired the imagination. Neither was it a courage they wore on their sleeves.

There were many acts of gallantry which justly merited the public honours bestowed on the individuals concerned, but let it be remembered that there were countless deeds of unsurpassed heroism which never saw the limelight of publicity and went unhonoured.

I had a very firm conviction in those days that the city and not individuals should have been honoured. Individual recognitions, well-earned as most of them were, left too many gaps. Besides, those honours are but transitory. They are not imperishable, as an honour to the city would have been.

An honour to the city could have been handed down to posterity. It would have lived as an inspiration to the generations to come. But Plymouth certainly, in those days of awful terror and destruction, enriched her great traditions and added another chapter to her glorious history through the manifestation of a spirit which so many people had chided us had become decadent.

Yet, there will be a memorial – the new Plymouth that will one day arise, Phoenix-like, from the ashes and rubble of the old.

All I say is, let it be a worthy memorial, for the people earned it.

The new Plymouth will be, above all, a memorial to the "little man" and his wife – the "little man", John Citizen, who discarded his bowler hat for steel helmet, his umbrella for the stirrup-pump, who set aside his mild manner and rolled up his sleeves when the supreme job had to be done, who hour after hour when danger was about, patrolled the dark streets and back lanes grimly alert, who during the raids would call at this house and that house giving a reassuring word to the women and children and particularly the old folk, who, when high explosives and incendiaries came hurtling down and jagged bits of exploded shells whistled through the darkness, was always ready to tackle a dangerous job, and who when the raid was over was still not too tired to give a hand with the cleaning up; and the wife and mother who when the sirens sounded, often left in the house, quietly collected the sleeping children, shepherded them to the shelter, kept them comforted and unafraid while terror was loose all around, and who, when a lull came, would quietly slip back into the kitchen and make the inevitable cup of tea.

John Citizen ... "who discarded his bowler hat for steel helmet."

These are the men and women to whom that memorial of a new and fairer city must he dedicated. Just the ordinary people, the common stock, who defied the worst that a ruthless enemy could vent, and who gave to Plymouth in her greatest hour a new and imperishable glory.

Can you deny them the right to that memorial? But again let me repeat and emphasise - let us see that the memorial is worthy of the occasion.

This, then, was the character and the spirit of the people in those great and, so often, fearsome days. They stood firm.

I know I shall be challenged with the fact that there were some who left the ship when danger threatened and were not in Plymouth to play their part during the intensive raids. But they were a small proportion, and it was inevitable. Let us be charitable in our criticism

– we who went through the fire can afford to be – and, remembering that physical and mental attainments differ with people, just say that the strain was too much.

I may even be reminded of the fact that after the heaviest raids in March and April, 1941, the city was depopulated to the extent of 75,000 people. Yes, but the vast proportion of them were driven out because their homes were destroyed, and there was no alternative accommodation within the city.

Some pile onto lorries, seeking sanctuary outside the city as night approaches, others are looking for their mothers or fathers.

These "refugees", if I might be forgiven for so calling them, poured over the surrounding district, into town, village, and hamlet, like a human flood. They had no alternative. They had to lay their tired – oh, so tired! – bodies somewhere; their weary feet could not go on for ever. And so they found sanctuary in the quiet countryside.

But even from there at night they would look back through the darkness. They would see the long slender fingers of the searchlights sweeping the dark sky, they would hear the ominous throbbing of bomber engines and the distant crash of explosions, they would see the fearsome glow in the night – and they would shudder.

But, driven out as they had been, they had still left behind a vast army of citizens and fighters who would never give way. They would still look after Plymouth.

And the Plymouth front line held firm. It was mauled, battered, mangled, shapeless in parts, bleeding from gaping wounds, reeking with the stench of fire, overhung with a heavy pall – but it did not yield.

Until the war came right to Plymouth's door – and that really began in the serious sense after Dunkirk and the capitulation of France, which left the enemy free for action on the opposite side of the Channel – the life of the city had flowed as evenly as was possible in the changes brought about by the imposition of war conditions.

Our streets were still bright with the display of varied merchandise, uniforms of all types increased and multiplied with the progress of the war and the marshalling of man-power and woman-power, our womenfolk, smart in their seasonal clothes, gave colour and animation to every gathering, the cafes were always crowded for morning coffee and afternoon tea, it was still "the thing" to go "down town" in the morning, there was no serious hardship or shortage, save perhaps for such things as "No. 8 batteries" for torches.

Life drifted along quite evenly while we were "waiting" for the war to come to Plymouth. There were, of course, irksome little inconveniences, but they were accepted quite cheerfully with the remark, "Oh, we must just put up with that in war-time! After all, we are at war, you know!"

We soon developed "cat's eyes" for the blackout, although there was a strange eeriness and emptiness in walking through streets which had no particle of illumination from either the familiar standard lamps or the brightly-lit shop-windows. Remember how we were advised to "wear something white"? The edges of the pavements, the lower parts of tree-trunks and other street obstructions which were a danger to the unwary pedestrian in the blackout, were painted white.

Motor cars and buses had restricted lighting. Their lamps had to be screened and the small side-lights so that they would not be visible at more than three hundred yards. At first only one headlight was. allowed, and that heavily masked, but later two masked headlights were permitted. Both walking and driving were rather trying ordeals in those early days, but we gradually got used to such conditions.

Plymouth observed the blackout regulations with strict watchfulness. It was generally a £2 fine even for a first offence when a citizen was hauled before the magistrates for showing an unscreened light, and later he was also fined for waste of fuel.

No excuses were of avail. The light was a potential danger to the entire community, and even the slightest negligence could not be tolerated. In the course of the war years many hundreds were fined, and in every street police and wardens maintained an alert vigil during darkness. "Put out that light!" became a familiar cry.

Neither the rationing nor the fact that everyone had to carry a National Registration Identity card for production if called on to do so by an authorised person, unduly disturbed people. They were conditions of war which were accepted quite calmly.

"At the outset of the war everyone was issued with a gas mask."

Plymouth was a protected area, which meant that there was a particularly stringent watch kept on aliens coming into the place. There was one period when the police carried out a few raids on public assemblies such as dances, fun fairs, greyhound racing and cafes, demanding the production of identity cards by every person present, and at the same time Ministry of Labour officials checked the registrations for war work. These raids caused a bit of a flutter among the negligent few, but generally Plymothians were anxious to conform to regulations.

At the outset of the war everyone was issued with a gas mask. Those concerned with the Services and the police had the heavy Service type of respirator; Civil Defence workers had what was called the civilian duty respirator, and the ordinary citizens had the small civilian respirator. For a while these were most conscientiously carried by everyone everywhere they went, but in the later years such carrying became the exception rather than the rule. It was felt that there would be a certain amount of warning if attacks with gas were impending, and so people were advised just to keep them somewhere reasonably handy and to make periodical tests to see that they were effective. By 1943 it was a rare thing to see a respirator being carried, save by Service men and women going on long leave.

I think the police were the most faithful to the respirator drill. At least, until well into 1943 it was a regulation for all policemen on duty to wear their respirator for half an hour every Tuesday afternoon. The traffic "cop" looked a rather grotesque figure as he carried out his duties at the busy crossings. For a long time the police tried to get the public to participate in this regular practice, and on occasions tear gas was released in busy thoroughfares to add realism, but the public did not respond too well, and the appeal eventually died a natural death.

The ladies did not relish disarranging their hair without good reason, and the men seemed very self-conscious that their looks were not enhanced by the respirator. Only the kiddies seemed to get any fun out of it.

The general attitude towards respirator practice seemed to be "We'll be alright when the time comes", which was not altogether reassuring to the officials responsible for public safety. But they had to be satisfied, and hope for the best if any such emergency as a gas attack happened. Many people, however, went to pains to ensure that their respirator was maintained in an efficient manner. Yet, I am very much afraid that had you made a complete canvass of the city in 1943 for an inspection of gas masks, a rather alarming position would have been found, and in the event of such a ghastly attack there would have been a heavy responsibility. Happily, no such test was necessary.

Fortunately, Hitler thought discretion the better part of valour, and heeding the warning which this country gave about the use of gas – and you can take it from one who saw something of the preparations for chemical warfare that there was no bluff about this warning – had another correct "intuition" that he had better not attempt it. So suffice it is to say that the respirators were never needed for their sinister real purpose.

The rationing system for food and clothing was, on the whole, smoothly organised, and while there were inevitable inconveniences at times and distribution could have done with a bit better balancing, there was really little about which serious complaint could be made. "Under the counter" trade and "black market" traffic touched Plymouth as it touched everywhere. Unscrupulous people are to be found in every walk of life, and I am not pretending that they were all saints in Plymouth. Human nature is the same everywhere.

But the rationing was, in the broad sense, well administered, and perhaps one of the best features was the very strict control which was maintained with regard to prices. There were heavy fines for those who offended against the price orders which were issued with regard to many commodities.

Supplies were good. They fluctuated, but after five years of war Plymouth, with the rest of the country, was living amazingly well. A feature of the war-time feeding was the establishment of what became popularly known as British Restaurants. These were organised in many parts of the city. One of the first was at the Girls' High School, North Hill, but this was later closed and others operated at such places as the Lecture Hall (Guildhall), Hyde Park School, Keyham, and St. Budeaux. They were introduced immediately after the heavy raids in 1941, when so many people were homeless and others were deprived of cooking facilities by the absence of gas and electricity. Then, too, many hotels, cafes, and eating houses were destroyed. Some such form of communal catering, where hot meals could be obtained at a small economic charge, was absolutely essential.

So many mouths to feed ...

The British Restaurants and kindred organisations filled the need. If my memory serves me aright, I believe in the initial stages it was possible to obtain a good hot midday meal – meat with at least two vegetables and a sweet – for eightpence. Later, to make the meals an economic proposition, the charges were slightly increased. The restaurants became a permanent war-time feature, and many people used them regularly particularly those who had had to make their homes outside the city and had to come in each day to business.

The catering was done by a special staff, and the improved methods of cooking and serving ensured meals being on the table in good condition appetising and of good quality.

While on this question of feeding, it might here be mentioned that. Plymouth was also in a position to meet any serious emergency that might arise from further bombing. In various parts of the city there were emergency feeding centres, which were manned by voluntary workers immediately a serious raid started.

Queen's Messengers Flying Food supplies set up camp in Central Park.

There was, too, an enormous increase in the number of midday meals which were served to children in the schools. These ran into thousands every day. It required considerable organisation by the Education Authority, and while at times there was criticism over the lack of variety and the cold condition of meals, these defects were readily, remedied as more up-to-date equipment was obtained.

The question of public transport became one of the major problems of the war as far as the travelling public was concerned. With the complete suspension of private motoring it was inevitable that a far heavier demand would be made on public transport. During the blitz in 1941 the Corporation bus depot at Milehouse suffered heavy damage. It was, in fact, one of the targets. Some fifty buses were destroyed, others damaged to the extent of being off the streets for some time. I remember seeing the Milehouse depot the morning following the heavy damage. It was a very sorry spectacle, and the sight of one complete bus lying on its side on the roof of the main shed, where it had been lifted by explosion, was a grim reminder of the power of the German bombs.

With so many buses out of commission the resources of the department became over taxed owing to the difficulty of getting replacements for those completely wrecked or spare parts for those damaged. Then again, there was the insistent clamouring for rigid economy in petrol, oil, and rubber, to say nothing of staffing problems.

Fortunately, although Plymouth had decided before the war to scrap the trams, which had given such long and faithful service, certain portions of the track, notably from the centre of the city to Peverell, remained intact. And so the good old dependable trams continued to rumble and rock their way over this route.

There was also the enormously increased demand for public transport to serve the outlying thickly populated areas such as Plympton, Plymstock, and Crownhill, which hitherto had been outside the Corporation service and had been served exclusively by the Western National Omnibus Company.

The great demand had to be met somehow or other, and so it came about that in the autumn of 1942 an agreement was reached between the Corporation and the Company for a joint and greatly accelerated service to these places adjacent to the city.

This arrangement did not come about without considerable criticism and prolonged discussions. There were those who saw in it the thin end of the wedge for the loss to public ownership of the Corporation undertaking; others, however, viewed it in the broad sense of the wider and imperative need.

In due course the joint service became an established fact, and proved a tremendous boon to the very considerable population just adjacent to and beyond the city boundaries, and who had to come into the city daily for work and shopping.

Another recollection of the city war-time transport service was the 9-30 p.m. "curfew" which came into operation during the latter months of 1942. This was entirely dictated by the urgent need for rigid economy in the use of rubber and petrol. In most places the "curfew" was at 9 o'clock, but Plymouth managed to get the half-hour extra, and this was a considerable boon, especially to so many people who were living outside the boundary. After 9-30 at night Plymouth became a city of walkers. There were still taxis to be obtained, but people grew to find the exercise of walking was not without its advantages. Entertainment houses brought their performances into line so that patrons were out in good time to catch their last bus. Theatres and cinemas finished about 9 o'clock, and very soon the streets in the main part of the city were deserted save for the late pedestrians and Service men and women returning to their quarters.

The public houses still kept open until 10 o'clock, and that "last one for the road" was responsible for many a long walk. But, here again, in the matter of transport Plymouth adapted itself without any grumbles. They appreciated that the position was inevitable, and was dictated solely by war conditions.

The wonderful way in which women adapted themselves to men's jobs solved many anxious labour problems for distracted managements. They came into every walk of life, from sweeping the streets and the hard manual labour of demolition tasks with pick and shovel to driving every type of vehicle. There were women porters and women taxi drivers, women linotype machinists and women publicans, women wardens and women ambulance drivers; there were women on the land and in factories, where previously they would have been regarded as interlopers. And, of course, there were thousands in Plymouth in the smart Service uniforms of the WRNS, the ATS, and the WAAF. Women took over men's jobs in business management. Their accustomed peacetime ways of running the household, shopping, a game of bridge, and a spot of gossip just went by the board. They were in the war effort up to their heads just as the men, and the faith which Mr. Ernest Bevin put in them as Minister of Labour was never misplaced.

Their answer to the question "Can you do it?" was an unmistakable "Give us a chance and we will show you." They were given that chance and they did show us.

"The wonderful way in which women adapted themselves to men's jobs solved many anxious labour problems."

There was a Women's Auxiliary Police Corps, in the smart dark blue of the police force, helping in administrative work and as drivers, there were hundreds in the National Fire Service doing similar work, no less attractive in their dark blue with scarlet piping. There were the auxiliary nursing services, the women wardens, and other organisations such as the Women's Voluntary Service, in their distinctive green uniform with red decorations.

Yet in the welter of all these women's services there was one section which always aroused my admiration – the section which wore no uniform, but which did most vital and essential work at the benches of our war factories, and those thousands who gave part time to release others for the full war effort.

Neither let us forget the thousands of hard-working and patient housewives and mothers who so wonderfully kept the wheels of domestic life turning sweetly.

Aye, they were all a grand lot. There was a job for everyone, and Plymouth women responded to the call in force and with enthusiasm. If there were dodgers, they were a meagre minority. They can be left to their consciences.

Sometimes we were perhaps inclined to wonder how all this woman labour would be sorted out when the war was over. They had assailed every one of man's citadels. They were definitely in man's domain. But it is not my task here to anticipate the future; simply to pay my tribute to their tremendous contribution to the war effort.

Yet Plymouth did not believe in all work and no play. People made the most of their periods of leisure. At the Plymouth end of the city the big cinemas marvellously escaped the wholesale devastation all around them. Those modern buildings like the Royal, Odeon, and Gaumont, and the "ever faithful" Palace Theatre, received only slight damage and were able to continue their full programmes within a short time of the heavy raids in 1941. But at the Devonport end such popular old houses of entertainment as the Hippodrome, the modernised Electric, and the old Alhambra – formerly the Metropole – were destroyed, leaving the Forum in Fore Street, badly damaged but repairable, to carry on.

The surviving houses, with their tremendous seating capacity, did their work well. Plymouth was still able to enjoy first-class cinema entertainment, despite the loss of some seven cinemas, large and small, in the 1941 raids. We were able to see all the best films.

Top left opposite page: the NFS ladies training at Bickleigh. Middle, boys and girls in uniform. Bottom, Inspection time. This page, top, the Odeon, cinema and concert venue, survives. Middle, American bandleader, Glenn Miller plays one of his last ever concerts (at the Odeon) signs autographs for fans. Bottom, a couple read the posters outside the Royal Cinema, another Blitz survivor that had opened just before the war.

The greatest enterprise was shown by Mrs. Hoyle, the owner of the Palace Theatre. Traditionally a variety house in the old music-hall sense, it broadened its programme to cater for all tastes. For instance, we were able to enjoy the Gilbert and Sullivan light operatic gems by the famous D'Oyly Carte Company, a week of Noel Coward's popular plays, with the personal appearance of that great artiste – remember how at the close of each of his performances he came before the curtain and honoured citizens by reciting Clemence Dane's delightful tribute to Plymouth's war-time courage, "Plymouth Hoe" – Richard Tauber with his glorious voice, in Old Chelsea, a week of classical music by the National Philharmonic Orchestra, with famous guest artistes either conducting or contributing, and visits by the International Polish Ballet.

I know that Mrs. Hoyle went out of her way to secure these great performances, because she knew the tonic effect they would have on a people which had had such a raw deal in the war's holocaust. If ever there was any doubt as to whether Plymouth was sufficiently classically-minded to appreciate such entertainment it was well and truly dispelled by the way in which audiences booked in advance and packed the theatre. Those doubts had existed, but the experiences pointed very clearly that Plymouth did merit in the "scheme of things to come" a first-class theatre for the best of the national entertainment. Plymouth can look back with considerable gratitude on what the Palace management did to bring pleasure to the battered life of the city.

Neither let us forget that almost throughout the winter months of the war Mrs. Hoyle placed the theatre at the disposal of the authorities every Sunday night free of charge, and the staff gave its services, in order that there should be free concerts for the Forces.

Plymouth took its war-time pleasures happily. The sun still shone in the hearts and minds of the people to a wonderful degree. They did not sit down and weep in the midst of their ruins, and they were never averse to snatching a full measure of diversion when the chance came.

There were plenty of dances for the young folk, and quite a happy feature was the introduction after the heavy raids of the alfresco dancing on the Hoe promenade on summer evenings. It was a sight to stir the heart, and it was one which prompted Clemence Dane to compose the moving lines of "Plymouth Hoe". There were occasions when such distinguished visitors as the late Duke of Kent – he had developed a sincere affection for Plymouth, as Plymouth had for him – and Lord and Lady Astor were happy minglers with these dancing crowds. How this spirit reflected the mood of the people! Drake played his historic game of bowls while waiting for the enemy; the twentieth-century people of Plymouth danced while waiting for the German air attacks!

Dancing on the Hoe. Right Lady Astor steps out with a sailor.

There were gala days, too, when Plymouth had the company of Their Majesties the King and Queen, when Mr. and Mrs. Churchill came, when other distinguished visitors from the Colonies, from America, and from the Allied countries came and saw and marvelled. There were the returns of H.M.S. Ajax and H.M.S. Exeter in all the glory of their victory in the naval battle of the River Plate; there were days when we had ceremonial parades of the Civil Defence services and the Armed Forces. Plymouth reacted to these occasions in a manner which truly reflected the unquenchable flame that burned within the hearts of her citizens.

There was sport, too, which gave glimpses of happy days gone by and, we hoped, of even happier days to come. The great football clubs had gone out of existence with the start of the war. Plymouth Argyle and the excited Home Park crowds became only a memory, but often an old-time argument over some outstanding incident of a specific match would burst into flame.

Home Park was one of the targets when the Nazis wreaked their fury on the city in 1941. It so happened that the grandstands were packed with furniture salvaged from the houses damaged in the earlier raids. What an appalling bonfire it all made as the raiders' incendiary bombs got their hold and the high explosives dropped into the furnace to blast what was not burnt!

The Plymouth Argyle headquarters were a sorry mess after that onslaught. The great grandstand, stretching the length of one side of the ground, with its offices, dressing-rooms, and training rooms underneath, was reduced to a shambles.

For a while the grass grew long and rank on that once well-kept pitch where we had watched twinkling feet and quick brains match their skill in the national game. Then the game got a small measure of revival through the formation of the Plymouth City Club and the Plymouth United Club. Some good games were seen against Service teams, which often included players from the greatest professional clubs in the country. But the old keen competitive spirit of Plymouth Argyle in League football was dead, at least for the war.

Then one day in 1943 there was a rather sad procession into Home Park, and the ashes of Mr. Robert Jack – Bob Jack to the football world – for so many years the manager, were scattered over the ground he had known and loved. Mr. Jack had given up the management of the club a year or two before the war and had gone to live in London. He remembered Home Park only as he left it; the well-kept home of a famous club. He never saw the shambles which the enemy bombs made of it.

The well-known Rugby clubs, Plymouth Albion at Beacon Park, and Devonport Services at The Rectory also put up the shutters when war broke out. They, too, became silent memorials to happier days.

But Rugby football was kept alive in the highest fashion by the Royal Naval Engineering College at Keyham, and several first-class games were seen there each season. The College team was never at greater strength than in the years 1941-42-43, and many well-known international players serving in the district were seen In the teams which opposed them.

Another club which immediately closed down for the war was the Plymouth Cricket Club at Peverell Park. This, I think, was rather a pity, because there were more cricketers than ever in the district through the Services, and quite a number of the local players were still about. A cricket match on a pleasant Saturday afternoon was a welcome diversion, and we were grateful for the fact that a good programme of fixtures was available at the Ford Park ground of Plymouth College.

A new feature in the local world of sport which was introduced into the district was the American baseball. This was played by the American soldiers stationed in the garrison in such large numbers from the summer of 1943, but the game had only a very limited popular public attraction.

This was because the game is not played in normal times in this country, at least, by the British. But just as it is said that the Scotsman always packs a football in his bag for a "kick about" wherever there is a bit of waste ground to be found, so the Americans seem to pack their baseball kit.

When the American Army became such a substantial part of the garrison in 1943 they did their best to educate the citizens in the matter of baseball. They had a first-class side known as the Plymouth Yankees, and they played regularly at the Pennycross Greyhound Stadium on Saturday evenings. The "education" process was helped by a running commentary and explanation of the finer points of the game through loud-speakers as play proceeded. With typical generosity the Americans gave the "gate" to local charities. But I don't think baseball, fast and exciting as it is, will ever oust our national football.

The school that stayed put, providing regular sporting entertainment Plymouth College remained at Ford Park throughout the war. Above, an big crowd for a schoolboy game. Below the 1942 cross country starts off.

CIVIC LEADERSHIP

Future generations will no doubt ask who were the people on whose shoulders rested the responsibility of "running Plymouth" during the war years. The responsibilities were heavy, especially when Plymouth became a front-line town.

The city was fortunate in its choice of leaders. It has always been said that the occasion finds the man. This applied to our city, for never was inspiring leadership, influence, and personality more desired than in the many anxious months through which Plymouth passed.

When war broke out there was general agreement that politics as far as municipal government was concerned should be relegated to the background "for the duration", leaving a "work together" unity for the common end. Up to that time the three parties – Conservative, Liberal, and Labour – had had an understanding regarding the office of Lord Mayor. They took the office in turn.

On September 3, 1939, when the war storm broke over the world, the Lord Mayor was Mr. G.S. Scoble, a Labour member of the City Council, and he completed his term of office on November 9 of that year. For two months in the early anxious days of the war, when there was so much initial work to be done, Mr. Scoble worthily upheld the highest traditions of the office, and he was energetically supported by his wife in the office of Lady Mayoress.

Left, Lord Astor with the Duchess of Kent, May 24 1940. Above, his predecessor as Mayor, GS Scoble with the Duchess on an earlier visit.

He was, however, the last for five years of what I might call the politically-elected Lord Mayors. The leaders of all three parties looked around for the man who would typify unity at the head.

Their choice immediately fell on Lord Astor, and to the general gratification the unanimous invitation was at once accepted, which meant, of course, that his wife, the irrepressible Lady Astor, Member of Parliament for the Sutton Division of Plymouth since 1919, would be the Lady Mayoress.

Viscount and Viscountess Astor chosen as Plymouth's Mayor and Lady Mayoress

Lord Astor's election at the Mayor Choosing on November 9, 1939, in the historic Guildhall, was a memorable, colourful, and happy occasion. The city without distinction of class, creed, or politics, wholeheartedly acclaimed the choice. Lord Astor at once appointed Alderman W.J.W. Modley as the Deputy Lord Mayor.

It was a date to be remembered, for it marked the establishment of a combination at the head of Plymouth's civic life which was to provide the city's five hundred years of incorporation with a new mayoral record. It was the combination of Lord and Lady Astor as Lord Mayor and Lady Mayoress and Alderman and Mrs. Modley as the Deputy Lord Mayor and Deputy Lady Mayoress – a combination which was to last almost for the duration of the war.

In the trials and tribulations which beset Plymouth in the ensuing grim years it was a stimulating thing to have Lord Astor at the head of affairs. He gave Plymouth every ounce of his great ability, his energy, his tremendous influence in high places – yes, and a very big slice of his health. The strain was heavy, and twice he had to take spells of several weeks' duration completely away from the work and the worry to recuperate his health. That strain of being the civic head was heavy enough in itself but when it is recalled that Lord and Lady Astor never neglected their important Parliamentary and other duties, the measure of the demand on their time and health can well be appreciated.

During these very difficult years, and especially after Plymouth became, as Lady Astor used to describe it, "the worst blitzed city in the country", the influence which Lord Astor was able to bring to bear in responsible and important quarters will never be fully known among the ordinary public. Only those charged with the responsibility of the municipal government knew the true assessment and value of Lord Astor's work.

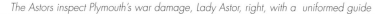

The Astors inspect Plymouth's war damage, Lady Astor, right, with a uniformed guide

In the course of my newspaper work it was my privilege to often "contact" Lord Astor on a variety of public matters, and it gave me a great opportunity of appreciating the depth of his work and his tremendous sincerity in helping Plymouth.

By the great influence he was able to bring to bear, by the complete determination he showed, by his foresight and wisdom, he was able to ensure that the city gained and maintained her rightful place, particularly in regard to the consideration to which she was entitled after her blitz ordeal.

I always felt that Lord Astor was looking at the then distant horizon and in his mind saw the new Plymouth, the new Plymouth "worth fighting for". One of the occasions on which I saw him most excited was after he had spent the greater part of a day going through the secret plans for the re-planning and re-building of the post-war Plymouth. It was safe to say that he was positively "bubbling with excitement".

And who will deny that in Lady Astor he had a faithful first-lieutenant? Who will deny that she ever tired of "advertising" Plymouth? There were times when in her criticism of things which she thought were wrong she was bold to the point of daring. She often drew vitriolic criticism on her own head, but no one could ever deny her loyalty to Plymouth or the sincerity of her actions. It was once said, and not without reason, that when Lady Astor died the name of Plymouth would be found engraved upon her heart. Next to her own native and beloved Virginia there was no place for which she had greater affection. Often when I heard complimentary people try and say what Plymouth owed to her she would retort by saying "I owe everything to Plymouth", and she was sincere.

Be all that as it may, everyone will agree that she was a tireless worker for Plymouth, and her admiration for the courage of the ordinary people in the heavy raids was something which came from deep in her heart.

When distinguished personages, even that popular member of the Royal Family the late Duke of Kent, came as the guests of the Lord Mayor and Lady Mayoress, nothing delighted Her Ladyship more than to break away from the formalities and take them on a tour through the poor parts of the city through some of the back streets, through the crowded market, where she could show them the ordinary people and let them talk to them.

Lord and Lady Astor were not content to be missionaries for Plymouth wherever they went, but the list of distinguished people they brought "to see for themselves" was limitless. Through the doors of their home at 3 Elliot Terrace, with the Hoe promenade in the immediate foreground, and the broad expanse of the Sound and Channel unfolding beyond, there was an endless stream of war-time notabilities, mostly British and American, but with a fair sprinkling of representatives of the Allied nations. Lord and Lady Astor always gave practical expression to their determination to promote Anglo-American friendship. They regarded it as the basis of future world security.

Royalty in the personages of Their Majesties the King and Queen and other members of the Royal family, especially the late Duke of Kent, famous politicians, including Mr. Winston Churchill when Prime Minister, the Archbishop of Canterbury, the Lord Mayor of London, ambassadors, diplomats, well-known authors and journalists of international reputation, town-planners, and many others who had any contribution to make to the war effort or social advancement, were all induced to come to Plymouth.

And when they came it was no mere fleeting visit to see the highlights of a badly-blitzed city they were brought into close personal contact with those responsible for city management and with the everyday lives of the citizens.

The Duke of Kent with Lord Astor inspecting Head Wardens on Plymouth Hoe.

Around the luncheon and dinner table at Elliot Terrace there were many informal chats which were to have material bearing on the future life of Plymouth. I remember one such occasion which describes what I mean. Mr. W. S. Morrison, who at that time was Minister for Town and Country Planning, came to hear what was being done regarding the replanning of the city. He spent the best part of the day with the Lord Mayor and officials, seeing areas, seeing plans, hearing the proposals. I wanted to get a statement from him for The Western Morning News, particularly in relation to certain legislation which the Government was being pressed to pass regarding the acquisition of sites for development. Lord Astor came to the door. With a handshake and characteristic smile he said, "Come in. We are just having tea and an informal chat about things. You'll be able to hear for yourself." I went in and joined the party, and when it was over I said to Mr. Morrison that I wanted a statement. He forthwith wrote it out himself and handed it across the table. It was just the summary I wanted. That was the way Lord Astor worked. Always behind the scenes there was continuous activity for public welfare, of which the ordinary people knew little save when they saw results.

Not the least of the war-time responsibilities which fell to Plymouth's war-time Lord Mayor and Lady Mayoress were those which charged them with the care, welfare, and entertainment of the thousands of Service sojourners, both British and Allied, which the war brought to the city. That word "welfare" was to assume vast proportions as the years passed, and Lord and Lady Astor were always exercised as to what should and could be done. Many welfare schemes, hostels, entertainments like concerts, dances, and parties owed their inception to suggestion and practical help given by these civic leaders.

Neither can we forget the enormous wave of sympathy and the generous gifts of money and in kind which flowed to Plymouth during her great agony from the other side of the Atlantic. Behind that lay the personalities of Lord and Lady Astor.

At the same time no record of Plymouth's war-time Lord Mayoralty would be complete without due tribute to the untiring work of Alderman and Mrs. Modley as the Deputy Lord Mayor and Deputy Lady Mayoress. Whenever Lord and Lady Astor were away from Plymouth, as was often the case, with their Parliamentary and other duties, these deputies assumed the mantles and discharged the Mayoral obligations — they were many and varied — in a manner which won for them not only gratitude but affection. Lord and Lady Astor paid frequent tribute to the energetic support of their deputies. It was well deserved.

As far as the civil management of Plymouth was concerned it was, as usual, vested in the permanent Corporation officials under the direction of the City Council. In this connection the various departmental heads found their duties enormously increased by extra responsibilities imposed by war-time regulations and conditions.

As I have already indicated, the City Council decided in a general way to side-track politics for the duration of the war. The ugly head did, however rear on occasions, but for the most part the truce was honoured.

An interesting feature was that the members of the City Council served "for the duration" without re-election after their normal term of office had expired. In other words, there were no Council elections. Vacancies which occurred were filled by nomination from the party to which the former member belonged. So the balance of the political parties

Lord Astor with the First Lord of theAdmiralty

The City Council meet in the Museum, with newly elected Mayor HG Mason centre, his deputy on his left and Town Clerk, Colin Campbell on his right.

remained static.

The various Committees of the Council continued to function regarding municipal business and management. There was, however, one important addition. This was the War Emergency Committee, which, as its name implied, was wholly concerned with war matters as they affected the city, particularly civil defence. This latter item became the most expensive in the city's yearly budget, involving an annual expenditure of about £600,000.

For the first three years this Committee, with the Lord Mayor always ex-officio, comprised the leaders of the three political parties in the City Council: Alderman L.R. Dunstan, Conservative; Alderman J. Churchward, Labour; Alderman Solomon Stephens, Liberal. Later Alderman Stephens retired, and his place as the Liberal representative was taken by Alderman G.W. Cummings. Then, in January 1944, Alderman Dunstan died, and his place as the leader of the Conservatives was taken by Alderman Sir Clifford Tozer, and on the Emergency

Committee by Alderman Modley.

In passing, it must be mentioned how great was the loss to public life caused by the death of Alderman Dunstan. He was the type that the city could ill afford to lose, particularly at this momentous stage, when there was so much leadership required, not only in the immediate management but in future planning. Almost immediately came another loss to public life by the death of Alderman Churchward. Like Alderman Dunstan, he was a former Mayor and had given great service to the city. His position as leader and member of the Emergency Committee was taken by Alderman H. G. Mason.

The civic life continued to flow, with Lord Astor at the helm until the Lord Mayor Choosing in November, 1944. Then the record was broken. There were many who felt that Lord Astor should have carried on until peace was proclaimed, but it was decided to make a change, and the honour fell on Alderman Mason of the Labour Party and an employee in Devonport Dockyard. His election was the reward for many years of service to the city.

Incidentally, Lord Astor's fade-out from civic life was the subject of some controversy. When it became obvious that he was to be no longer Lord Mayor there were many who felt that his association with the City Council should be continued. To that end Alderman F. C. Roach offered to resign his aldermanic seat if Lord Astor would accept. But immediately the ugly political head reared up. This was a Conservative aldermanic seat, and the party would only agree to Lord Astor taking it if he would come in under the party label. This he very definitely declined to do. He, however, agreed to continue as a co-opted member of the Reconstruction Committee, which was dealing with the replanning of the city. This position, of course, precluded him from taking part in Council discussion of and voting on the replanning.

There was no change in the political representation of Plymouth during the war, the three members being Lady Astor for Sutton Division, Mr. L. Hore-Belisha for Devonport Division, and Col. Henry Guest for

Colin Campbell, Town Clerk and ARP Controller, pictured (centre) at Pounds House.

Drake Division.

The chief official in the management of Plymouth was, of course, the Town Clerk (Mr. Colin Campbell), and he had the added responsibility of being the ARP Controller with all its important duties relating to Air Raid Precautions. Bombed out of the imposing municipal offices facing the Guildhall Square in the 1941 blitz, with a, loss of all his records, his department found a new home at Pounds House, in the north-west corner of Central Park. It was here that the Air Raid Precautions control was established – the nerve-centre of all activity during raids – when the original control centres under the Guildhall and Devonport Market were burnt out. Plymouth was fortunate in its war-time chief officials, and not the least in the cool, level-headed, courteous, and efficient Town Clerk. Nor should it be forgotten the part which Mrs. Campbell played in the many war-time organisations and social activities of the city.

Finance in war-time, especially in the midst of such upsetting influences as Plymouth experienced, must have been a positive headache.

But I never once found the City Treasurer (Mr. John Ainsworth) unduly perturbed by the tangle of things. Perhaps, too, it was that I never fully appreciated the extent of the Treasury responsibilities until, in the fifth year of the war, I happened to have a long interview with Mr. Ainsworth, and he took me behind the scenes and let me in on many financial secrets. The financial business of a city the size of Plymouth is a big enough job in peace-time when things flow normally, but when it has been jolted so badly by war's vicissitudes the position to the layman becomes bewildering. In that interview I learnt to appreciate the complications of the Treasury – rates imposition and collection, wages for the thousands of Corporation permanent and temporary staffs and ARP personnel, superannuation, income-tax deductions, salaries made up to personnel on service, claims for war damage to Corporation property, and, in fact, the whole range of Corporation finance.

The Treasury at the east end of the burnt-out Guildhall was not wholly destroyed by the 1941 air attack. Three rooms were affected, They were in the basement, and a lot of damage was done to records. The Treasury was, however, able to continue in occupation, as it did on two other occasions when damage was sustained. One of the biggest losses sustained by the Treasury was when the Old Guildhall in Whimple Street was destroyed, with all the Valuation Lists for the

City and Stores records.

With the destruction of so many properties in the raids there was a disastrous drop in rate revenue, so much so that had the remaining ratepayers to find the money the rate would have had to be increased from 10s. 4d. in the pound to 15s. 6d. in the pound. Representations were made to the Government, and they immediately came to the assistance of the distressed city by making good the deficiency and continuing to do so until such time as the rate could be restored: The yearly grant amounted to £225,000, and this enabled the rate to remain fixed at 10s. 4d. in the pound. Of that sum 75 per cent was by way of grant, the balance of 25 per cent an interest-free loan.

In addition to being the City Treasurer Mr Ainsworth was also the Food Officer for the city, and in this he proved as fine an organiser of the feeding of the city as he was in high finance. Plymouth never went hungry – no, not even in those dire days after the devastation in 1941, when everything was so badly disorganised. The feeding of Plymouth, the British Restaurants, the emergency feeding was a fine piece of organisation.

Another important office was that of City Engineer and Surveyor, held by Mr. J. Paton Watson, and this, too, involved heavy responsibilities and organisation. Then again, Mr. Watson was one of those officials who was seriously concerned with the future planning of Plymouth. In conjunction with the famous national town planner Professor Patrick Abercrombie, he produced the Abercrombie-Watson report and plan for the rebuilding after the war. He was a man with bold vision in regard to these matters.

The health of the city, a most important matter, as well as the casualty services connected with Air Raid Precautions, was in the capable hands of the Medical Officer of Health (Dr. T. Peirson). His department was bombed out of the Stonehouse Town Hall, and then found new quarters at Seven Trees. Various hospitals also came under Dr. Peirson's control, and, like the heads of other departments, he knew what it was to have his staff, especially the doctors, reduced to saturation point by the greater national calls.

The Water Engineer, until just before hostilities ceased, was Mr. Alan Atkinson, who combined with that office the duties of Fuel Officer, the Electrical Engineer was Mr. H. Midgley, and the Gas Engineer was Mr. F. Blackburn. For the first three years of the war Mr. W.A. Clegg was Education Secretary. He was succeeded by Dr. Andrew Scot-

Lord Astor surveys the model for the reconstruction with City Engineer Paton-Watson. Below, the Minister of Health, Mr E Brown, tours the bombed city with the Town Clerk.

land. The responsible position of Transport Manager and Engineer was held by Mr. Clement Jackson, who was also in command of that

Members of the Special Police Reserve of Plymouth being inspected by Mr GS Lowe (Chief Constable) and Mr F Edgar Bowden (Commandant) at Greenbank. Below, the Matron of the RN Hospital (Miss DW Beale) being presented to HRH the Duchess of Kent, with Admiral Sir Martin E Dunbar-Nasmith, watching, far left with stick. Bottom, The Duchess of Kent, with the C-i-C, Sir Charles and Lady Forbes, at Mount Wise.

department's detached unit of the Home Guard.

Plymouth had the rather unique experience of having three wartime Chief Constables, When war broke out Mr. G.S. Lowe held the appointment, but in 1941 he became Chief Constable of Sheffield and was succeeded at Plymouth by his Deputy, Mr. W.T. Hutchings, who had served all his career in the Force, Within a year, however, he was taken ill, and after some months died. The appointment then fell to Mr. J.F. Skittery, a Divisional Inspector of the Metropolitan Police, a much younger man, who came with a first-class record. Under the last two Chief Constables Mr. J. Hingston was Chief Superintendent and Deputy Chief.

In view of Plymouth's very close association with the Services and the part which the port, garrison, and air station played in the events of the war, the record of leadership will not be complete without reference to those who were at the head of those bodies.

As far as the Navy was concerned Plymouth had three distinguished officers as Commander-in-Chief. When war broke out Admiral Sir Martin Dunbar-Nasmith, V C., was in command, and in 1940 he was succeeded by Admiral of the Fleet Sir Charles Forbes. His tenure of office expired in the autumn of 1943, and he was succeeded by Admiral Sir Ralph Leatham.

The Admiral Superintendent of Devonport Dockyard was Vice Admiral Sir Arthur N. Dowding. He held the appointment throughout the war, and it was in the New Year honours of 1945 that he received his knighthood.

For the greater part of the war the military control of Plymouth rested with Colonel G. Thomson as Garrison Commander. This was, of course, an appointment which held serious responsibilities regarding the defence of Plymouth and the very extensive plans relating to meeting possible invasion.

The Air Officer Commanding for the area was, until 1943, Air Vice-Marshal G.R. Bromet, who, when he left, was appointed to an important position at the Azores, then recently loaned by the Portuguese for use by the Allies. In the latter part of the war the Air Officer Commanding the area was Air Vice-Marshall. R. Maynard.

Regional authority played a big part in war-time Plymouth as it did in other parts of the country. The South-West Region into which Plymouth came had as its chief at the Bristol headquarters Sir Hugh Elles, and he had as his two deputies Major-General G.L. Lindsay and

Mr. H.M. Medland, the latter a member of Plymouth City Council, a former Labour Mayor of the city and an employee in Devonport Dockyard.
There was also a Ministry of Information branch at Plymouth, and the Man-Power Board for the south-west had its headquarters at Burleigh House, Peverell, with Mr. W.H.J. Priest as the Chief Officer.
The Plymouth station of the British Broadcasting Corporation was in

Right, His Majesty the King, with President Truman, and the US Secretary of State (Mr Byrnes), and Sir Ralph Leatham, on board HMS 'Renown' in Plymouth Sound. Below, forced out of the Guildhall and Council Chambers, the Council meet in Methodist Central Hall, Plymouth.

SOCIAL LIFE

What was the social life of the city like in those changed conditions brought about by war? That is another question which generations to come might well be expected to ask.

The war brought limitations, if not the end, to certain normal peace-time activities, and with the widespread destruction and general up-heaval caused by the 1941 blitz, people found themselves flung willy-nilly and with some degree of violence out of their accustomed grooves. People and friends became widely scattered. Those with whom you had been accustomed to associate socially almost every day, just passed out of your circle. You did not meet them again for months.

These separations were sudden and violent, and the reasons were twofold; firstly because so many people had to find new homes and in the scramble had found sanctuary here, there, or anywhere away from the city, and thus had had to build entirely new social circles, and secondly because so many of the social centres, clubs in particular, were wiped out of existence in the war storm which swept the city.

Take the number of clubs that were destroyed, and the second point I have made will not need any greater emphasis. These included the Royal Western Yacht Club facing Plymouth Hoe, the Plymouth Club in Lockyer Street, the Masonic Club in Princess Square, the Conservative Club in Princess Square, the Devonport Conservative Club in Fore Street, the Devonport Liberal Club in Chapel Street, the Minima Yacht Club on the Promenade Pier, the Promenade Pier itself, the Central YMCA in Bedford Street, the YWCA in Lockyer Street, the Devon County Social and Billiards Club in George Street, the Ballard Boys' Club at Millbay, the Sutton Division Conservative Association headquarters in Lockyer Street, the Drake Division Conservative Association headquarters in Bedford Street, the Drake Chambers in Drake Circus. Then, again, there were all the numerous social centres which were attached to the churches, the Guildhall, and such well-known hotels as the Royal, with its popular Assembly Rooms, the Westminster, the Farley, the Lockyer. Altogether about 150 public-houses were destroyed, and whatever one might say for or against the trade, these houses, great or small, were part and parcel of Plymouth social life.

Left and above the Pier on Plymouth Hoe, a popular resort for over sixty years.

Some of the clubs and other organisations restarted in fresh premises as soon as they could, if only to keep them "alive" until there could be complete re-establishment after the war. Others just remained in abeyance.

The Royal Western Yacht Club, above, stood alongside the Grand Hotel prior to the Blitz. To the right the Plymouth Social Club just off Princess Square in Notte Street.

The destruction of the Guildhall, the Stonehouse Town Hall, and the Royal Hotel robbed the city of three of its main halls for social functions. Another very serious blow to the social life of the place was the total destruction of the Public Free Library which was gutted by fire together with something like 80,000 volumes, many of them of great value, the Proprietary Library in Cornwall Street, with hundreds of priceless volumes, and the Athenaeum, in which Plymouth Institution housed its valuable antiquarian collections.

Even the City Fathers were homeless. The imposing Council Chamber was reduced to a burnt-out shell by the raging fire which swept through the Municipal Offices in the Guildhall Square. With it also went the Lord Mayor's Parlour, the Lady Mayoress's Parlour, and the many well-appointed Committee Rooms. In passing, it might be mentioned that the only part of this block of municipal offices which escaped destruction was the Muniment Room, in which so many valuable documents were kept. The Lord Mayor's chain of office, which dates from the time of Drake, the Lady Mayoress's chain, and the maces, were fortunately all saved.

The City Fathers found a temporary war-time home in one of the largest rooms at the Museum and Art Gallery. They met here regularly for their monthly meetings, but one must confess that the atmosphere, in more ways than one, was not the same as in the old impressive Council Chamber. The Muniment Room was cleaned out and renovated to make a Committee Room, and another Committee Room was reconstructed amid the ruins at the east end of the building.

The Town Clerk's department found a new home at Pounds House in Central Park. This former mansion, which became the property of the Corporation when Central Park was purchased for the City, came in quite handy for this and other purposes during the war. It became the main control during air raids, the "nerve centre", as it were, of the entire ARP organisation which sprang into activity the moment raids started.

One well recalls the pre-war criticism which so often cropped up as to the use to which Pounds House might be put. It was going almost derelict in those days. It certainly became a useful asset during the war.

With the loss of the Stonehouse Town Hall the Public Health and the Water Engineer's departments became homeless. The former found new quarters at Seven Trees, a large private house standing in its own grounds near Beaumont Park, and the Water Engineer went into Portland Square.

The loss of the Guildhall, and the consequent deprivation of its use for all that variety of civic and public functions which grace the normal year, was the most serious. Fortunately, there remained one building with the requisite available accommodation – the comparatively new Central Hall, which had taken the place of the old Ebenezer Church in Saltash Street. So it was that important meetings, as when Sir William Beveridge came down to speak about his famous "free from want" social scheme, when Professor Joad, of the BBC Brains' Trust, gave a lecture, and such historic ceremonies as the annual Mayor Choosing, found accommodation in this building.

Such organisations as the Plymouth Mercantile Association, Devonport Mercantile Association, the Plymouth Chamber of Commerce, the Rotary Club, and others, all continued what might be called their business activities, but dropped most of their social events, such as annual dinners and kindred gatherings. Such things did not seem to quite fit in with the war years. It was as if people were all the time conscious of the bigger calls and the more important claims on their money and their time. But at the back of their minds there ever lingered that "celebration to come", when the lights would once more blaze both indoors and out, when the war passions had died down, and mankind was once again in possession of freedom to work and to play as the mood dictated.

Meanwhile Plymouth, like other parts of the country, got on with the job of war, realising that the sooner that was ended the sooner would everyone be able to gather up the lost threads of happy social intercourse.

Beaumont House in the bottom left-hand corner of the park and Seven Trees, another large private house towards the top on the other side of the road heading to Lipson.

CHANGED FACE OF PLYMOUTH

Apart from the actual mutilation which was caused by the raids, nothing served to change and disfigure the face of Plymouth during the war more than when the ornamental railings and gates of private houses, public buildings, and parks were taken in 1942 for the national melting-pot.

The call went through the country for every ounce of scrap metal that could be salvaged. Guns, munitions, bombs, shells, tanks, and countless other war equipment were the priority claim.

I do not know whether Plymouth was any better ornamented by railings and gates than other places, but the fact remained that it was one of the first places where this salvage drive took place. From street to street, road to road, terrace to terrace, park to park, the workers

King Gardens in 1940, note the railings still in place - almost. Left the Hoe Bandstand is scrapped for its metal.

went. As fast as the railings were cut from their bases and the gates lifted from their hinges so they were taken away for transit to the great smelting centres. There was no sentiment in this business; neither was there any option. They were just taken.

There was slight compensation payable after the war, if the owner so insisted, but I do not know of any Plymouth people who were not ready givers, even if there was at times the privilege of a "moan".

After all, it was not exactly a very heartening sight to see the despoilers at work on the fancy railings which had for so many years been an attractive ornamental defence of your front garden to the ravages of every passing dog, and watch calmly the smashing with cold chisel and sledge-hammer those decorations which had given a touch of "class" to your road.

Yet Plymouth was a city of cheerful givers. I think that perhaps at the back of the "generosity" was the feeling that those railings and gates would one day be hitting back for the wanton destruction that had been caused by the enemy raids. And, incidentally, many hundreds of tons of splendid steel were salvaged from the blitzed buildings in the city.

I remember standing beside one of the city's "cheerful givers" one day as we watched a military procession pass during a war weapons "Week". A monstrous tank came lumbering along. He watched it for a moment, and then with a grim smile remarked, "I wonder how much of my gates and railings went into that?" Probably none, but it gave him a kick to think so.

Looking back, one remembers how naked some of the streets and parks looked without their railings. But we got used to it, as we did to the far worse sights which were ever before our eyes in a city mauled as Plymouth was. After all, it was a small price to pay for the building up of our war resources, for which every scrap of metal was vital.

Another wartime feature came from the "grow more food" campaign. It was wonderful to see what vegetables were produced from even the smallest patches which previously had grown nothing more than carefully-tended grass and flowers. Even many of the neat little front gardens of proud suburbia had tomatoes, beans, and lettuce where once flourished the flowers. It was, perhaps a small contribution in the great pool of the national demand. Nevertheless, it reflected something more than a mere expression of patriotism.

Plymouth householders, by making good use of the small plots attached to their houses and by more than doubling the number of allotments provided by the Corporation, did a lot to help the food problem.

Top, sorting salvage. Bottom, Land Army girls pulling turnips. Right, off duty Rescue Squad preparing Hoe soil for vegetables.

Vegetables were grown even on the historic Hoe – probably the first time in history. The fairly large patch selected was near the spot where Drake was supposed to have played his famous game of bowls while waiting for the Spanish Armada. Previously part of the grass-covered slope facing Citadel Road, it was ploughed and tilled with great success by the Corporation gardeners. Many tons of potatoes were grown each year in the Corporation public parks and in grounds attached to hospitals, while in the Corporation greenhouses, which in days of peace provided the seedlings for the flowerbeds and the floral decorations for the "great occasions", heavy crops of tomatoes were grown each year.

All these things seemed to change the face of Plymouth tremendously in those war years, even apart from the disfigurements caused by the raids.

These changes, like others more drastic and violent, were, however, quietly accepted.

There were many others. Take, for example, the salvage. Like other places in the country, Plymouth was soon to realise the valuable "waste" that in previous years had been scrapped. Paper, tins, rags, rubber, metals – these were the by-products which were salvaged in thousands of tons; even the grass in the parks was constantly cut, dried, and baled for sale as feeding stuffs. Even these did not complete the salvage efforts. In every street the Corporation placed refuse bins, and into these householders placed all their kitchen and table edible waste. It was valuable pig food; indeed, the Corporation themselves maintained a piggery in the old farm in Central Park. From all these sources there came a considerable revenue to the assistance of the rates.

But its value did not altogether lie in the financial gain. Small though these salvage efforts might have looked when applied to individual homes, the accumulation from the entire city was enormous, and in the course of twelve months ran into thousands of tons. Paper, tin, rags, bones, rubber, metals, were all kept separate from the ordinary rubbish of the refuse bin, and the collectors did their part in conscientious collection. Indeed, it paid them to do so – they got a bonus.

A fuller appreciation of what this meant can be gathered from the fact that to the end of 1944 the value of salvage recovered and sold by the City Engineer's and Surveyor's Department totalled nearly £200,000. Most of this was from household edible waste.

SELF-RECOVERY

The raids on Plymouth during the war years form a separate story. Yet, I think – after the bombs had fallen, the guns were silent, and tragedy hung so poignantly over the city – it was then, in the aftermath, that another kind of splendid courage was shown. So much was irretrievably lost in the devastation, that one wondered how the threads of life could be again gathered. Yet they were.

The gathering of these threads of broken lives was a marvel in self-recovery. How they conducted themselves – "managed" would, perhaps, be the more applicable word – when deprived of so many of the ordinary everyday amenities, public services like water, heat, and light, was a striking example of resourcefulness, enterprise, and often ingenuity.

The women of Plymouth were never beaten. There were long periods after the raids when large sections of the community were without the use of the "tap". We knew what it meant to be without all those conveniences which time had somehow made us accept without questioning the why and the wherefore. We had all got so used to simply turning on the tap for gas and water, and pressing the switch for electricity, that we had never seriously thought we might one day be without it and have to improvise to overcome the inconveniences.

I well recall that many days after we had been deprived of gas and electricity, the habit was still so strong that I found myself quite involuntarily turning on the tap or pressing down the switch.

But I think we rather prided ourselves on how we managed. It certainly did not get us down. Somehow or other the housewife always managed to produce a meal – and a hot one at that! The improvisation was remarkable, and neighbours "swopped" ideas. Sometimes, when conditions were favourable, ovens were constructed Boy Scout fashion in the garden, and the Womens' Voluntary Service had a team of demonstrators who could make a marvellous oven in the back yard out of a few bricks and some clay. The Primus stove-lucky were the people who had these souvenirs of their happy picnic days in good condition – worked overtime, even electric fires were "converted" and used for frying and boiling. It was really astonishing what could be accomplished when deprived of the ordinary everyday services which we had so come to accept without question.

The feeding of a city after those very heavy raids in 1941 was, however, a pretty serious problem, yet – deprived as we were of what we had regarded as essentials – we were never without our meals.

Adequate feeding was, of course, very necessary, and realising all the difficulties in so many of the homes that the raiders had left standing, the authorities came to the rescue in, I think, quite commendable fashion. Added to this problem of the homes was the fact that there were many hundreds of people who, coming into the city from the surrounding district, had been accustomed to having their midday meals at a cafe or hotel. These places were so wiped out of existence by the destruction of the city centres that there was a complete inadequacy of facilities for meals.

It was this state of affairs that gave birth to the British Restaurants and the emergency feeding centres.

Food and entertainment the fare here in this British Restaurant. Left, the Queen's Flying Food squad in action in Central Park.

Fresh fish is sold from handcarts, meanwhile Mutley becomes the new place to shop.

One of the major problems after the heavy raids, which so completely gutted the main business centres, was the everyday shopping. George Street, Bedford Street, Old Town Street, Cornwall Street, Frankfort Street, Fore Street, Devonport, and a number of other streets, were gone so far as shopping was concerned, and with them went the big stores which had supplied most of the clothing, food, and other necessaries of life. True, some of these had branches in the suburbs. I think there was a lot of credit for the way in which the big firms tackled this extreme position. They did not sit back and reflect on their loss, they just jumped straight in with something akin to a stampede to get in wherever they could to start business again. They seemed to take the view that they were the servants of the public, and it was their job to get going again with the least delay. They wanted to keep that goodwill which in so many cases had been built up in generations of service.

These firms did not fail the public, and let it be said that the authorities helped all they could. It was amazing how so many of the "quart" and "gallon" firms squeezed themselves into pint pots wherever the pint pot presented itself. One thing the authorities did which I thought was full of good common sense was that they allowed people to shop where they liked until things settled down. By that I mean they were not tied down to getting their goods from the particular firms with which they had registered. They had to get the rations on their ration books, either their regular ration books or emergency ration books, but these could be presented at any shop.

Thus it was that in a night the erstwhile "white elephant", Mutley Plain, became the city's main shopping centre, and so it was to continue until the new Plymouth arose.

The immediate effect of the blitzing of the main shopping centres was a scramble for business accommodation in Tavistock Road, North Hill, Mutley Plain, and in the big houses fronting the main road through Mannamead. There must have been a good many awkward covenants in leases and property agreements which went by the board in those frantic days. But "Business as Usual" was the city's slogan. It was interesting to reflect how force of circumstances had at long last brought the "despised and rejected" Mutley Plain into such prominence. Previously it was very largely just a "funnel" through which traffic passed from the residential to the "down town" shopping centre.

The Germans changed all that for us, and henceforth you did your main shopping along Mutley Plain. Never before had the pavements of that thoroughfare been so crowded with shoppers as they were in the post-blitz days.

In the old centre of the city the great firms like Messrs. E. Dingle & Co., Messrs. Spooner & Co., Messrs. Pophams, Messrs. John Yeo & Co., and others, had had their departments concentrated in one great building, or series of adjoining buildings. Now we found them widely scattered from Mannamead to Drake Circus in a whole series of little shops. But they all got going again with wonderful enterprise. It was one of the features of the immediate post-blitz days. There were few, if any, vacant properties left in those areas after the rush. There was no haggling over letting prices. One of the big firms that did manage to retain its scattered departments down near the old centre was Messrs. Spooner & Co. The reason was that they had a flying start over their rivals. They were blitzed out twenty-four hours before the rest. They went up in smoke on the first night of the heavy raids, and they were able to step in and get the first option on a number of "down town" places, which kept them within fairly short distance of their old site. The others had to go farther afield.

Even this amazing transformation straightened itself out in a few days. Customers and firms were soon again in contact, and the whole city settled down to "getting on with life" with amazing adaptability.

Now and again one had to pause and ask, "Let me see, where are So-and-so now?". But throughout all this difficulty the tradespeople did show splendid initiative, and the people a commendable patience. What applied to shops also applied in hundreds of instances to offices.

Solicitors, insurance firms, brokers, accountants, banks, and other such business and commercial firms were burnt out or blasted away in wholesale fashion. But they all managed to squeeze in somewhere. "Carry on" was the invariable rallying cry. And carry on everyone did. The limit of human endurance was truly beyond comprehension.

Temporary shopping facilities are erected in town - welcome to Tin Pan Alley - for small traders. Far right, Marks and Spencer have moved!

NOTABLE EVENTS

It was in the cold grey dawn of January 30, 1940, that hundreds of the citizens, emulating their sixteenth-century ancestors, rushed to the waterside to honour yet another glorious epic of the sea. The cruiser Ajax, first of the British warships that had accounted for the German pocket-battleship Graf Spee in the stirring naval engagement to be known to history as the Battle of the River Plate, had come home.

How the whole nation had been thrilled by that encounter, the tenacity of the smaller British warships in forcing that memorable fight to such a dramatic climax! The British cruisers primarily concerned were the Chatham-manned Ajax, the Devonport-built and Devonport-manned Exeter and the New Zealand Station cruiser Achilles. Plymouth's welcome to its own ship was yet to come, for Exeter was delayed owing to her casualties and serious damage. But here was the Ajax, and she was just as much a part of the British Navy.

For days rumour had been in circulation that the victors of the Graf Spee were on their way home, but for obvious reasons the date and time of the Ajax's arrival were closely guarded secrets. How the German U-boat commanders would have gloated had they been able to "pick up" the Ajax as she steamed steadily through the Western Approaches.

But the voyage was safely accomplished, and dawn revealed the cruiser safe at moorings in Plymouth Sound. She had steamed up Channel and into the security of the heavily-guarded harbour under cover of darkness. The first definite news Plymouth had that the cruiser was in the Sound was when it was announced over the local Rediffusion wireless service. Although the Ajax was an Eastcountry-manned ship, it did not detract from the welcome which was accorded when later in the morning she went up to Devonport Dockyard.

Almost as soon as light was breaking over Staddon the tugs were fussing around her, and soon she was in tow for her passage up harbour.

Crowds were at all the points of vantage along the sea front. The cheering, started by a large party of the Royal Air Force and the Roy-

A Civic reception for the crews of HMS Ajax and HMS Exeter in Guildhall Square

al Australian Air Force on the Mount Batten breakwater, was taken up by the people gathered on the slopes of the Hoe, and carried on like links in a chain from Rusty Anchor to Devil's Point, from Mount Wise to the Dockyard. It was an inspiring homecoming.

Thousands of Dockyardsmen dropped their tools and rushed to the Dockyard sea wall to join in the welcome.

Ajax wore her battle honours proudly. The scars were still visible even to those standing on the foreshore, and there was a salt-water hoariness about her paintwork and rusty patches about her superstructure which told dramatically of her fight not only with the enemy but also with the elements over a long voyage.

One of the features which caught immediate attention was the stunted mainmast; it had been cut in half by a shell from the Graf Spee. It was, incidentally, one of only two shells which struck the cruiser during the engagement. Most of her wounds had been patched up, and in reality the Ajax looked more as if she was just returning from a "dirty trip" than a naval battle which had stirred the whole world.

One of the two shells which struck her was responsible for killing seven men and wounding twenty-two as it sped on what was a freak course through the ship. It was a 11-inch shell from the heavy armament of the Graf Spee. It entered the ship on the port side, passed through the cabin of the captain's secretary through the captain's cabin, through a bulkhead, through one of the barbettes, and finished up in the admiral's cabin, where it exploded.

It was an amazing course, and the damage was considerable.

When the Ajax was approaching the English Channel on her voyage to Plymouth the Commander-in-Chief (Admiral Sir Martin Dunbar-Nasmith, V.C.) signalled a welcome from the officers and men of the Western Area Command, and yet another signal was from the escort ships of the Western Approaches Command.

I had the privilege of being among the first to board the cruiser when she "tied up" alongside the sea wall at the North Yard, and it was here that Plymouth extended its official welcome through the persons of the Lord Mayor (Lord Astor), the Deputy Lord Mayor (Alderman W.J.W. Modley), and the Town Clerk (Mr. Colin Campbell).

Members of the ship's company told their story with characteristic naval modesty, but there was nevertheless an underlying pride in the part the ship had played.

There in the security of Devonport harbour we left her. In a few hours her ship's company were homeward bound for well-earned leave, while at Devonport skilled craftsmen immediately set about the task of repairing the Ajax for further service.

Return of H.M.S. Exeter

The gallant part which the cruiser Exeter played in the battle of the River Plate will always "live" in the annals of the British Navy's great deeds. It was not without tremendous pride that Plymouth anticipated her homecoming. She was in many ways our own ship. Apart from the fact that she bore the name of the "ever faithful" city capital of Devon, she had been built at Devonport by Devonport hands, and she was manned by a Westcountry crew.

It was in the very early hours of February 15, 1940, that she arrived safely within the sanctuary of Plymouth Sound. Like the Ajax, she came in under cover of darkness, and during the latter part of her voyage through the U-boat infested waters of the Western Approaches she had been under close escort. When her anchors were dropped it closed one of the most thrilling chapters in the naval history of this war.

After her part in the memorable engagement, the badly-battered Exeter limped southwards to the security of the Falkland Islands. There she healed physical wounds that had been of well-nigh mortal severity. The wounded members of the crew had been landed and taken to hospital.

Then the patched-up Exeter put to sea again, and came home. Once

again the exact date and time of the arrival were kept a close secret. There were rumours, as there were concerning the Ajax, but it was not until the cruiser was actually in the Sound that any announcement was made to the public. Certain newspaper representatives had been more or less let into the secret. I had the happy privilege of being among them. It was our job to describe the return of the ship – the sort of assignment which gave one a thrill and tremendous scope.

No ship ever received a more stirring welcome. It was a proud day for everyone, and great and spontaneous as was Plymouth's welcome, it had to be shared with the nation.

So memorable was the occasion that such distinguished personages as Mr. Winston Churchill, then First Lord of the Admiralty, Admiral of the Fleet Sir Dudley Pound, the First Sea Lord, and Sir John Simon, the then Chancellor of the Exchequer, came specially from London to convey the nation's official welcome.

No sooner had the cruiser dropped anchor than the following message was received on board from the Admiralty:

"Their Lordships welcome the Exeter back to her home port, and congratulate you all on bringing your ship safely home in spite of the damage received during the Battle of the River Plate in which you upheld the best traditions of the Navy. We hope you will soon enjoy well-earned leave."

The news "The Exeter has arrived" spread like wild-fire throughout Plymouth, and was further made public by being "put out" on the local Rediffusion in the early morning service. It was as though history was again repeating itself, with a flash-back to the sixteenth century when the early morning cry was "Drake is home again". And, as in those days, so on this memorable occasion the people rushed to the waterside. Every point of vantage from Mount Batten to Devonport Dockyard was black with people, and the early-morning air was filled with their cheers, the music of bands, and the answering cheers of the Exeter's ship's company as the ship slowly passed up harbour. For an hour the Exeter had ridden at her moorings in the Sound. It was a grey, bleak, winter morning, but though the weather was bad enough to chill the waiting throngs to the bone, their hearts were warm with excitement.

In the half-light it was some time before the ship could be seen with any clear distinction from the shore, but when the mists cleared there she was, with tugs and other small craft fussing around her. I had the opportunity of being in one of the ships that went specially into the Sound to join her procession up harbour. In fact, so great was the occasion that two naval drifters were placed at the disposal of the representatives of the Press – one for the reporters and the other for the cameramen. Throughout the world the home-coming would be recorded in word and picture.

Night after night the cynical German broadcaster had asked "Where is the Exeter?" The British Admiralty knew, but they did not fall for the obvious German bait.

We knew where she was this February morning – safe again in the welcoming arms of "Mother Plymouth". Actually when the ship steamed into Plymouth Sound, she had completed something like 8,000 miles since her engagement with the Graf Spee.

When the escorting ships shepherded the Exeter into the safety of Plymouth Sound one of them laconically signalled:

"There you are, safe and sound. Hope you all have very fine leave, and your fine ship will soon be ready to have another go at them."

Another ship "which passed in the night" signalled:

"Hearty congratulations and sincere admiration for your magnificent victory. We are proud to belong to the same port division."

Messages like these were showered on the Exeter from all directions, but her greatest moment was when she passed up harbour, and the heartfelt pride and gratitude of the nation was expressed in the cheers which echoed and re-echoed across the historic waters of Plymouth Sound and rumbled into the silence of the grey sheltering hills of Devon and Cornwall which flank the harbour.

Bands on shore and afloat played familiar airs, lusty voices sang and cheered. It was the scene to send the blood pulsating, and the cruiser was wearing her battle-scars with tremendous pride.

The eyes of every spectator searched the hull and superstructure of the cruiser. The scars were there by the hundreds: holes through her funnel, grim patches on her hull.

Curiously enough the guns seemed to be intact.

"Surely," we said, "some of them were shot away. She has got refitted pretty quickly."

In point of fact those "guns" only looked the part.

"Don't lean too heavily on them," I was warned almost as soon as I went on board. Yes, with one exception they were magnificent dummies. The ship's carpenter, the artificers, and the painters had accomplished a striking piece of make-believe.

"Well, we had to make a show, in case we met anything; we had to look businesslike, even if we were not," one of the officers remarked when I discussed this piece of work with him.

The biggest surprise for the Exeter's crew was when the ship got abreast of Mount Wise. A naval barge, with the Admiralty flag at the stem, came nosing out into the fairway.

Who was that sturdy figure in peaked cap standing amidships? Glasses were focused on him. It was none other than Mr. Winston Churchill, First Lord of the Admiralty, who had come down in person to bring the nation's official welcome. Little did we know then of the inspiring part which this bulldog personality was to play in our subsequent fortunes as the nation's expression of dauntless spirit.

But the Navy knew him then for their leader, and the quick recognition was followed by cheer after cheer from the ship. He waved back enthusiastically.

All the way up harbour the tremendous welcome followed the ship; nothing was more impressive than the scene at Devil's Point, where the Royal Marines, from the Plymouth Division, Stonehouse Barracks, turned out in strength, with their band, to join in the tribute. Some of their own comrades were members of the gallant returning crew.

Yet another stirring incident was when the ship steamed past the South Dockyard – past the cradle in which she had been fashioned.

Left; Battle-scarred Exeter comes home. Below & over, Churchill addresses the crew.

The Dockyardsmen who built her dropped their immediate work to join in the welcome. They cheered her as they had when she had slid down that slipway at the launching, and high up on the "cradle" in which her hull had rested their message of welcome was boldly displayed.

Mr. Churchill was the first man aboard the Exeter when she was safely moored alongside the North Dockyard wall. As he stood on that quarter-deck and looked around the ship and spoke to the captain, there was pride and emotion in his voice.

A little later, when the members of the ship's company were assembled on the quarter-deck, he stood on a capstan and voiced the nation's pride in the ship's accomplishment and joy in her safe return.

How we were to get to know that voice and the inspiring words it always carried. On this occasion he told them how in the grey, sombre winter days their brilliant action in the Plate had come "like a flash of light and colour on the scene, carrying with it encouragement to all who are fighting".

"This is a great occasion, and will long be told in song and story," he told them. Then, with that characteristic touch of colour, he said how the shades of Drake, Raleigh, and the sea-dogs of olden times, must have watched their homecoming. Finally, his tribute ended with these words:

"In the hearts of your fellow-countrymen you have come back with work nobly and faithfully accomplished in a worthy cause, with your honours gathered and your duty done."

There were others who also came to offer their official welcome – the Lord Mayor and Lady Mayoress of Plymouth (Lord Astor and Lady Astor, M.P.) and the Mayor of Exeter (Mr. R. Glave Saunders).

Yet amid the glamour of this homecoming there was withal a tinge of sadness. The ship's company mourned the loss of gallant comrades. I see that I wrote in my notes at the time:

"To some the return of the Exeter meant a joyous family reunion, but there were others who saw through the mists of their tears only a grey ship, and a memory over sixty shipmates are sleeping in the blue waters of the South Atlantic."

The punishment which the ship received in the River Plate action was inevitable in the gallant action which she fought so successfully against a bigger and more heavily-armed enemy. She had been battered mercilessly. Her decks were strewn with dead and dying, five of her six big guns were out of action, but her flag was still flying.

Now she was home, with kindly hands to once more nurse her back to her old fighting strength. As I went on board that morning there were everywhere grim reminders of the battle. The grimmest spectacle of all was in the petty officers' mess-deck, where a big shell had torn on a mad, erratic course, causing death, devastation, and fire. The pluck of the ship's company in action was only matched by the courage with which they fought the fires and took the heavily damaged ship first to the Falklands and then home to Plymouth. So, here again, as with the Ajax, we left her in the hands of the healers.

But while we left the Exeter in Dockyard hands after her proud homecoming, there was to be much more limelight and feting for the officers and men who had so illustriously added new honour to British naval history.

On February 16, 1940, the day after the ship had returned, Plymouth was given the opportunity of welcoming the ship's company in her own warm-hearted fashion.

They marched through the streets of the city to the historic Guildhall, where they were entertained to luncheon by the civic authorities. It was one of the most memorable events ever held in this shrine of Plymouth's great men.

In the centre of the great hall was prominently displayed one of the most treasured and historic of the Westcountry's links with the nation's sea power, Drake's Drum – specially lent for the occasion by the present owner. For years this drum had rested at Buckland Abbey, the home of Sir Francis Drake, at Buckland Monachorum.

Officers and men of the Exeter looked at it and touched it – almost reverently. Truly they had upheld the finest Drake traditions – victorious battle against the odds. I heard one of them quietly saying Newbolt's familiar lines:

"Take my drum to England, hang et by the shore,
Strike et when your powder's runnin' low;
If the Dons sight Devon; I'll quit the port o' heaven,
An' drum them up the Channel as we drumm'd them long ago."

The central figure at this luncheon was Captain F.S. Bell, the Exeter's commanding officer. He spoke with sailor-like modesty about their achievement, but there was a touch of wistfulness in his voice when he referred to their comrades who had been killed in the action.

16.02.40 Civic Dinner in the Guildhall for the crews of HMS Ajax and HMS Exeter.

"I only wish that I had been able to bring them all back home," he said, adding, "but some we left behind."

"But," he continued, with a ring of pride in his voice, "I would like all those who are left to know that their husbands and their sons died gloriously, and if they had not done that for us, I think we might not have been here to-day."

Subsequently the ship's company was entertained at Exeter, and in due course the flag which she carried throughout the action found a resting-place in the shrine of the historic city whose name the ship had borne.

The climax to this homecoming of the Exeter was when the entire ship's company marched through the City of London together with the ship's company of the Ajax, and together they were entertained to luncheon at the Guildhall, where the chief speaker was Mr. Churchill.

Evacuation of French Troops

No record of Plymouth's notable war-time events would be complete without recalling the stirring scenes which centred around the middle of June, 1940, when between 70,000 and 80,000 French troops, evacuated through the miracle of Dunkirk, were re-embarked at Mill-bay Docks for France.

Let it be remembered that there was no indication at this stage that the capitulation of France was to take place within a few days, and so it was that their departure was in the atmosphere of under-standing that they were going back to be reorganised in the further defence of their land as part of the Allied armies.

These embarkation scenes were spread over about eight days. During this time Plymouth Sound was crowded with French ships of all sorts and sizes for the work of transport. I remember how I, in common with other citizens, used to look at those "armadas" with some concern in our minds. What a target they presented for air attack. But, fortunately, the Germans were apparently so busily occupied with the overrunning of France that they missed this target. At all events the embarkation was carried out in a complete absence of any untoward happenings.

There was an endless procession of these transports. Big ships they were. The embarkation was carried out alongside the West Wharf – a spot more familiarly associated with the little French strawberry boats than these mighty transports.

I had the opportunity of watching these daily scenes. There was something very tragic about the whole business, but again I thought of Plymouth with a proud heart.

The citizens worked untiringly and gave generously to send these weary soldiers back to their native land with encouragement and hope, and their gratitude in return was something which could not fail to touch one deeply.

The first contingents to arrive at the docks for embarkation bore all the evidences of their grim ordeal – weary, bedraggled, plodding, dirty, unshaven. Yet with their hearts still brave and strong, and even a song on their lips, they went from train to ship. How little we or they knew of the unhappy collapse which was to take place within a few days.

At the head of one regiment marched a woman refugee who had

been found on the sands at Dunkirk. When on board the rescue ship off that beach she had repeatedly dived overboard to save soldiers from drowning. And the regiment had adopted her.

One distinguished French officer was so overcome by what was being done for the welfare and comfort of his troops that he took two medals from his weather-stained tunic and gave them to two girl canteen workers.

As the days passed the later French contingents had a better appearance. Food, hot baths, and sleep had given them new life. The French troops were inspired, too, by the daily presence on the quayside of the band of the Plymouth Division Royal Marines, under Major F. J. Ricketts, which played stirring French airs and marches and excerpts of popular music.

As each transport drew away from the quayside the band played the "Marseillaise", and cheers and answering cheers echoed between ship and shore until the transport was swallowed by distance and joined the great convoy in the Sound.

One magnificent feature of this great re-embarkation will always be remembered by the Frenchmen who passed through the docks – the voluntary canteen service which was called into action at an hour's notice. This was organised through the Lord Mayor's Welfare Fund, with the aid of an untiring band of workers.

French troops heading back to France, below left, waiting at Millbay.

To meet the emergency two temporary canteens were fixed up in the docks. One of these canteens alone distributed 100,000 cigarettes. Buns and biscuits were ordered daily in 5,000 lots; lemonade was made 100 gallons at a time; 3,000 oranges and apples were given away each day. Cake was cut up from 500-lb. slabs; there were stacks of chocolate, and tens of thousands of sandwiches.

Every man was supplied, and not once but thousands of times one heard these war-weary men say they would never forget the kindness and hospitality shown by Plymouth.

Many gardens were that week denuded of their flowers; the blooms were handed to the French troops as they went up the gangway of their transport. Some of these were tenderly deposited in pocketbooks to be kept as a souvenir and memory, others were stuck jauntily in the barrel of a rifle.

The Frenchmen were touched by this simple gesture. Many an English flower, plucked fresh from a peaceful garden, was tenderly carried back to France in those grim days – a simple, lovely flower which, somehow, seemed to strikingly express just the things for which these men were fighting.

Eventful days followed in quick succession, and Plymouth was to experience the full weight of these terribly anxious times.

Within two days of the departure of the last of the French troops I was again at Millbay Docks, to see the departure – as we thought, of the First Canadian Division for active service in France. But, as I elsewhere record, the transport never went farther than Plymouth Sound, for the same night the Canadians were disembarked again. Their services in France were not then needed. The situation in France had become untenable. Within a week France was to capitulate.

June 18, 1940, and several succeeding days, witnessed more stirring scenes at Millbay Docks. On this day thousands of British, French, and Belgian refugees streamed across the Channel to the safety of these islands. They came from France and the Channel Islands. Plymouth was one of the chief ports through which they made their entry.

There were pathetic scenes, and again the voluntary canteen service, with its willing helpers, toiled day and night to afford some welfare and comfort to these unhappy victims of aggression. Many of them came with just the things in which they stood and without money. Not one of them sought help in vain, and for weeks after the Lord Mayor's Welfare Fund was receiving letters of gratitude from refugees who had passed through and had been helped.

But these scenes at Millbay Docks did not end with the army of refugees. Following them came the British troops evacuated from France. Mostly they came home from Brest and other ports of western France. Constantly driven westward by the avalanche of the German attack, there was but one outcome – final withdrawal. Plymouth was the gateway through which tens of thousands of these men came home. Shipload after shipload steamed into the Sound. Ships that had once sailed into this port as proud and spotless liners, merchantmen, dirty little tramps, warships of all sizes, and small craft of varied assortment, had again been pressed into the great hazard of evacuation. It was on one of these mornings I went up on the Hoe. Surely never in history had there been such a remarkable scene as the mixed ship-

Left and above French and Moorish troops on baord the Sir Francis Drake.

ping which seemed to fill Plymouth Sound; craft of every conceivable sort were there. Between seventy and eighty I counted.

And this was the daily scene for the best part of a week. Harassed by enemy aircraft at the embarkation ports on the other side, dive-bombed and attacked for most of the voyage across, they eventually found safe anchorage at this port.

Here, again, was surely the most amazing target that an enemy could have desired. It was like serving it on a plate; yet, as was the case with the French troops' departure, there was no attack.

The bulk of the stores and heavy equipment had to be left behind in France, but these precious seasoned troops were saved. Their amazing confidence and unbroken morale stood out. They were tired, hungry, footsore, bedraggled. But they were unbeaten, like the men of Dunkirk, and they came home to form the nucleus of the new British strength that was to arise and be fashioned into a victorious army.

They, too, enjoyed the welcome and hospitality of a wonderful canteen service at Millbay Docks.

Thus in the month of June, 1940, Plymouth had been the gateway through which all these forces had flowed – the French troops, the refugees from the other side, and the British troops. Yet the whole organisation, much of it hastily improvised to meet dire emergency was magnificent. It was a supreme test, especially in the matter of transport and feeding, and it was handled with great efficiency.

This story of June, 1940, would hardly be complete without recording the dramatic climax – the capitulation of France on the 25th. The grey forebodings of the past few weeks had reached finality.

The "Cease Fire" had been ordered in France; she had laid down her arms. It was eighteen months later that the Prime Minister let us peep just a little behind the scenes of the drama.

The British Government had pleaded with France to carry on the fight, to take their Government to North Africa. But it was of no avail.

Britain was left to fight alone. A highly-placed French officer had predicted that in six weeks the enemy would wring Britain's neck like a chicken.

Remember the biting reply of Churchill – "Some chicken; some neck".

But Britain was alone.

And war came to Plymouth's door.

Above, French and Moorish troops leaving Mount Batten for France. Right, top; The Sound after Dunkirk, right Major Ricketts, the Royal Marine bandleader whose music kept many troops entertained at Millbay. Far right British troops back from France.

Other Naval Epics

Plymouth was not without being linked with two notable naval victories which marked the closing days of the year 1943, for some Westcountry ships and men were in the memorable engagement which took place in northern waters and led to the sinking of the German battleship Scharnhorst. The formidable warship, which in recent months had been lurking in one of the fjords of the far north of Norway, went out to destroy a vital convoy on its way with precious supplies to Russia, but was not aware of the trap which was being laid by the British Navy. After being skilfully "played with" by cruisers and destroyers, she was finally brought up against the mighty new British battleship, King George V and was sunk. Broadside after broadside was poured into her, and in the closing stages of the engagement the lighter ships closed in and sent her to the bottom by torpedo.

Within a few days of this the nation was again thrilled by another notable naval victory in the Bay of Biscay, and it was in the early morning mists of December 30 that the two cruisers Glasgow and Enterprise steamed into Plymouth Sound after having engaged eleven destroyers in a running engagement of several hours, sinking three of them and badly damaging a fourth.

It was a clean-cut victory which once again demonstrated British naval supremacy, even against the odds. The destroyers were of the latest German types, armed with guns of little shorter calibre than the 6-inch which the cruisers mounted. Here, again, the destroyers had ventured out from their hideouts on the west coast of France, and the cruisers were looking for them. It was a grim and exciting fight.

The two cruisers operated independently in the action, but so skilfully were they employed that ultimately the eleven destroyers broke their formation and raced back to their bases – save the three which were sunk.

As against the damage which they inflicted on the enemy, the cruisers escaped lightly. Although shells were falling all around, the only material damage to the Enterprise was the shooting away of the wireless aerial, and there was only one casualty, the fifteen-year-old Marine bugler who had sounded "Action stations" being hit in the arm with a piece of shell splinter.

The Glasgow was not quite so fortunate. She got a shell through the signal deck, and seven men were injured. But this was slight damage and negligible casualties compared with the cost to the enemy. The officers and men of these ships had been hunting this enemy all through the Christmas, but they had no regrets over this when they counted their success against the enemy.

I had the opportunity of going on board and chatting with the officers and men as soon as the ships came into harbour. There was a grand feeling of exhilaration on board, and yet there was that same modesty in telling the story that I have encountered so many times in the Royal Navy.

For many of the men it was their first real action, and both captains were loud in their praise of the efficiency shown, and they were particularly mindful of the men "down below", whose only knowledge of the trend of the battle was from what came over the loud-speakers. On board Glasgow the torpedo officer gave a running commentary over the loud-speaker system as the battle proceeded.

Left, HMS Enterprise in 1938, above King George V

Premier at Plymouth

It is not without interest to recall how intimately Plymouth was concerned in the goings and comings of the Prime Minister, Mr. Winston Churchill, on those historic and memorable trips when he journeyed by ship and by aircraft to meet the President of the United States.

Plymouth had seen Mr. Churchill when as First Lord of the Admiralty, in the early days of the war, he came down specially to welcome home the battered cruiser Exeter from the memorable naval victory against the Graf Spee in the River Plate battle, and, more intimately when he came with Mrs. Churchill after the heavy raids in 1941, saw for himself the damaged city and brought a message of reassurance and confidence to the citizens.

But the events in connection with his long trips to America and the Middle East came within another category altogether. They were for the most part shrouded in secrecy, necessary secrecy, of course, bearing in mind the importance of his missions and the fact that the movements of such an important personage had to be concealed.

It was on a January morning in 1942 that a mighty flying boat made a perfect landing on the waters of Plymouth Sound, taxied to its moorings and landed a number of passengers. Among them was the familiar figure of Mr. Churchill. He had flown the Atlantic, by way of Bermuda, the last lap of 3,287 miles, from Bermuda to Plymouth, then constituting a record for an air liner. Part of the way Mr. Churchill had himself been at the controls. The journey was safely made without any interference by the enemy, but it can now be said that for the last phase of the trip there was a pretty substantial air umbrella watching the skies for any hostile aircraft. Mr. Churchill stepped ashore from this long and adventurous flight as though he had just been for an hour's pleasure cruise. He went from Plymouth to London by train, and when I saw him at North Road Station he was in the mood of a schoolboy who had just "pulled a fast escapade and got away with it".

The next time Plymouth was concerned with the Prime Minister's long voyaging was when, in November, 1943, he went to the Middle East for the conferences with President Roosevelt, Premier Stalin, and Generalissimo Chiang Kai Chek at Cairo and Teheran. He and his formidable party sailed from Plymouth in the battleship Renown, and it was a particularly "hush-hush" departure. Well do I remember that secrecy, because although we at The Western Morning News office

Winston Churchill on board HMS Exeter in Plymouth, 1940.

had the knowledge that he was leaving, it was like "throwing David to the lions" when we approached naval headquarters for any information. Talk about the "cat among the pigeons". It was a decidedly awkward moment. We had no right to even a glimmering of the knowledge, and, well knowing the penalties, we made sure that we kept the information to ourselves. In due course we hoped we should get release for our story.

That secrecy was almost equally pronounced when in the very early morning of January 18, 1944, Mr. Churchill reached this country again, landing at Plymouth from the battleship King George V. It will be remembered that after the conference with President Roosevelt and Premier Stalin at Teheran, Mr. Churchill was taken ill with pneumonia, and after recovering from the illness at Cairo he went for a period of convalescence at Marakeesh in Morocco, Mrs. Churchill having gone out to join him.

Again we got to hear that he was due to land at Plymouth, but this was another occasion when we had to talk with our finger on our lips. We made no attempt at official enquiries, but just watched points. We knew that the battleship had steamed into the Sound with her escort of the cruiser Glasgow, destroyers, and submarines, and that there had been substantial air cover. The ship came into harbour under cover of darkness – a really filthy night, with driving rain and as black as pitch. We knew, too. that a special train had been shunted into the Millbay docks to convey the party to London.

But it was as much as our lives were worth to squeak a word or hope for a story.

The train steamed into Paddington at 10 o'clock the next morning, and it will be recalled how Mr. Churchill, suddenly emerging from behind the Speaker's chair, made a dramatic reappearance in the House of Commons. Most of the members were unaware that he was even back in this country.

But so far as the landing at Plymouth was concerned the story was very effectively "spiked", for with the public announcement that he was back in this country came also the instructions that nothing was to be said as to where he landed or the ship in which he returned.

Indeed, there was an interesting sequel to this secrecy. The Daily Express, with the pre-knowledge that Mr. Churchill was arriving, had sent a reporter specially from London to cover the story. He was telephoning this through to his paper from a kiosk in the Continental Hotel, giving the names of the King George V and Glasgow, mentioning Mr. Churchill by name, and giving other details about the homecoming, when he was overheard by two naval officers and the hall porter. They reported him to the police, and subsequently he was charged in the police court with communicating to certain persons information with respect to the movement of certain of His Majesty's ships. He was found guilty and fined fifty pounds and ten guineas costs.

Which all goes to show how difficult was the path which had to be trodden by newspaper reporters in war-time.

Still, even at this distance of time there is a certain reflected glory in the knowledge that Plymouth did play an important part in those very momentous journeys which the Prime Minister so boldly took during his war-time leadership.

A Plan For Plymouth

"A Plan for Plymouth". Under that very simple title is hidden a vision of the city beautiful which planners hope will one day arise a fitting memorial to the agony of total war and the start of a new chapter in the centuries-old history of the Westcountry metropolis.

How far the Plan, which was produced jointly by Professor (later Sir) Patrick Abercrombie, one of the famous town-planners of the day and the City Surveyor and Engineer (Mr. J. Paton Watson), will be implemented in its entirety is something which only the future can determine.

It is a plan which in its bold conception has enthralled not only the citizens but planning idealists all over the world. But when the keen edge of the first excitement had been taken off there were those who questioned its practical value, and, above all, doubted whether Plymouth could possibly shoulder the financial burden which loomed the more onerous the more deeply one considered all the implications and schemes.

It was in the spring of 1944, three years after the city had been so ravaged by enemy bombs, that the Plan was presented by the joint authors in impressive book form. For some time its contents had been a close secret of the few, for fear that without the necessary Government legislation there would be those rushing to seek material gain from the situation.

Then it was presented to, and accepted in principle by, the City Council. A Reconstruction Committee was set up to consider the whole aspect of the plan, to hear the representations of the many interests vitally concerned with the rehabilitation of the city, and to submit its recommendations to the City Council for final approval, amendment, or rejection.

Quite obviously, the implementation of such a vast scheme in its complete form would take many years. But there were urgent priorities connected with the re-establishment of Plymouth, the first of these being housing and the second the business centre.

The housing problem was acute. Most of the 75,000 people who had been driven out of the city because of the destruction of their homes were anxious to return, and, in addition, there were many hundreds of war-time married couples naturally desirous of setting up their own homes as soon as they were released from war service.

It was varyingly estimated when the Plan was produced that Plymouth needed between 10,000 and 20,000 new houses to meet post-war requirements. But even on this matter there was divergence of opinion, for while the planners saw the solution in overspill into satellite communities outside the city, others felt that there were sufficient undeveloped sites within boundaries to accommodate the need.

The Plan provided for a completely new layout for the city centre – elaborate shopping rendezvous, precincts for public buildings, cultural activities, entertainment, residential, and industrial areas, with a wide vista approach sweeping from the top of North Road right down through the shopping centre and up to the Hoe, and for the old part of Plymouth to be preserved behind its own formidable wall.

The idealists said, "Here is the great opportunity: let us plan boldly and with vision." The realists – at least, that is what they desired to call themselves – said, "It is a grand plan, but the financial burden

Far left, Paton Watson and Abercrombie examine their model for the New Plymouth, above Abercrombie delivers his plan to the Council with the Lord Astor in the chair.

would make it impossible of fulfilment; let us proceed with caution and modification."

So it was that many of the "visions" as presented by the authors of the plan became controversial matters; there was a wide gulf between the idealists and the realists.

Meanwhile the plan had captured imagination both in this country and on the other side of the Atlantic, which seemed to emphasise that the responsibility on the shoulders of the builders of the new Plymouth was indeed a heavy one. Future generations would either praise them or condemn them.

At the time of writing this chapter it is still "A Plan for Plymouth" – accepted only in principle. Certain it is that the city could not itself bear the financial burden of fully implementing the "vision of the city beautiful" as painted in the planners' book. Much would have to depend upon the measure of financial aid forthcoming from the national exchequer, and in this connection there was strong feeling that generous treatment was merited.

One can at this stage only hope that ways and means will be found to carry as much of the Plan as possible into effect, with due consideration for the many interests involved, and that generations to come will be able to point to their city and say with pride, "That is the memorial to Plymouth's great triumph over terror and destruction; the memorial to her finest hour."

THE SERVICES

While there was always the strictest supervision of all civilian aliens coming into the protected area of Plymouth – Military Security Police and the Aliens and Special Branch departments of the City Police handled this matter with great efficiency - it could be said that the city was able to extend hospitality to representatives of practically all the Allied armed forces. In this respect Plymouth became quite a cosmopolitan city.

Officers and men of the Allies who became quite familiar in the streets of Plymouth included airmen from Australia, in their neat dark blue, naval men from New Zealand, Newfoundland, and Canada, contingents of the Royal Indian Army Service Corps, with their mule transports and picturesque turbaned head-dresses, the Polish, Swedish, Free French, and Dutch navies, and later, in 1943, when the American troops virtually took over the area and large forces were stationed at Crownhill, where they occupied both the Seaton and Plumer Barracks, with Divisional Headquarters at Tavistock, the city was flooded with soldiers from across the Atlantic.

We knew, too, that the intrepid Polish and Czech pilots, who had so much to avenge, were often in the skies above Plymouth, alert for every chance to strike at any raiders. Incidentally we recall how it was a Polish night fighter pilot, from a station fifty miles away, who provided Plymothians with one of the most thrilling night spectacles of the war when he made a successful attack on a raider over the city and sent it crashing down in flames near Roborough. And as, on his lone patrol, he accomplished this feat, the people, unseen by him but with their eyes searching the sky, saw his bullets streak home with unerring marksmanship, and the enemy raider burst into flames. Neither did he know how the people surged into the streets from their shelters to watch this grim climax to a raid, and how they cheered with the excitement of a football cup-tie.

Do we not also remember that during the sharp raid on Plymouth in June, 1943, one of the four enemy victims of the defences was shot down by a New Zealand fighter pilot.

In the main the Allied forces stationed in Plymouth were under their own immediate commands, although, of course, they were part and parcel of the mighty force engaged against a common enemy.

Pilots pose at Mount Batten, 1945. Above, Australian boys on the Hoe taking a stroll on the Promenade stop, with friends, by the Armada Memorial. Looking up the Plym across RAAF Mount Batten, 1940, temporary home of many young Aussie airmen.

The officers and men of the Royal Australian Air Force were very popular. They were our own kith and kin, sons of the Empire, who had come, as their fathers did in 1914-18, all the way from "down under" to help the Motherland. They took over the Mount Batten Air Station, and, as part of the ever-growing and invaluable Coastal Command, flew the gigantic Sunderland and Catalina flyingboats, patrolling the great wastes of the Atlantic and Bay of Biscay in search of enemy air and sea craft, particularly submarines, convoying and protecting along our exposed sea routes, searching for survivors of sunken merchantmen, and maintaining frequent air service for supplies and passengers to Gibraltar.

I hope some day that someone will write the story of Coastal Command operations from Mount Batten by the Royal Australian Air Force. It will be an exciting story crammed full of action. Many of these lads who came from so far gave everything. They paid the full price of war but whether their bodies lie where the surging main they so faithfully patrolled murmurs its everlasting requiem, or in the peaceful corner of an English churchyard, where the breezes sing through the cypresses and the yews, we render simple and sincere homage.

I know from personal experience something of the work of these Australians, because there were occasions when I had the privilege of flying with them as a War Correspondent on long operational patrols. On one occasion I flew in F for Freddie Sunderland flyingboat 1,400 miles on a thirteen-hours' patrol, which took us right down across the Bay of Biscay and away out into the Atlantic. It was not many months after that F for Freddie went out on another such operational flight – and did not come back.

They were grand lads to fly with, those Australians. They had the supreme carefree bearing typical of Australia. They were splendid comrades at work and at play, and the camaraderie which existed among the members of a crew was something to be experienced to be fully appreciated. Flying over those miles of monotonous sea, their keen eyes searching every fleck of spray breaking the surface, one sensed the supreme adventure which must have surged in their hearts to have brought them so far from home. They took you into their good comradeship, made you feel that you were one of the company, made you feel supremely safe and confident – and they did it all with that easy – friendly way which had no trace of patronage.

Flying boats and their crews became a very familiar sight in and around the Sound. Left, an aeiral view of Mount Batten and Plymouth - May 1944.

I remember having had the same experience in the previous war. There were occasions in France when the artillery battery in which I was serving was on loan to the Australians for a particular action. We had no blankets that winter; the Australians saw that we had some from their own supplies. Yet the gesture was simply in keeping with their natural outlook.

More than a quarter of a century later I was to find from the sons of those men I fought with in France the same natural friendliness expressed in seeing that I was properly equipped for my flights from Mount Batten.

I was sitting in the officers' mess, sort of "waiting on edge" for instructions regarding my first flight, when a slim young Australian wearing the rings of a Flight-Lieutenant came across and quietly remarked, "You're flying with me in the morning". We chatted with that free and friendly atmosphere which is so characteristic of the lads from "down under".

Then a little later the Squadron-Leader came over to ask if I was "all fixed up". Suddenly his mind turned to kit. He looked around the mess and his eyes lighted on a burly Australian about my build. "Say, Bill, you're not flying tomorrow, are you?" he asked. " No," was the answer.

"Well, lend Mr Twyford your kit, will you?" he continued. "O.K.,"

replied Bill, without hesitation. "I'll have it sent up to your room," he said to me. And then, with a happy jest, added, "But make sure you bring it back!"

It was, perhaps, just a small ordinary act of hospitality, yet behind it all was that same spirit which induced the Aussies in France in 1916 to give us some of their blankets.

Yes, the Australians from Mount Batten added a glorious chapter to their nation's war record. Even when their own country was in such dire peril with the threat of Japanese invasion, when there was some anxiety in their hearts for the safety of their folk at home, they still carried on with the job they had been given at Plymouth. Some were drafted home to give the benefit of their experience to the building up of the home Air Force, but there were always others who came to Plymouth to take their places.

There were a good many flying-boats which flew out from Plymouth Sound and did not return, but there was always another machine and another crew to go out on the next patrol. The Royal Australian airmen who served at Mount Batten had a distinguished record. They had a formidable list of U-boat "kills" they had many thrilling fights with the fast-flying German fighters, and many sea survivors owed their salvation to the efficiency and daring of these keen-eyed young airmen.

Top left, A Sunderland on a mission passes the Eddystone. Above, 8 January 1944, a 10 Squadron RAAF Sunderland takes out a German U-Boat.

Of the splendid Canadian army which came to this country Plymouth had only fleeting glimpses. In point of fact, they came and they went all in a day. It was a rather remarkable experience. June 14, 1940, was the day.

Christmas Day 1944 and a couple of young Australian airmen experience an English Christmas in Mount Gold. Top right, July 1944 an RAAF man marries a Plymouth girl. Near right and below, Canadian fireman Sam Posten. Far right, Dec 1944, Lord Mayor Mason bids the Canadians a fond farewell.

It was not without reason that Plymouth had a special affection for the Royal Australian Air Force. I think that warm feeling was reciprocated. The future will certainly hold many close ties, for not a few of these young Australians selected their brides from among the young women of Plymouth.

June 1940, the Canadians come to Plymouth.

On that day the First Division of the Canadian Army was to embark at Millbay Docks for France. Among them were the famous Toronto Scottish.

In my job as War Correspondent I was assigned to witness their departure and write the story. I spent practically the whole day at the Docks. Major-General A. McNaughton came down specially to see them off. As the Officer Commanding the Canadian Forces in this country he was to follow them to France in a few days. They were in grand spirits; it was inspiring to be in their company.

But that day the war atmosphere was rather tense. Things on the other side of the Channel were shaping to a dramatic climax. Everyone was worried - that was, save these fine Canadians who sang their war songs with a lustiness which was really heartening.

Yet there seemed to be a hitch somewhere, although no one at the Docks seemed to quite know what it was. General McNaughton stood for hours on the dockside chatting with the troops as they leant over the deck rails of the transports. The suspense over the departure was lessened by the Plymouth Division Royal Marine band. The presence of this band was a happy thought on the part of someone, for

quite a few of the Canadians had heard it during a Canadian tour which was interrupted by the war.

At last, somewhere about four o'clock in the afternoon, the mooring hawsers were slackened off, the transports eased away from the dockside and left the docks for moorings in the Sound.

The crowd at the Docks waved and cheered the Canadians until distance swallowed them up; the cheers from the troopships came echoing back across the ever-widening stretch of water.

I returned to The Western Morning News office and wrote my story of the departure of the Canadians. This was duly put over to London for the necessary censorship.

Two hours later I received the rather staggering information that the Canadians had disembarked again, and were moving out of Plymouth immediately for a camp "somewhere in England." The transports had gone no farther than the moorings in the Sound. The dramatic collapse of France had intervened. These gallant Canadians were not yet wanted on the other side. Our own troops were coming home.

I think here it might be mentioned that there was one force of Canadians, not an armed force, which did come to Plymouth, and remained with us for two or three years. They were men who wore a flash on their sleeve "Canadian Fire Fighters to Great Britain". Yes, they were firemen, and they had come across to help the National Fire Service. Quite a strong force was allocated to Plymouth, and in the intermittent raids of 1942 and 1943 they did gallant and efficient work at fires.

They were a self-contained force, and at first had their headquarters at the Torre Home for the Blind, which was taken over for that purpose. Later on they were provided with their own headquarters on that same Torre Estate, with up-to-date station and the most modern fire-fighting equipment. This new station was officially opened for them by the Duchess of Kent in the early part of 1943.

While these were the only two official links between Plymouth and the Canadians sent to this country, there were many Canadians who visited Plymouth in their periods of leave. Some time after the heavy raids of 1941 I remember meeting two as they were looking over the ruins of St. Andrew's Church. Actually they had come west to search out records of their ancestors. They were of Westcountry stock.

The grim spectacle of Plymouth shocked them enormously.

New Zealand Premier, Peter Fraser, inspects the New Zealand troops in the Dockyard

Arrival at Plymouth of the body of the Polish Prime Minister and Commander-in-Chief, General Sikorski.

Neither the New Zealanders nor the Newfoundlanders came very much into the public eye. They were entirely confined, as far as Plymouth was concerned, to the Royal Navy and when they had completed their training in the depots here they were drafted, and so we never had any great association with them as a body.

The only occasions on which I saw them parade as composite units was when they had some special visitor. I remember one such occasion when the Prime Minister of New Zealand, the Hon. Peter Fraser, was visiting Plymouth, as did most of the leaders of the Dominions and Colonies when in this country. He paid a special visit to the Royal Naval Barracks and delivered a message from the homeland to the New Zealand naval ratings, and promised to take back messages from them to their families.

A considerable force of the Polish Navy operated from Plymouth throughout the war; in fact, Devonport was their main depot. They manned their own destroyers and rendered brilliant service, particularly on convoy duty and in operations against the U-boats in that infested area known as the Western Approaches. They were a gallant force, and had some good hunting.

In the early days the Polish Navy which escaped the Nazi net was only a nucleus of the force which was ultimately built up. They were accommodated in a depot ship, the Gdynia, which was moored in the Hamoaze off the North Dockyard. Later, when their numbers grew considerably, especially after Russia's entry into the war, they had a shore headquarters at Stoke. They took over the United Services' Orphan Home for Girls, which institution had been evacuated to Cornwall for the duration of the war.

As more and more Poles found their way to this country to join the fighting forces, their naval strength grew appreciably. They were fine sailors, and, like their airmen, who, operating from a nearby fighter station, were often in the skies over Plymouth, had their whole outlook animated by revenge for what the Germans had done to their country.

The Poles became quite a familiar part of the Services at Plymouth. Many of them enjoyed the warm hospitality of Plymouth homes, and there were a number of marriages between Polish naval men and Plymouth girls.

One always had the feeling that there was an understanding sympathy between these war exiles and Plymothians. They were men without a country, and, what was worse, were without knowledge of the fate of those they loved.

There was a great courage in their hearts, but if you talked to them about their country there was a wistfulness in their voice and a faraway look in their eyes. As one of them said to me: "We fight to forget. If only we knew what had happened to our homes and our people, it would not be so bad. Many of us have beard nothing since we escaped and the Germans overran the country. And that was a long time ago."

A small Allied force which was always popular in Plymouth was that provided by the Norwegian Navy. Like the Poles, this was composed of the elements which managed to evade the Germans. The Poles were distinctive from the British in appearance, but with the Norwegians there seemed to be something of an affinity in appearance and manner.

These fair-haired, blue-eyed men came mostly from the Norwegian fishing industry. They brought with them their sturdy fishing trawlers and their splendid seamanship. A number of their powerful boats, used mostly for mine-sweeping, operated from Millbay Docks over the Western Approaches, but their shore depot was at Stoke, where they took over a large private house at Penlee.

I had the privilege of being there when they were visited by King Haakon and the popular Crown Prince Olaf. The royal visitors also visited the minesweepers at Millbay. These visits did much to inspire the Norwegians to work for the day when their country would be liberated. Like the Poles, they were exiles and without much knowledge of their homes and families. They were men with a grim resolve.

Several times I had the opportunity of visiting their ships at Millbay Docks. Officers and men were charming company, overwhelmingly hospitable, but always one sensed their thoughts turning to that land across the North Sea, and their eyes would look with affection at the photos and souvenirs which decorated the cabins - their only links with home.

After the capitulation of France there were several French warships at Plymouth. Among these was the very old battleship Paris, which turned out to be of no more use than for a depot ship alongside the dockyard wall in the harbour at Devonport. There was also the submarine Surcouf the world's largest underwater craft, and a destroyer and one or two small craft.

Tension was very great at that time, and matters were very much in the air as to who was with us and who was against us as far as France was concerned.

These French warships naturally were kept under close watch. There was an unfortunate clash soon after these ships came to Devonport. On July 3, 1940, an armed British force surrounded the basin at the North Dockyard in which the French destroyer No. 141 was berthed.

The crew of this ship surrendered without anything untoward happening. But the same good fortune did not prevail when a boarding party went to take charge of the submarine Surcouf. The first British rating to step aboard, a leading seaman, was shot dead by a French officer, but he paid the penalty, being promptly clubbed with a rifle. He died shortly after. The crew of the submarine were disarmed and marched ashore under strong escort.

Above members of the Free French Army march through Plymouth.

Later all the French ships at Plymouth were taken over. The French crews were taken away from Plymouth. It will be remembered that about this time the British seized French ships lying at Oran. Many of the Frenchmen belonging to these crews were in complete sympathy with the Allied cause and later became part of the Free French forces. Only occasionally, however, did Plymouth see members of the French armed forces again.

French submarine Surcouf - the world's largest underwater craft, in Devonport Dockyard.

United States Force

It was not until the spring of 1943 that Plymouth made real acquaintance with the great American Army which was accommodated in this country. They had been in this country some time before they overflowed into the South-West, and, with the true American tradition for the bigness of things, their arrival was an avalanche. They came as an army.

An entire division – the 29th – moved down into Devon and Cornwall from Salisbury Plain, and took over many stations previously occupied by British units. As far as the Plymouth Garrison was concerned, they occupied the entire Seaton and Plumer Barracks at Crownhill and Raglan Barracks, Devonport, and from then on they became even more familiar in the streets of the city than were our own British soldiers.

These Americans were wonderfully equipped, smartly dressed - unless one was familiar with the markings, it was difficult to distinguish officers from men – and, bearing in mind the thousands who were stationed at Plymouth, their general behaviour and conduct in public gave satisfaction.

The American troops were kept under very strict discipline, and any breaches were dealt with by their own commanding officers, or their own special courts, according to the character and gravity of the crime.

It was not a picnic for the Americans here. They were here for a purpose – to train intensively for the invasion of the great European fortress. In this training they made good use of the adjacent moorlands. Their divisional headquarters were at Tavistock.

Often to be seen helping in this training were American reconnaissance aircraft based on Roborough and Yelverton. The distinctive white star on the fuselage easily picked them out from British machines.

Whenever we think of these Americans we shall recall that snappy little runabout "truck" which they used – the American jeep. You saw it everywhere, a handy little vehicle, with a four-wheel drive; a real utility job. The American motors have, of course, a left-hand drive, but the drivers accommodated themselves remarkably well to driving on the left-hand side of the road, thus conforming to the rule of the road prevailing in this country.

Many of the Americans were keenly interested in the historic side of Plymouth and the links which connect the city with their own country. Both Lord and Lady Astor, in their official positions as Lord Mayor and Lady Mayoress, did everything possible to foster the good fellowship that permeated the association from the very outset of their coming to Plymouth.

These Americans saw the famous Mayflower Stone on the Barbican which commemorates the sailing of the Mayflower with the Pilgrim Fathers to found New England, they saw the Door of Unity leading to the ancient Prysten House, given a few years ago by the Daughters of America, and at which spot each year a simple service is held.

They liked Plymouth and they quickly made friends. They had not been stationed in Plymouth long when they experienced their first air raid. "Not at all pleasant," one of them remarked the next day adding, "But I guess it was only a fleabite to what you had a while ago."

And I liked these Americans for the way in which they came in to lend a hand when those later raids were giving us trouble.

One thing which did impress Plymothians was the way in which the United States forces got on with a job of work, especially if it happened to be a big one. In fact, the bigger the job the more strikingly did it seem to reveal their powers of organisation.

Plymouth was the centre of their activity, both for the Army and the Navy, and in many parts of the city and the surrounding countryside there were the evidences of their presence and resourcefulness. They adapted and applied themselves to construction with a "get-on-with-it" atmosphere which was most significant.

If the Navy or the Army had a big job of construction to do, they went right ahead. There was no dallying about between a score of different Government departments. They had their own Constructive Battalions, which carried out the entire job, from preparing the sites to the finished camps or establishments.

A striking example was the naval hospital for 250 beds in the dip at the bottom of Manadon Hill. In two months they put in the foundations, built the camp, and equipped the hospital. Every single section, nut and bolt, stores and equipment, for that most modern hospital came across the Atlantic. It was just like sending a mail order.

Left, The Astors receive a plaque from Col. Sherman L Kiser.
Below, US Naval Hospital at the bottom of Manadon Hill.

Top, The entrance to Shapter's Field Camp. Middle accommodation at Shapter's Field. Bottom, The US Camp at St Budeaux.

Foundations on this low-lying ground were a problem at first. But bulldozers and loaders removed thousands of tons of rubble from the blitzed sites in the city to provide the necessary ballast. Once that was down the hospital accommodation went up like mushrooms. The same thing happened at Coxside, where, on the rough ground at Queen Anne Battery, they constructed a camp complete with a most up-to-date laundry, and at Efford, where they built another camp.

In passing it might be mentioned that although the United States Army occupied the big hospital at Plaster Down, just on the edge of Dartmoor, above Horrabridge, that was laid out and built by the British. It had capacity for between 700 and 800 beds, and was very largely occupied by the United States troops, wounded and sick, between the invasion of the Continent and the termination of European hostilities.

Gradually the momentum of the United States' activity in and around Plymouth grew, and it was soon apparent that Plymouth was to be an important base and jumping-off place as far as their part in the invasion of the Continent was concerned. Their activity at many points along the foreshore, particularly at Saltash and in the Cattewater, was revealed at hards, wharves, slipways, basins, and beaches.

Hamoaze House at Mount Wise was their naval headquarters, but they had an important Naval Advance Base in the Cattewater, where they occupied almost the entire frontage from Sutton Pool to Laira Bridge.

Some of the United States' biggest warships came to Devonport Dockyard for repairs after the Normandy landings. These included the battleships Texas, Nevada, and Arkansas, all of which had taken part in the preliminary bombardment of the German defences.

The Stars and Stripes – Old Glory, as the flag of the United States is familiarly called – could be seen at many points. It flew for their Navy from the old Admiralty House at Mount Wise, it flew at the entrances to the Seaton and the Plumer Barracks at Crownhill, it flew from the stem of scores of ships in Plymouth Sound and in Devonport Harbour.

United States soldiers and sailors, on duty and on leave, crowded our streets, shops, and social centres to such a degree that their presence completely swamped the comparatively few British still in the area; their vehicles, all carrying the insignia of the "white star" were the heaviest part of our traffic. Their police, conspicuous with their white helmet, white gloves, white belt, and white gaiters, were familiar at our street corners; their patrols, each man armed with heavy truncheon, were a constant deterrent to unruly behaviour

Yet, I think, with all these evidences of war so apparent, it will be the friendliness of these men from the other side of the Atlantic which will linger in memory the longest. They had a very profound respect for Plymouth and the people who had endured so much before they came. They read the signs without having to be told.

It became a reciprocal friendship. They belonged to what I suppose was the most highly-paid army in the world. I remember one of their staff-sergeants – incidentally he held a position of considerable prominence in the American newspaper world in that he was the literary editor of The New York Times – telling me that his pay was something like £8 a week. And that, of course, was spending money, because they were generously provided for in the matter of clothes, accommodation, and feeding. Thus, they had plenty of money to spend, and they spent lavishly. Their hospitality was generous. They were received into many Plymouth homes with characteristic Westcountry warmth, and they in turn, responded to this with great sincerity. I think one of the best expressions of their appreciation, and also perhaps their sympathy with a people who had been heavily hit, was the lavish way in which they entertained thousands of the schoolchildren at Christmas parties in 1943.

I had the opportunity of attending one or two of these parties. They fetched the children in their jeeps and lorries from the schools and transported them back again at the end of the party. Their hospitality was wonderful, and their characteristic sentimentality where kiddies are concerned was expressed in many ways. The men themselves subscribed the cost of the parties. They went without their rations so that there should be plenty of candy, chocolate, and chewing-gum, and every child attending came away hugging some sort of toy or doll.

But there were also other aspects of their sojourn which we shall not soon forget. In the weeks that immediately preceded the invasion, when it was strongly felt that Plymouth, by reason of its importance in the "scheme of things to be" would be most likely to receive special attention from the enemy, the United States Army increased the city's defences by manning light anti-aircraft guns at strategic points.

At this distance of time it is easy to recall the picture of such a gun

An American anit-aircraft unit stationed in the ruins to the west of Charles Church.

and its team settled into a site amid the rubble of the cleared area at the corner of Old Town Street and Treville Street. Yet again, I can see two more guns "sitting" in the outfield of the Plymouth College cricket ground, quite adjacent to the Ford Park Road boundary. These were but two of many places where the United States Army set their anti-aircraft guns in and about the city.

Week by week we watched the growing strength of the invasion force. Week by week we watched the building up of the enormous organisation that goes hand in hand with the modern army, week by week we watched the impressive convoys pass through our streets. It all became so common a sight that no one bothered to ask the why or the wherefore. These Americans certainly brought the bigness of their way of doing things and their organising ability to the southwest corner of this tight little island.

As someone very aptly put it when one day we were discussing this enormous weight of men, materials, and organisation from across the Atlantic – "I should say that this island is loaded well below the Plimsoll line."

Yes, we certainly admired their organising ability, their bigness of things, the way they got on with a job and just strode over obstacles, and it was a frequent expression from the British onlooker – "Well, if these Americans can fight as well as they can do these jobs, Hitler hasn't got a chance." Now we know that they could.

With such a big force of American troops in the district, it was obvious that considerable attention would necessarily have to be given to their "out-of-barracks" welfare. Here, again, they showed the same big and vigorous action. The powerful American Red Cross took charge. They took over no fewer than five of the big houses in Elliot Terrace – the terrace in which Lord and Lady Astor had their Plymouth residence – and equipped them as a hostel. In another part of the city there was another well-equipped hostel for coloured members of the United States forces.

Plymouth being such an important centre as far as the United States' spearhead of the invasion was concerned, it was not surprising that we should have several important military visitors in the immediate pre-invasion days.

General Dwight D. Eisenhower, the Allied Supreme Commander-in-Chief, came on several occasions; in fact, his military cavalcade huge, powerful military car, with armed motor-cycle outriders became quite well known. There were times when he came with General Montgomery, because "Monty", too, was a fairly frequent visitor in those building-up days. Lord and Lady Astor, because of their positions as Lord Mayor and Lady Mayoress, and also because of their links with the United States, took a very keen interest in the welfare of these visitors, Lady Astor often visited the barracks, and there was one special occasion when a battalion from Her Ladyship's home state of Virginia held a special parade in her honour. At the close of the parade Lady Astor was presented with the certificate and badges of a corporal in the United States Army – souvenirs which, I think, she has retained with considerable pride.

Left, American anti-aircraft guns outside St Andrew's Church. Top right, General Dwight D Eisenhower, Supreme Commander of Allied Forces, with Maj. Gen. Charles Gerhardt and Air Marshall Sir Arthur Tedder, visit the American 29th Infantry Division. 4 February 1944. Middle, US Ambulances with Lord and Lady Astor outside the Guildhall. Bottom, American preparations for 6th June 1944 at Queen Anne Battery.

Devonport Royal Dockyard

During the five years and eight months of the European war Devonport Royal Dockyard, by virtue of its geographical position and its first-class facilities, became Britain's No. 1 Naval Repair Establishment. Throughout hostilities it was commanded by Vice-Admiral Sir Arthur N Dowding as Admiral Superintendent.

There was only a limited amount of new construction on the slipways at the South Yard, including some submarines, but the definite Admiralty policy was to utilise to capacity the great resources in repair, maintenance, and "modernisation".

In all these directions the Yard accomplished much with an industry which worked right round the clock, and if ever the word "impossible" had elimination from Britain's war-time vocabulary it was in connection with some of the jobs done here – not only in the actual character of the work but also in working against the clock.

Only at the end of the European operations was it possible to lift the veil on the activities and tell something of the contribution which the Devonport Dockyard "matey" made to victory.

Throughout the war that much-maligned individual had worked behind the high walls of security. The fighting services had their spots of limelight; the Dockyard just carried on, but, as the Navy will tell you, it delivered the goods.

Now, too, it is also possible to give something of the picture of damage which was caused by German high explosive and incendiary bombs on this big, vulnerable target. It was never comparable with the exaggerated German claims, and while it caused some interference and inconvenience – or as one woman industriously plying a broom, said to me, "a devil of a mess to clean up" – it never meant any very serious check on the flow of works. Certainly the Devonport Dockyard was very far from being put out of action.

It was in the heavy raids of March and April, 1941, when the whole city was so wantonly blitzed, that the heaviest damage was done at both the South and North Yards.

Among those very old buildings at the South Yard there was ready material for disastrous fires. The Mould Loft and the ancient Ropery were among the burnt-out buildings on what I might call the working side of the Yard. But there were also two other scenes of notable destruction. That lovely terrace of houses which for generations provided the official residences for the Admiral Superintendent and the principal officers was gutted almost from end to end. Only the two end houses were repairable. The Dockyard Church was also destroyed. Antiquarians were glad to know that the Scrieve Board, that 150-year-old building, with its single-span roof of 103 feet, in which so many of the famous ships built on the nearby slipway had been modelled, was saved by the magnificent efforts of the then voluntary fire-watchers. There were fifty incendiaries on that roof, but they were grimly tackled and beaten out.

At the North Dockyard where, of course, the "shops" are much more modern, there was a considerable amount of damage to roofs, but here again the work of the passive defence was very efficient, and after a bit of clearing up and first-aid repairs had been executed the motto was "carry on". Men and women worked in "tin hats" to protect them from falling debris, as roofs were being repaired, and were provided with clogs as protection against glass on the floor.

The increase in Dockyard personnel for the war was not as large as in the last war, something about 15 per cent. But the manpower problem was one of the big headaches. This was no "umbrella" for the unskilled man. Many hundreds of the young labourers were called to the fighting services, and labour was diluted with many women. They were largely employed in cleaning up the yard, but in the skilled trades they did splendid work as welders and drillers.

This man-power problem was intensified by reason of so many of the skilled men going to establishments overseas and in the north, while scores of the best men of the foreman type went on overseeing duties with the big Admiralty contracting firms.

Most of Britain's best-known warships, from the modern Anson, Howe, King George V, and pre-war battleships down to the smallest craft, were at one time or another at this Dockyard during the war. Ships had to be constantly "modernised" to keep them equipped with the latest scientific devices, sometimes when they were but a year or two old. Others had to be refitted. It was, however, in repair work to ships damaged in action, by mines, torpedo, or aerial torpedo, that the record of Devonport Dockyard makes proud reading. Take as an example Admiral Lord Mountbatten's destroyer Javelin, which was brought back to the Dockyard with both bow and stern just masses of twisted metal. The damage was so extensive that you just wondered how on earth the middle kept afloat. But it did, and the Dockyard did a wonderful job of "ship surgery". They fitted a new bow and a new stern. And there were many other ships where the craftsmen of the Dockyard showed equal skill. Rightly, too, there was a measure of pride in these achievements.

As one remembers this enormous contribution to the war effort, it is gratifying also to know that the Admiralty are – at any rate, at the time of writing – attaching so much importance to this Westcountry establishment that they are planning extensive extensions in the post-war reconstruction of the city. Much that was familiar in pre-war Devonport will vanish with the 240 acres which they are acquiring from that residential and business area which lay adjacent to the Dockyard from the Naval Barracks to Mount Wise. From these definite indications there is the bright prospect of Plymouth's assured future prosperity.

Women at work - "in skilled trades they did splendid work as welders and drillers."

A COSTLY EXPERIENCE

The greatest experience Plymouth had to buy and buy very dearly, was in dealing with fires. I do not know whether it has ever been estimated how much was destroyed by fire compared with what was actually blasted into ruin, but it must have been a very high percentage. I think a safe figure would be 75 per cent.

Some of this, no doubt, was due to the fact that so much of the property destroyed was very old – ready fuel for the mass burning which would result from the dropping of thousands of incendiary bombs on congested areas.

Yet, while admitting all this, there was unquestionably the fact that the fires were of such a widespread character, so big and so violent, that they were beyond the capacity of the existing fire-fighting organisation. Bluntly, we had neither the men nor the equipment to deal with such conflagrations as gutted Plymouth in those heavy 1941 raids. However gallantly the fire-fighters and volunteers worked – and let us honour the personal bravery which was shown in countless incidents – this was something beyond their efforts.

Until the National Fire Service was inaugurated on a completely reorganised basis and equipped on a nationally standardized method in the middle of 1941 – that was after the Plymouth blitz – fire brigades and their war auxiliary forces were a local concern. In Plymouth the fire brigade was part of the Police Force, and came under the authority of the Chief Constable and the Watch Committee of the City Council. It was a completely efficient brigade for dealing with the normal calls of peace-time.

With the heavy raids, however, it was found that the great weakness of the British fire service was lack of uniformity in both equipment and training. Fire-fighting is a highly skilled job. There is much more in fighting a big conflagration than the mere unloading of tons of water on to the flames. It requires a very high standard of specialized training.

The weaknesses emphasized themselves when the fire service had to tackle something almost beyond imagination.

Thus it was that in the blitzes of March and April, 1941, the greater part of Plymouth was burnt to destruction because the means to tackle fires on such a scale were wholly inadequate.

Left, firemen tackle the blazing offices of the Western Morning News. Above, Old Town Street

Hundreds of fire brigades were rushed to Plymouth from all parts of the country. Along the great arterial roads from the north, east, and west the fire engines and trailer pumps raced to the city's assistance.

I remember talking to members of one brigade which came from the other side of Salisbury, and how I was told by their leader, "There was no need to ask the way. The tremendous glow in the sky was our signpost all through the night."

Yet with all these brigades ready to help, anxious to help, desperate to help, the city burned with tragic completeness. The fact was that many of the brigades could not be used for the very simple reason that their equipment was of a different standard to Plymouth's. They were helpless, and virtually had to stand idle.

It is a grim picture to recall. Here was Plymouth, with all the wide ocean washing her front doorstep, two broad rivers lapping her flanks. Yet she burned in the most appalling fashion because there were not the means to fight the fires. Hundreds of the fires just had to burn themselves out; the efforts to extinguish them were puny by comparison. The fire-fighters had to rely on the ordinary water-mains and the limited equipment which would fit.

A costly and bitter lesson was learnt from the Plymouth experience. Perhaps it was that no one had ever quite visualized what intensive fires could come from heavy raids. But that was not an excuse. It was, as someone said, "like trying to put out a blazing warehouse with a stirrup-pump."

The experience was, I think, in no small measure responsible for stirring the authorities to the realisation that nothing short of complete reorganisation on a national scale of the fire-fighting services of this country was the answer. If it did not mean the actual start of the National Fire Service it certainly hastened its development. The utmost speed was essential if raids of a similar character were to be efficiently handled in the future.

And so the National Fire Service came into existence – a force organised and equipped on national lines under the direct control of the Home Office, like the Police Force. The whole country was zoned into areas and regions, personnel was enormously increased, modern equipment became a priority job in the nation's war production, the training became intensified and standardised, with specialists in charge. Plymouth, in common with the rest of the country, was fully

All hands to the pump, but sadly the pumps couldn't always be connected.

embraced into this scheme. There were those who in subsequent criticism declared that in the reorganisation of the fire service the authorities went from one extreme to the other – that whereas before it had lacked national organisation it now became over-organised. But this is not a criticism of the fire service, but rather the record of events and changes which came with the experiences of war.

For the purposes of this record it is sufficient that Plymouth came fully within the new organisation. It forthwith ceased to be a local police responsibility.

Plymouth came within an area, the headquarters of which were established at Yelverton. That was the fire-fighting nerve-centre, and while in the city itself the main station was still at Greenbank, there were sub-stations in various parts of the city, all well equipped. Then, too, the scheme provided that automatically with Plymouth being attacked there would be a closing in of the services from other areas, so that there was always immediate help within close call in the event of the city services being inadequate.

Whereas in the heavy raids of 1941 the water supply for the fire-fighters came from the water-mains and ordinary street hydrants – where the fires were very close to the foreshore the harbour water was, of course, used – the available supply was materially augmented immediately afterwards. Throughout the main thoroughfares many miles of surface 6-inch pipes were laid - although to what extent these would have been destroyed in a heavy bombardment was a matter for serious conjecture – and scores of static water tanks were constructed at various key points in the city. These were always ready with many thousands of gallons of water for pumping.

Above, static water tank outside the Guildhall. Right, the Post Office burns out.

POLICE AND CRIME

It was only to be expected that war conditions would impose fresh and important duties on Plymouth City Police. With the influx of Service men of so many nationalities, there could have been few places in the country where a more cosmopolitan population existed, and while these foreign elements came under the rigid supervision and discipline of their own respective authorities, their presence did at times give the police more than a passing "headache".

There had of necessity to be a very close liaison between the police and the Services. The major extra work which was thrown on the police came from the imposition of war regulations, which had to be the more stringently applied because of Plymouth's importance from the war point of view, and the fact that it was a protected area and a target of significance to the enemy. The Special Branch department at police headquarters, which dealt with aliens and any question of subversive activity, had a job of extreme importance, and worked in the closest possible alliance with the War Security Police, which had its headquarters at Millbay Docks.

Then there was also the very intimate liaison between the police and the military in the matter of defence, and this meant the establishment of another department. Yet again there was the fact that the Wardens Service was under the direction of the Chief Constable, and so specially trained officers were seconded from normal police duty for this purpose.

So enormously did the duties of the police increase that the normal peace-time force would have been hopelessly inadequate to meet the demands. Consequently the personnel was about trebled. This was achieved from three sources – the First Police Reserve, which was composed of recalled pensioners; the War Reserve, which was a whole-time paid force recruited from the civilians; and about three hundred Special Constables, part-time and voluntary, whose service was not less than forty-eight hours a month. In five years the "Specials" did over 700,000 hours of duty.

The last-named proved a force of ever-growing value, especially when under de-reservation many of the regular police up to thirty years of age, and War Reserve men up to thirty-three years of age, were taken for the Armed Forces or for essential industry in the trades in which they had been trained before joining the police.

Plymouth had the rather unique experience of having three different Chief Constables during the war. Mr. G.S. Lowe was in command when the war broke out, and saw Plymouth through the heavy raids of 1941, in the autumn of which year he was appointed Chief Constable of Sheffield. He was succeeded by his deputy Mr. W.T. Hutchings, who had grown up with the force and was for many years an oft-commended Chief of the C.I.D. He held the office for only a year when his health failed, and he died in the spring of 1943, after several months' absence from duty.

For nearly six months the responsibility was undertaken by the Deputy Chief Constable (Chief Superintendent J. Hingston) until Mr. J.F. Skittery was appointed to the position in June, 1943. Mr. Skittery thirty-five years of age, was a Chief Inspector of the Metropolitan Police, and came with a first-class record.

The Special Constabulary was under the command of Mr. F. Edgar Bowden as Commandant; it was organised in divisions and subdivisions on the same basis as the regular force, but with the addition that it had a strong mobile section attached to the regular Traffic Department, which did traffic patrol and also provided important transport for the police during raids.

There were also two other police auxiliary forces. One was the Women's Auxiliary Police Corps, about thirty strong, who were employed in the administrative offices and as drivers, and later as policewomen; the other was the Police Auxiliary Messengers Service. All these auxiliary services were uniformed.

1944 Plymouth's WAPC office staff, far left a policeman stands guard at Peverell.

There was, of course, an increase in crime, although I do not think anyone would be justified in saying that it was a serious or alarming increase. I think the greater concern was in the matter of juvenile crime. Many children seemed to be lacking in the old-time home discipline. This was perhaps understandable to some extent, because so much former parental control was missing by reason of fathers being away in the Services and mothers often engaged all day on war work.

General crime was, however, not more than one would expect, bearing in mind the wholly abnormal influx of "strangers" which the Services and other industries brought to the city.

In dealing with this I think I am right in saying that the "blackout" was the biggest obstacle with which the police had to contend. It had a baffling influence in more cases than one. During the war there were four unsolved murders, two of the victims being women, one a Polish petty officer, whose body was found in an empty raid-damaged house at Devonport, and the fourth a fourteen-year-old Egg Buckland girl, whose body was found on the grass verge of a military road near the village. She had been asphyxiated.

"The police primary job of 'preserving life and property' covered a very wide field." Above, an inspector inspects a bomb crater. Right, a crime incident at Manadon, far right, daily duties - in Devonport and St Judes.

The police worked untiringly on every slender clue that came their way, hundreds of enquiries were pursued to their bitter end, but without avail.

Apart from these unsolved murders, most of the serious crime was in relation to warehouse and shop breaking, and at some of the Quarter Sessions there were heavy calendars of this type of offence, with both thieves and receivers in the dock.

But the ordinary police duties were multiplied a hundredfold by the war conditions. The maintenance of "law and order" and the police primary job of "preserving life and property" covered a very wide field.

The enforcement of the blackout regulations, traffic problems, the responsibility of controlling all raid incidents, apart from fires, were just some of the extra duties which fell on the "man in blue". As I have already mentioned, the Chief Constable was responsible for the training and organisation of the Wardens Services, and during actual raids "incident posts" had to be organised and supervised by the police, who were also responsible for evacuating areas where unexploded bombs were located, and for solving the difficult problems of traffic when thoroughfares became blocked.

The policeman's lot was anything but a happy or an enviable one during the war in Plymouth, but they did their work - both regulars and auxiliaries - with that discipline, efficiency, and courtesy which could not fail to have a marked effect on the morale and general conduct of the public. The public did not look in vain for the "strong arm of the law" in their great distress.

SINEWS OF WAR

Earlier in this record of the war years in Plymouth I mentioned that the citizens gave generously to pay for the war. In the first five years of hostilities savings and investments totalled over £23,000,000. People were, of course, earning more money than ever before, and while there was lavish spending, the savings were on a very substantial scale. Many of the young people outside the Services had money to burn. There were times when people seemed not to know what to do with their money.

Yet there was an encouraging amount of thrift. War Savings Groups increased enormously. "A group in every street" was one of the objectives, and it could not have been far short of being realised. In schools, churches, clubs, workshops, stores, and factories there were active savings organisations, and in parts of the city there were "offices" voluntarily staffed where war savings stamps could be purchased with odd money after shopping.

In the larger national efforts Plymouth did well, and in friendly rivalry with Portsmouth and Oxford walked away with the honours during the special "Weeks". The savings invested by Plymouth in the five big annual efforts were:

	TARGET	TOTAL
(1941) War Weapons	£1,000,000	£1,110,080
(1942) Warships Week	£1,200,000	£1,433,395
(1943) Wings for Victory	£1,500,000	£1,556,428
(1944) Salute the Soldier	£1,250,000	£1,610,016
(1945) Thanksgiving Week	£1,250,000	£1,384,588

While, of course, such colossal sums included a number of very substantial cheques from banking houses, insurance societies, and other bodies concerned with big finance, a splendid feature of all four efforts was the volume of small savings.

Plymouth raised money with tremendous enthusiasm, and there was a keen spirit of competition between local kindred organisations to head the lists. There was even this healthy rivalry between sub-stations of the police force, between wardens' posts, between first-aid posts.

Left, Wings for Victory march - 1943, above right, Warships Week march 1942.

With each of the "Weeks" there were impressive parades and demonstrations by the three Services and the Civil Defence organisations, which revealed the ever-growing strength and efficiency which year by year was being brought to the war effort. These Services, both armed and civil, were a heartening sight as each year they swung past the saluting base. They showed how the 1939 "slumbering lion" was completely aroused. In these processions the British forces were joined by contingents of the various Allied forces which were in the district.

Another way in which Plymouth showed a generous war mind was in respect of what was known as the "Lord Mayor's Services Welfare Fund", to which was subsequently added "Air Raid Relief Fund".

This Fund was inaugurated by Lord Astor when he first became Lord Mayor in November, 1939. He realised the possibility of a variety of funds being started for an equal variety of objects, but mostly for

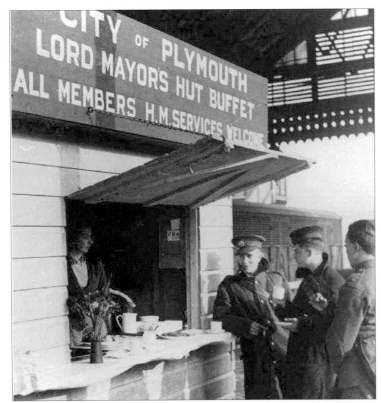

the comfort and welfare of the men and women in the Services. His suggestion was that they should create one central fund to which all appeals for monetary gifts or gifts in kind could be sent. His suggestion was promptly and heartily agreed to.

Mr. Arthur Brunyee, Manager of the Midland Bank, became the first Secretary and Treasurer of the Fund, the ramifications of which grew far beyond what was at first visualised. It was well organised, well publicised, and the response of the public was such that there was throughout the war a steady stream of money flowing into the Fund.

There was, of course, a possibility that when the first rush of subscriptions stopped the Fund would be lacking in money to carry on, and so Lord Astor appealed for what he called "an assured income." He did not appeal in vain. The assured income came in the way of regular weekly or monthly subscriptions from firms and staffs. From their pay packets staffs voluntarily agreed to a small regular deduction, and in thousands of instances that was continued throughout the war. Sixpence a week was a small unnoticed deduction, but in the aggregate it swelled into an enormous figure.

The Fund rapidly grew, and in the first four years of its operation a total of £121,000 was subscribed for the welfare of the Services in the district, Plymothians serving away, or prisoners of war, and for air raid relief.

As an example, from this Fund large donations were given to the British Red Cross in order to ensure parcels being sent regularly to Plymouth prisoners of war. Canteens, hostels, clubs were liberally financed for the benefit of Service men and women, entertainment and recreational facilities were provided for even the most isolated units in the district.

The work became so vast that a permanent staff had to be employed in self-contained offices, but Mr. Brunyee continued to be the Honorary Treasurer, with the Lord Mayor as President. There was an Executive Committee under the chairmanship of Sir Clifford Tozer, and this Committee was thoroughly representative of the various social bodies, denominations, and voluntary organisations in the city.

Then when the heavy raids came, bringing acute distress among so many bombed-out families, it was obvious that Plymouth would need to help its own people. While the authorities had the organisation to deal with what might be called immediate necessities, there was that inevitable gap when a little prompt extra help, given immediately and without any shadow of publicity, made a world of difference.

This was where the Lord Mayor's Fund stepped in, and in a quiet way, which only the recipients and those actually concerned with the distribution knew it accomplished a grand work.

For this purpose the Lord Mayor's Fund added to its title "Air Raid Relief Fund". Partly, this addition to the title was also necessary because money flowed into the Fund specially earmarked by the donors for air raid relief. This money came in large and small contributions from all parts of the world. Cities, towns, and villages in this country especially in the western counties, sent generous contributions, but no less heartening was the practical sympathy which came from overseas from the Dominions and Colonies, and, in particular, from the United States of America. Many of Plymouth's daughter towns - "full forty scattered up and down the world" - did not forget the agony and distress of the "mother".

"Mother Plymouth", old, tired, bleeding from a hundred wounds, did not beg; rather she sat, as ever, proudly by the sea. But wherever she looked, north, south, east, or west, there seemed to be tender hands anxious to soothe her brow, words to console her anguish, encouragement to meet and overcome her difficulties, and practical sympathy in money and in kind to relieve the burdens of the hour.

Plymouth will never forget that sympathy. It was something which touched her deeply, and it did much to help the flickering flame of hope to gather strength and once again regain steadiness.

And, I think, the enhanced value of this help lay in the fact that in the giving and in the receiving there was never a thought of charity. Never before in her long history had Plymouth been made to realise that she had so many true and solid friends in every quarter of the world.

But do not let it be thought that Plymouth was solely dependent on this outside aid; she helped herself as well. Neither let it be forgotten how the thousands of men and women in the Services themselves gave practical expression of their gratitude and affection for Plymouth in her hour of trial.

Let us honour, too, the hundreds of Service men who risked their lives in the "Battle of Plymouth" when they came into the city in voluntary parties fighting the fires, rescuing people from bombed buildings, driving any cars they could beg, borrow, or "commandeer" for emergency work. I know of more than one party of officers, non-commis-

sioned officers, and men which on those nights of terror went to their commanding officers and begged permission to "go into the city and help". That permission was not denied. It was a wonderful expression of their gratitude for what Plymouth did for them.

And these men and women of the Services gave generously to the Fund which was created to provide them with comfort and welfare. Take as an example the buffet which was provided at North Road Station to provide a free cup of tea and a bun or sandwich to weary war travellers.

If ever you have been such a traveller you will know the value of that hospitality. No man or woman was asked to pay for that refreshment, and it cost the Lord Mayor's Welfare Fund something in the region of £40 a week to keep it running. But the price was small compared with the value of the work done. The buffet was open night and day. A million cups of tea were served in one year and the buffet was maintained for the duration.

There was a collecting-box on the counter of that buffet. No recipient of refreshment was asked to contribute, but the box was there if they

Far left top, Lord Mayor's hut buffet, for all members of HM Services, North Road Station, bottom, Queen's Messangers provide a tonic for the troops. Below, Canadian canteen, outside the bomb-damaged Treasury.

so desired. So many of them did so that it was generally something in the region of £15 to £17 which was emptied at the end of the week. In further reference to the Lord Mayor's Welfare Fund, it might be as well to give some indication of other activities which were carried out under the heading "Services Welfare and Comfort".

Not the least of these was the provision of a hostel in St. Michael's Terrace; close to North Road Station. Here Service men who were journeying by train could spend the waiting period in warmth and comfort and at the same time obtain a light meal. This was run, under the auspices of Toc H., but the Lord Mayor's Fund financed the scheme. Thousands of Service men utilised this place every year, instead of having to put up with the cold discomfort of a dark railway station.

Then, again, there were numerous hostels and canteens which the Fund financed, although in some instances the money was refunded when the concern reached the profit-producing basis. Among the most important was the assistance given to the Y.M.C.A. This made possible the acquisition of premises formerly known as the Hoe Mansions Hotel in Elliot Street, close to the Hoe, where meals, entertainment, and sleeping accommodation were obtainable.

Then, again, there was the King George VI Officers' Club, close to the main entrance to the Hoe. These premises, acquired and run by the Y.M.C.A., provided a place where officers could have meals, and there was limited sleeping accommodation. This was the first experiment of such a club for officers in the country, and it was an unqualified success. Incidentally, the official opening of this club in 1942 was one of the last public ceremonies performed by the late Duke of Kent in Plymouth.

Altogether, when one looked around, it could be seen on every hand what a truly magnificent work was performed by the Lord Mayor's Fund. Plymouth could say with all sincerity that despite her own troubles she had extended hospitality to the war sojourners with traditional Westcountry generosity. Perhaps the Service men and women were the best judges; they expressed themselves freely. Many letters were received by the Lord Mayor and Lady Mayoress from Service men and women who had participated in that hospitality. For Plymouth it was sufficient that the city had regarded the provision of that hospitality as a serious responsibility; it would have been a sad reflection had she done otherwise.

Queen's Messenger Convoy Canteen facilities at St Budeaux station.

EDUCATION AND RELIGION

No record of Plymouth in the war years would be complete without some reference as to how the schools carried on. Things proceeded fairly normally until the heavy raids of March and April, 1941.

As I have stated earlier those who saw the way in which the storm was beginning to gather had pleaded with the authorities in London that, as far as the children were concerned, Plymouth should be an evacuation area. It was of no avail, and thus it was that many schools were destroyed and many Plymouth children were among the Nazi victims of mass murder of civil populations before there was a change of official mind.

Then, of course, it all had to be done in a hurry. The evacuation even then was quite voluntary. I do not think much more than about fifty per cent of the children went into the country, and as things grew quieter the greater proportion of these came back again.

For the most part they went into Cornwall. I saw many of the special trains off at North Road Station. The evacuees went off very cheerfully, but I do not think I shall be wrong when I say that there was some pining in the homes which had thus become hushed of the sound of children's voices and laughter.

The evacuation of the children was properly organised. They went in parties to special reception areas, where arrangements were made for their billeting with foster-parents and education in the local school under their own teachers, who accompanied them into "exile".

By the middle of 1943 of the total of 12,000 children who had been evacuated, no fewer than 8,000 had returned to Plymouth.

This flow back into the city created a very serious problem for the Education Authority, both from the point of view of accommodation and teaching staff.

The accommodation worry can best be appreciated when I say that about ninety Plymouth schools were either destroyed completely or severely damaged by enemy action. Fortunately, all the damage was caused during night raids, so that there were no casualties among children while actually attending school.

As far as evacuation was concerned, there were only a few schools which went away as complete entities. Among these were Devonport High School, which was evacuated to Penzance, and there, singu-

Smeaton College, Citadel Road, one of many Plymouth schools to be destroyed.

larly enough, enjoyed a period of outstanding success as far as academic results were concerned. Sutton Secondary School migrated to St. Austell; Devonport Girls' High School to Tiverton; Plymouth Girls' High School to Newquay; Mount House private school to Tavistock; St. Boniface College to Buckfast Abbey; Headland Girls' College to Gunnislake; St. Dunstan's Abbey Girls' School sent the boarders section to Newquay, while retaining the day school at the Abbey, North Road. Later the full school, as a day school only was at the Abbey. The United Services' Girls Orphanage, Stoke, was evacuated to their old-time summer residence at Newquay.

Among the educational establishments which "stayed put" in the city was Plymouth College. While there were many bombs that exploded in the vicinity the College, which must have been quite a conspicuous target for an enemy which obviously had an eye for public buildings, it went through the war unscathed. The Ford Park cricket ground was quite a sportsman's "oasis" during the summer months, especially as the Plymouth Cricket Club had put up the shutters at Peverell Park with the outbreak of the war. Other private schools which continued in Plymouth included Warrans and Moorfield.

Left, Summer 1944, the athletes of Plymouth College sports day negotiate two American anti-aricraft guns on the school field at Ford Park.

It was, however, the flow back into Plymouth of the evacuee children which created the problem for the education authority. Much accommodation had to be improvised to meet the demands of the children already in Plymouth. Classes in the existing schools became swollen to a far greater extent than normally laid down as practical. Nevertheless, the full curriculum was maintained, and the examinations for the higher schools continued to be held. By the middle of 1943 the position had materially improved, as by that time several of the lesser damaged schools had been repaired.

While Coventry lost its historic cathedral in the first of the very heavy and concentrated raids which fell on the big provincial cities and towns of this country it is, I think, doubtful whether any place had its ecclesiastical gems more ruthlessly destroyed than Plymouth. The long list of churches which were destroyed, either by the blast of high explosive bombs or gutted by fire, included some which were associated with the earliest organised religion in the city and there were, of course, priceless historic ties.

Left, Headland College opposite Plymouth High School for Girls is hit, 21, March 1941. Above, Hoe Grammar School in Lockyer Street is also destroyed.

Heading the list was the lovely and beloved mother church of St. Andrew which was left nothing but a charred shell after the second of the heavy raids in March, 1941. St. Andrew's truly belonged to old Plymouth, but the modern Plymouth had daily swirled past her doors, standing as the church did adjoining the main shopping centre at St. Andrew's Cross. Its great sturdy square tower with the four-faced clock which every four hours had cracked out familiar hymn tunes for generations, had been dominating even amid the group of tall architecture provided by the much more modern Guildhall and Municipal Offices.

Alone in the centre of this ancient and modern architecture the St. Andrew's church tower withstood the shock of that terrific bombardment. In the days that followed the tower stood like a mighty sentinel watching over the stricken body of the church.

The clock stopped, the hands on two of the faces were bent and broken by the blast, but, miraculously, the works were found to be still in order, and after a few days it was again giving the city faithful time on its two sound faces looking down on the Guildhall Square, and towards the historic Hoe.

The bells, too, were intact, and when, after the long silence imposed on the ringing of church bells throughout the country save as a warning of invasion, the ban was lifted in 1943 – first in commemoration of the North Africa victory and then for normal resumption in calling people to worship – I do not think the People of Plymouth had ever listened to sweeter music.

The peals were like a message of hope; certainly a message that St. Andrew's was "living". Were we not reminded that it was the bells of St. Andrew's that Drake heard when he sailed into Plymouth Sound in the sixteenth century after his voyage round the world?

One could imagine the music of the 1943 peals going on and on into the great void of space until they reached every son and daughter of Plymouth in every corner of the world.

The intact tower, the bare, gaunt, fire-stricken walls and pillars were all that remained of the once lovely mother church when dawn, smoke- and dust-laden, broke after that final destruction.

Gone was the perfect barrel roof that had spanned the mighty nave for so long an architectural gem for the antiquarians – gone was every vestige of glass from the beautiful stained-glass windows, through

Nancy Astor in the ruins of St Andrew's Church, March 1941.

The congregation filter out of the shell of St Andrew's where services continue despite the exigencies of war.

St. Andrew's that next morning was just a shell, the floor piled high with the masses of burnt timber and broken masonry. Yet it seemed to stand as a symbol the body crushed and bleeding, but the spirit surviving.

There were many gallant workers in St. Andrew's during those hours of destruction, men and women. The valuable plate was saved. They saved all they could; they tried in vain to battle with the flames. The whole place was a fiery furnace.

Yet even in those terrible conditions the outline of the building never seemed to lose its dignity. Plymouth will get back its St. Andrew's one day, nobler and finer than ever before. Even as I write the initial steps have been taken towards raising the thousands of pounds that will be required to complete the work of restoration.

It was only a matter of hours before there appeared over the doorless north porch that used to look out on the Cross and well kept gardens the single word "Resurgam" ("I shall rise again").

Thus it was that as soon as facilities could be provided tender hands set to work to heal the wounds. The debris-charred wood, blackened and blistered masonry - piled high in the great body of the church, was removed. The stone aisles were bared. Where the pews had ranged grass was neatly laid, where the choir and clergy stalls led to the altar there were borders of scarlet geraniums. A simple altar, with its burnished, gleaming cross, was erected under a temporary cover against the elements. The main body of the church was, of course, still open to the sky. Birds flew in an out of the windows, empty save for the twisted lead that once held the "lights".

That was the scene when, in the summer of 1943, "garden" services were held there every Sunday evening, and were attended by thousands. The veteran organist, Dr. Harry Moreton, led the singing from a small manual organ at the foot of the pulpit. The congregations just stood, grouped in the "garden" that was once the body of the church. The pulpit was fitted with a microphone and loud-speaker. The services were simple – but St. Andrew's was "living" again.

With the loss of St. Andrew's the daughter church of St. Catherine, at the bottom of Lockyer Street, which had escaped the devastation all around, became the parish church of St, Andrew's, the new title being "St. Andrew with St. Catherine". Here the religious life of the parish continued with all its activities, even to the attendance of the famous St. Andrew's choir, and with Dr. Moreton at the organ.

which the sun used to send its delicate shafts of light by day, and which in the darkness of peace-time night during evensong would emit to the outside world a soft multiple glow of reds, blues, ambers, and other shades. Gone were all the pews, many of the ornaments, the gleaming lectern, the richly-carved choir and clergy stalls. Broken steps led up to the half-destroyed pulpit, from which in the centuries gone so many brilliant and distinguished ecclesiastics had delivered their spiritual messages.

Another old and historic church which Plymouth lost in the 1941 blitz was Charles, which was built over a period of years and completed in 1665. Yet another of the lovely old edifices which had come down through the centuries to be destroyed was St. George's, Stonehouse, concerning which there are valuable seventeenth century records. These were saved. The bomb which destroyed this church accomplished one of the most freakish incidents of the city's damage. It was as though some giant knife had sliced the square tower down in half. One half crumbled to the ground in a pile of debris, the other half remained standing. Viewed from the Stonehouse Bridge, this presented a rather remarkable sight.

Charles Church is left as just a shell. Above, the bells fall from their lofty height.

No list of the Plymouth churches destroyed would be complete without reference to the beautiful St. Peter's. It was much more modern than most of the churches in the city, and its appointments, vestments, and ornaments were a rich collection. This church was gutted by fire, but here again the fine distinctive tower remained standing. Similarly, St. James-the-Less, in the Hoe district, was a total loss from direct hits by high explosives and fire.

Above, the beautiful St Peter's. Top right, St James the Less on the Hoe.

At the Devonport end of the city the devastation among the churches was no less grievous. St. Paul's, old and mellow, which had stood four-square and solid at the corner of Morice Square; St. Stephen's, with its slender spire and colourful windows and rich ornaments, close to Mount Wise; St. Michael's, imposing and beloved, at Stoke; the Garrison Church; and St. Aubyn's were among the Church of England buildings lost or badly damaged.

To no less a degree the Free Churches of the city were destroyed. Some of these had been associated with the Nonconformist life of Plymouth for centuries. Foremost among the losses was the George Street Baptist Church, tucked away behind the busy main shopping thoroughfare, and dating from 1649; Courtenay Street Congregational Church; the spacious King Street Methodist Church; Norley Congregational Church; Sherwell Congregational Church; Greenbank Methodist Church; Salisbury Road Baptist Church; while quite a number of others at the Plymouth end of the city were badly damaged.

At Devonport the Nonconformist losses included Belmont, Gloucester Street, and St. Levan Road churches.

The Unitarians lost their old church in Treville Street, and Roman Catholics lost the Most Holy Redeemer in Ocean Street, Keyham.

The Salvation Army lost their famous headquarters in Octagon Street, Plymouth the Congress Hall.

These losses, which I enumerate by way of representation, show how all sections of the religious life were affected in the widespread damage, which showed neither class nor creed distinction.

Yet, in spite of these serious setbacks, the religious life of the city continued to flow at a high level. Many of the churches merged; those still standing took in their homeless neighbours.

Quite often the sirens sounded while services were being held. I was present on a few of these occasions. Never once did I see a person leave the congregation unless they were on air raid duty which demanded their presence. If the service ended while the "alert" was still in progress, the congregation was invited to stay on and sing hymns, or listen to short readings. The singing was often punctuated with the crash of the anti-aircraft guns as they engaged the enemy aircraft. It seemed as though the churches in those periods were indeed places of real sanctuary, and all the crashings and reverberations from outside were as from another world.

I remember on one occasion being at evensong at Emmanuel Church when the "alert" sounded. The vicar quietly announced that any who wished could leave, and paused in the service for a few moments to allow any departures. Then, quite coolly and calmly, he went on with the service. There were times when his sermon was completely broken by the noise of the warring elements outside. He would pause, smile, and then go on again.

The "alert" was still on when the evensong ended. The vicar suggested that the congregation should remain and have an impromptu service of hymns and readings. This went on for well over an hour, and then silence once more fell over the city, and the sirens wailed the "raiders passed" The congregation quietly knelt in silence for a few minutes and then went to their homes. This was another very striking example of how the people took the raids.

It was the sort of example that seemed to indicate that a powerful and sincere faith was beating in the hearts of Plymothians. It was a faith which gave them courage and hope. One saw it illustrated on other occasions, such as on those special days which were set aside as national days of prayer, when the churches were packed. The Christian spirit was far from dead.

Top, St Paul's, Morice Square. Right, A wartime service in St Andrews.

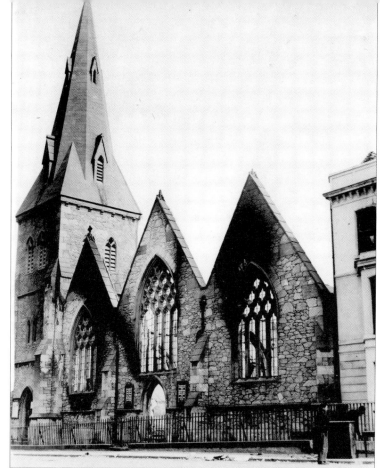

PLYMOUTH DEFENCES

There is no question that the south-west of England, with Plymouth as an all-important centre, held a prominent position in the German plans for any attempted invasion of this country.

How real was the threat of invasion was illustrated by the discovery in Brussels of a vast collection of maps, guides, plans, and a whole volume of other detailed information, prepared after years of painstaking collection by the Germans for the unquestioned purpose of attack.

I had the opportunity of seeing the "Guides" which had special relation to the south-west, and there was obviously not much that the Germans did not know about our coastline and all its features. Possible landings in Devon and Cornwall were clearly indicated.

On the other hand, those responsible for the defences of this country were quite alive to this danger of frontal attack by either or both seaborne and airborne forces.

It was against this threat that Plymouth, like other parts of the country prepared itself for dire eventuality. In this connection the setting up of an Invasion Committee was a matter of first importance. On its shoulders would fall a grim responsibility.

Anyone who has had the experience of towns over which the wave of war has surged with such fearful consequences to the lives of the civil population, will appreciate to the full how vital it was that there should be in existence to meet invasion emergency an organisation which could be the focal point to which people could look for guidance.

Preparations and plans made by the Plymouth Invasion Committee were most comprehensive and thorough, and had the occasion arisen one feels confident that they would have succeeded in a twofold way – reducing to a minimum the inconveniences and hardships of invasion conditions, and raising to the maximum the harassing and hampering of the enemy.

The Home Guard practice gun drill in the shadow of the Ballard Centre. Right, Evening Herald, 23 May 1940 "A view of public air-raid shelters constructed in the middle of the roadway in King-gardens, Plymouth. Next week work will begin on 44 new shelters on the highway in various parts of the city. They will be able to accommodate altogether about 3,500 people."

The "War Book" which contained all the details is most interesting in its directives and information, and now that the situation has permitted the disbandment of the Committee which was on a "stand to" footing for four years, one can to some extent remove the "red band" of security with its enjoinder "not to be allowed to fall into enemy hands".

In the main the Invasion Committee had three functions: to ensure co-ordinated action by the civilian interests affected by invasion; to secure appropriate action for the assistance of the Services' authorities if such demand was made to the Committee; and to act as the focal point to which the civil population could look for guidance.

The powers of the Committee were derived from the military and the Regional Commissioner.

During invasion civil administration would continue as long as possible. Military requirements would, of course, be paramount, but

that did not mean that civil administration would be superseded, but merely that the well-being of the civil population would necessarily be the secondary consideration.

To meet possible emergency the Committee was organised in two sections. There was the original Committee and a Shadow Committee, so that if the city became divided into two areas and one became isolated from the other they could function independently. Further than that arrangements were made for the functioning of the city even if it became divided into several pockets by enemy troops. This system was based on twelve centres of direct local action, each responsible for its own sub-area.

The main scheme was drawn up on the assumption that an attempt might be made to capture Plymouth (a) by airborne landings; (b) attack on the coast from the sea, with close aircraft support and gas; and (c) a combination of all.

It was assumed that the enemy, in fulfilment of this object, might bomb by day and night as a prelude and during invasion, with the object of destroying Services' resources, dislocating communications, and impairing morale.

Rightly, it was assumed that Plymouth held an important position in the plans of the enemy for successful invasion, but it can be said that

Lord Astor and Admiral Dunbar Nasmith inspect the men of the AFS on the Hoe.

The newly constituted National Fire Service at their HQ at Yelverton.

there was never any intention on the part of the Services to withdraw. Any attempt to capture Plymouth would be violently opposed.

And so the whole plans of defence were based on that determination. For instance, it was the instruction that all civilian services would stand fast to serve the needs of the civil population – a directive which would throw great responsibility on the Police, Civil Defence services, and the National Fire Service.

There were plans for the maximum functioning of public utility services, and at the same time every possible help had to be available for the Armed Forces. In fact, on this latter point the directive said, "This duty may well override everything else, even sometimes the call of humanity."

There was to be no general destruction of resources so as to deny their use to the enemy, but schemes were carefully prepared whereby important documents, papers, and vital machinery could be hidden. Special precautions were planned to ensure that, fake instructions by the enemy should be ineffective.

The plan emphasised that the civil population would not be without its responsibilities. It would be expected to stand firm except under definite orders, but not in a passive role. It was always expected that the people would offer united opposition to an invader, and there were certain well-defined instructions laid down.

Altogether, it can be said that as far as organisation and anticipation were concerned, Plymouth was well prepared for invasion emergency, and the entire build-up was on the Boy Scouts' motto of "Be prepared".

This way to the Air Raid Shelters

123

Home Guard

When, in 1940, this nation was left to face the avalanche of the Nazi aggression, and became the lone fortress of civilisation, when all other countries which had sought to arrest the onward sweep had become swamped and left under the heel of the tyrant, the greater part of the world conjectured that it would be but a matter of time before this country would likewise be overwhelmed. Remember the French cynic who declared that Britain's neck would be wrung like that of a chicken within six weeks, and how Churchill flung back the taunt with "Some chicken, some neck".

The world was to receive another astonishing lesson. There was only that strip of water, a mere ditch to fast seacraft packed with hordes of highly-trained men flushed with their success, a mere few minutes of hurtling through the air for the much-vaunted Luftwaffe.

The Prime Minister was quite aware of that narrow "moat" dividing us from the enemy. He knew the power of the enemy, he knew only too well Our own weakness, but he knew also the measure of the spirit of the British people.

Yes, our material defences were woefully weak, wholly inadequate, but there was a "something" about the people who manned the ragged battlements which made the aggressor pause and think.

This was a challenge which could not be left alone to the Armed Forces. It was a challenge to the entire manhood and womanhood of the nation.

So the call went forth to every able-bodied and home-loving man who could be spared from other essential work, and even those in their spare time, to enrol in the Local Defence Volunteers. There was a magnificent and instantaneous response. The Home Guard was born, although it was not to be known by that title for a few months longer. The force was open to men of all ages between 18 and 65. This age was subsequently reduced to take in youths of 17.

But it was one thing to recruit this force, another thing to equip and train it. When one paused and contemplated the gigantic and sinister military machine against which it might have to test its strength, one realised what a tremendous faith would have to be placed for the time being in the moral as well as the physical spirit of the nation. There was, however, no faltering. The citizen army, the like of which the world had never known, was created.

Fortunately, there was a splendid backbone of ex-Servicemen with experiences of the last war and even the Boer war. The scent of battle was in their nostrils; discipline and the handling of arms was their second nature. Too old for this war, by all the laid-down standards, here was their chance. They took it open-handed.

Left, Home Guard detachment at Plymouth College, Ford park. Above Colonel Bastard inspects a local unit.

In Plymouth the response was something of which the city could be proud. It was a stirring sight to see the early "fall in" of this force. There was no question of rank or class distinction. Britain needed every man for her home defences – ex-generals, colonels, captains, admirals, post-captains, and "other ranks", of all the Services, who had been languishing in "civvy" street and longing for something active to do in this war, fell in in a single rank.

A Home Guard battalion undergoes inspection at Radford, Plymstock.

The sorting out soon took place. Officers and non-commissioned officers were picked for ability as leaders in this new organisation, not for what they might have been. The squire and the farm labourer, the transport chief and the van driver, the bank manager and the bank clerk, the business director and the shop assistant, the man in morning dress and the man with the scarf around his neck, the youngster in flannel "bags" and plus-fours, whose face had never yet been scraped by a razor, and the grey-beards and bald-heads – these were the men of Britain who stood shoulder to shoulder in answer to the call.

At first glance it might have seemed a nondescript army as, without arms or uniforms, they rallied for their initial training. Their uniform was merely an armlet; they drilled with broomsticks. In the very early days there was no age limit, only physical infirmity as a bar to this service. There were not a few who found that while the spirit was keen and willing the flesh was woefully weak. And so age limits had to be laid down. War is no game for the old and infirm. And this was certainly no game.

A few months later someone had an inspiration. They altered the title to the Home Guard. What a fitting title that was!

Home Guard! That was just what the force was! Behind it lay that mossy-old claim "An Englishman's home is his castle". And now the Englishman's castle was being threatened.

Slowly, but surely the new and formidable defence force was built out of this great reservoir of the nation's man-power.

Plymouth raised and maintained two complete battalions within the city. These were the 16th Battalion, Devonshire Regiment, commanded by Lieut. Col. W.A.E. Northcott, which might more aptly be called the City Battalion, and the 17th Battalion, which was exclusively composed of Devonport Dockyard employees, confined its duties to that establishment, and was commanded by Lieut. Col. W.S. Cooper.

In addition, there were in the immediate neighbourhood two more battalions, one with headquarters at Plympton and the other with headquarters at Saltash.

It was specifically laid down in the early days – in the days when it was only a matter of conjecture as to how when, or where Hitler would strike this country – that the Home Guard, essentially a defence force, was for operation within the limits of its own immediate area. Thus the battalions mentioned above became an integral and vital part of the defences of Plymouth. Portions of these battalions were in detached units, but more about them later.

The provision of uniform and equipment was a painfully slow business. In the early days the weapons comprised all sorts of oddments, and there was a great deal of improvisation and not a little ingenuity. It was a case of the other and more important claims of the fighting services having to come first.

At the same time it was a striking tribute to the enthusiastic spirit of the members of the Home Guard, as well as their patience, that they never lost heart. They meant serious business, and they went on acquiring proficiency with the facilities that were available.

Steadily the Home Guard was moulded into a first-class army of defence, and while its responsibilities changed and increased with the altered war situations, and it was never used for its original purpose to resist the invader in combat on the shores of this land, they remained throughout the war a formidable and serious deterrent to any enemy ambitions.

One of the most stimulating features was the way in which the Home Guard enthusiasm was maintained. They trained assiduously, giving up their evenings, their Sunday mornings, and at times their entire weekend to advance their proficiency in real and serious soldiering. Once this army of the Home Guard had been established it was given an ever-increasing responsibility. It became something much more than a force to be called into action by the ringing of the church bells when invasion was imminent. It was given all-round-the-clock specific defence duties. It became almost the backbone of the defence of this country; a determined and solid backbone at that. At first they were trained almost entirely as infantry to deal with emergencies in their own district, and their intimate local knowledge of the countryside where they worked and lived was an important factor in their value as a delaying and harassing force.

They became uniformed, armed and equipped in due course on a par with the regular army, the discipline became strict, their training was no sinecure. Many an army has gone into the field less equipped, less experienced, less disciplined, and certainly less spirited, than the British Home Guard. Perhaps, because in the main they were never called into serious combat with the enemy, we never quite knew their full value, but it must inevitably go down with the history of this war that in the hour of Britain's greatest danger there was this mighty force, affording an ever-increasing confidence.

I had the opportunity of being with the Plymouth Home Guard during much of their intensive training, at weekend exercises and schemes, and during important combined operations with the regular forces. Sufficient for me was to hear the praise from highly-placed regular officers whose special responsibility was the defence of this country. They placed great reliance and confidence in the part which the Home Guard would have to play in emergency.

When the third anniversary of the inauguration of the Home Guard was celebrated in 1943, with parades and displays all over the country, there were no fewer than a million men in the force, highly trained in all phases of modern warfare, well equipped with the latest arms, and showing proficiency which gave the country justifiable pride. By this time we had Home Guard infantry, Home Guard artillery, Home Guard engineers, Home Guard anti-aircraft, and Home Guard commandos. By that date something like 1,400 of Plymouth Home Guard were in anti-aircraft and regularly manning part of the local defences against air attack. They were responsible for what were known as the "Z" batteries, rocket defences which formed a formidable part of the barrage. Some also did day manning.

The Harest is vital. Plymouth Home Guard help local farmers while still waiting and watching for the enemy.

One night when these batteries were filling the sky at practice with the flashes and reverberations of their rockets, someone very aptly remarked that they should not be called rockets but "rackets".

Certainly, when those batteries were in action, every window and door in the area was set rattling.

These Home Guard anti-aircraft batteries, commanded by Major J. Bedford and Major F.G. Fleury, had an advantage over their comrades who were still in the "P.B.I.". They did get real action in the later raids on Plymouth.

They had the satisfaction, too, of being among the first Home Guard in this country to bring down an enemy raider. That was in the 1943 Whitsuntide raid. They really claimed two of the four which were shot down, but officially they were credited with one and "shared" the other. For this they received commendation, and they were justly proud of their achievement.

There was another very important feature of the Home Guard which should be remembered. They provided a first-class initial training for the regular forces. Youngsters were admitted to the Home Guard at the age of seventeen, and so they had a minimum of a year's sound training before being conscripted into the regular armed services. I was frequently told of the enormous value which this proved.

Inspection by the Commander-in-Chief at the Hoe of the Home Guard Birthday Parade

It might also be remembered that while the initial force was voluntary, in the later years men were definitely directed for their part-time national service into the Home Guard. In this it came on a par with Civil Defence services, and men in the Home Guard had to accept their responsibilities seriously and attend the requisite number of parades or disciplinary action was taken, with possible severe consequences.

Save for the older men, the Home Guard was constantly changing in personnel. Unless a young man was in some reserved occupation, or engaged in essential production, he automatically passed into the regular forces on attaining the conscription age. Thus it was quite possible that during the war upwards of 5,000 men might have passed through a single battalion. Battalion strength at one time was 2,500.

The Home Guard wore the khaki battle-dress of the regular army, their officers held the King's commission, and there were generally some regular instructors and a regular army adjutant attached to each battalion.

I mentioned earlier the detached units of the Home Guard. There were a number of these in Plymouth, as, for instance, The Western Morning News, the Railway Companies, the Gas Works, the Corporation Transport, the Post Office, and others. They were composed entirely of the staffs of those undertakings, and their special task was the carefully studied defence of their own particular industry and buildings. At the same time they were part and parcel of the parent battalion.

It must be remembered that each of these undertakings which had its own detached unit of the Home Guard was what was defined as a "vulnerable point", or a "vulnerable undertaking", and as such was specially defended.

Thus the Home Guard was established, a fine blending of the extremes of manhood – age and experience, youth and new adventure. It was no crazy growth scrambled together on the alarm "Man the barricades!"; it was a powerful army, enthusiastic, proficient, and it marched down Hitler's ill-starred road of destiny with grim resolution. For four years it waited and watched; there was never a moment of slackening in its standard of alertness. Always my great admiration for the Home Guard was the way its enthusiasm and spirit of service was maintained. Its members never seemed, in Army parlance, to be "browned off" for lack of something to do beyond training. That was a great achievement. When, in November, 1944, the danger of invasion of this country had so far receded as to permit the "stand down" for the Home Guard being ordered, the standard of efficiency was just as high as at any period in the four years' training. I am pretty sure that among the general body of the members there was more than a passing tinge of regret when they handed in their arms and put away their uniforms for the last time.

Plymouth, however, did have its opportunity of saying "Thank you", and did so in generous fashion at the farewell parade on the Hoe on Sunday, December 3, 1944, when the Garrison Commander took the salute and the Lord Mayor expressed the city's gratitude.

It was an inspiring parade of between three and four thousand of the city's Home Guard – Plymouth men, full of military pride and precision – a striking fade-out.

Royal Observer Corps

One of the silent services of the war was the Royal Observer Corps, composed of both whole-time and part-time members. These were the men who throughout the war manned the observation stations on lonely headlands and isolated hilltops and maintained a ceaseless day and night vigil for hostile aircraft.

It was a service which played a vital part in the defences of the country, but it rarely was given any limelight. Its members wore a uniform of Royal Air Force blue, mostly of battle-dress style, but their head-dress was a beret with a distinctive badge depicting a "Watcher" of the Elizabethan days gazing out to sea, and with it the singularly appropriate motto, "Forewarned is forearmed".

There were few war occupations which demanded more intensive study, for these men had to have their eyes and ears so tuned that they could instantly identify any aircraft, hostile or friendly, which came within their zone of operation. Naturally this was easier by day than by night, but it was almost uncanny how in the darkness they could accurately plot and identify different types of aircraft. For the Royal Observer Corps, members had to qualify by examination, in which they were not only given a severe test at instantaneous identification of aircraft but had to be able to give the distinguishing features of construction and markings.

How very real this knowledge was I tested for myself on more than one occasion. I was handed a pack of cards, hundreds of cards in the pack. Each card gave a front and side silhouette of a different aircraft, and with a printed explanation on the back of the individual characteristics. I was invited to pick out any card and hold it up. The answer was always instantaneous – the type of aircraft and its particular features.

The immediate recognition of aircraft was most important. It often happened that an aircraft would be in range of sight or hearing only a matter of seconds.

In many ways the work was a flash-back through the centuries to the watchers of the Elizabethan period who similarly kept vigil against the approach of an enemy to these shores and who sent their alarm by beacon fire throughout the length and breadth of the country. Instead of being sea-watchers, the Royal Observer Corps were more vitally watchers of the sky and so carefully were the areas of adjoining sta-

A German pilot checks his map with Plymouth Pier and Royal Citadel below him.

tions overlapped,' that there was no stretch where the intruders could slip through unobserved.

The big difference was that whereas warning of the slower approach of enemy seacraft in Elizabethan days was given by beacon fire, the Royal Observer Corps had to match the modern speed of aircraft by telephone, or, failing that, by rocket. When it is remembered that the aircraft might sweep in at a speed of anything up to 400 miles an hour, the importance of speed of warning can be appreciated. But the plot of the machine would be passed from station to station and never be out of observation.

I had the opportunity of visiting some of the Royal Observer Corps stations in my capacity of War Correspondent, and so at first hand seeing the members at their work. The vigilance was unrelaxing. It was a job to test endurance. Of necessity the stations had to be in a commanding and exposed position, and observation had to be

The City was covered by a network of 135 wardens' posts, manned day and night.

maintained out of doors. Stand in the small "keep" of one of these stations on a bitter winter night, ears glued to headphones, eyes almost smarting with the knife-like wind and rain. Remember, too, that most of the members were of middle age or beyond it. But they were a hardy lot, and they were certainly proud of the Corps' efficiency. Nor was the job without its monotony. There were long and silent patches, but the vigil had to remain alert.

There were a number of these stations in the vicinity of Plymouth. And there had need to be, for if one took the line of coast from Looe to the Start, it was one of the busiest routes in the days of intensive air raids, not only for the targets which the enemy sought in the South-West, but for the West, the Midlands, and the North-West; the direct line, as it were, for the raids on Bristol, Swansea, Cardiff, Liverpool, Manchester, and Birmingham.

Let the mind go back to the nights when the heavy drone of enemy bombers on their way to those distant targets, and returning from them, was heard over Plymouth. The Royal Observer Corps was plotting every one of those 'planes, flashing the warnings to the defence nerve-centres.

It was a grand piece of work which the Royal Observer Corps did throughout the war; silent work, but tremendously effective.

This was, indeed, a service which never slept.

Air Raid Wardens

Several thousands of men and women citizens – ranging in age from their 'teens to an octogenarian, who was awarded the British Empire Medal for devotion to duty – formed the splendid air raid wardens' service as part of the Civil Defence organisation. It had a nucleus of full-time wardens, but the vast proportion of at least ninety per cent gave unpaid part-time service.

For the purpose of the wardens' service, which was organised and trained by specially selected and qualified police officers, under the direction of the Chief Constable, the city was divided into six divisions, each under a divisional warden, and the whole area was further subdivided into fifty-four groups, each under a head warden.

The city was covered by a network of 135 wardens' posts, manned day and night, and each in direct communication with the nerve-centre of the A.R.P. control at Pounds House. These posts were under the charge of a senior warden.

Some time before the outbreak of war the training of wardens was in operation as a precautionary measure, and, bearing in mind the strain which the city was to undergo from enemy bombing, it was well that this pre-war training was developed on a big scale. It was then, of course, an entirely voluntary organisation, but it did mean that when trouble came there was already available a strong nucleus of well-trained and well-organised wardens.

During the full period of the war something like 7,000 men and women wardens were trained in the most intensive fashion. It was no haphazard or casual business. As I have mentioned, in the early days it was voluntary service as far as the part-timers were concerned, but later, when the control of man-power became operative, men and women were definitely directed into the service as compulsory part-timers, and there was strong disciplinary action against any who persistently failed to perform their prescribed periods of duty.

The extreme measure of police court proceedings was rare in Plymouth, where the sense of duty generally called for commendation. Personnel, of course, fluctuated considerably. The peak period of strength was round about 1943, when there was so much directed service, and the wardens then totalled about 3,500.

But in 1941, when the heavy raids made such heavy demands on the city's civil defences, the available strength was about 2,500, of whom about 2,250 were part-timers.

It was a tribute to the conscientious way in which wardens responded to their calls that the city could rely on at least ninety per cent turn-out for actual raids. For the absentees there was generally some justifiable excuse, such as being away from the city, sickness, or work.

Wardens were highly trained for the grim work they were called on to perform during raid emergencies – anti-gas, incendiary bombs, high-explosive bombs, first-aid, intimate knowledge of all people living in the district, with a register of individuals in each house, fitting and examination of gas respirators, and the carefully organised action to be taken for each raid incident. Further, at that period when the danger of invasion was at its height, many of them were trained in the use of arms with the Home Guard. The wardens, with their valuable organisation and knowledge, would have formed an important part of the resistance activity.

Plymouth can remember with pride these thousands of men and women in their dark-blue uniform and gold badges. They did a grand job, and the organisation and training was such that whenever the raid warning sounded, every part of the city, from back lanes to front streets, were under their patrol within a few minutes.

During the intensive raids in 1941 many of them went days with only snatches of rest, doing their wardens duty and carrying on with their work in a spirit which tested their endurance but never knew defeat. There were times when they would have to turn out of their warm beds for as many as five "alerts" in one night; there were others when they would maintain their patrol for "alerts" of five or six hours' duration without any incidents to handle. But they were always at work next day. Neither production nor defence could be neglected.

Many wardens, both men and women, won decorations for gallantry. As a fine example of devotion to duty there was eighty-three-year-old Mr. G.H. Foster, of Mount Gold, who never missed turning out for a raid, and who in due course was called to Buckingham Palace to receive the British Empire Medal at the hands of His Majesty the King. There were, too, a number of casualties among the wardens. During the raids they were like other Civil Defence organisations, "front-line" troops, and Plymouth wardens can look to their roll of honour with considerable pride in duty faithfully performed.

Plymouth can remember with pride these thousands of men and women in their dark-blue uniforms and gold badges.

Neither should it be forgotten that they played a notable part in many other activities. In the War Savings Campaigns the posts competed with each other, and there were some posts which raised considerable sums for war-time charities, the hospitals, and welfare.

THE SECOND FRONT

There was a very natural impatience on the part of the general public to see the opening of what was commonly called the Second Front; in other words, the direct attack on the Continent from this country. Everywhere we had watched the terrific build-up of the force and equipment with which that task was to be attempted, particularly in the south of England, where the port of Plymouth played such an important part.

In this area we glimpsed - and I use the word glimpsed deliberately – something of big organisation on the part of the United States. The South-West was to a large extent their training ground, their assembly area, and their springboard.

As far as Plymouth was concerned, the city became almost Americanized with the vast numbers of American service men who, for their final intensive training and pending the launching of the invasion, were stationed in our midst. If Plymouth did not learn something for future use in the way of big organisation, then an opportunity was certainly missed. We saw how they got on with their jobs in a big way; that the bigger the obstacles, the bolder were the methods of tackling them. In the South-West we were, in every sense of the word, "occupied" by the United States' armed forces.

We watched all this enormous build-up through the summer and winter of 1943, and when the spring of 1944 came we were all hazarding guesses as to when the attack on Hitler's European fortress would be launched. We remained guessing to the very last; the secret never leaked out. But all the time we were witnesses to a gathering momentum.

In my position of War Correspondent, I moved about considerably and saw a great deal more than the average man and woman. I knew that I was to be among the correspondents to report the invasion. Yet every day we used to ask each other "How long?"

Plymouth Sound in those days of late spring and early summer was a scene to he remembered. Day after day there was an amazing collection of weird-looking ships of all sorts and sizes riding at anchor. What they were to be used for and what was to be their destination, we could only guess.

What we did know, of course, was that those fleets formed part of the build-up for the invasion. There were some evenings when I counted

In the South-west we were, in every sense of the word, 'occupied' by the United States armed forces. Left, in training for D Day at Slapton. Above, America comes to Devon.

as many as eighty or ninety odd ships, large and small, in the Sound. Next morning most of them would have gone where we knew not, but before nightfall the anchorage would be crowded again. Even the old seafarers used to gaze at some of those craft and shake their grey heads in complete bewilderment. They could not make head nor tail of them or their use.

Yet every one of those ships was to have a definite use in the great scheme of invasion, when the day came for the launching of the attack against that heavily-defended Normandy coast.

What a target for the Luftwaffe! Yet we never saw as much as a reconnaissance plane over Plymouth in those momentous days. What was wrong with the German air force to be missing such a target? There was hardly a citizen who did not look very apprehensively at that target day after day and wonder how long it would remain unmolested?

I think it was in those days that I began to develop a growing conviction that we in Plymouth had seen just about the last of the Luftwaffe. It seemed to me common sense to argue along the line that if the Germans were unable to take advantage of such a sitting target of shipping and stores at the assembly port, then there must be something wrong. What gave the point emphasis was that Plymouth's experience was also the experience of other assembly ports even nearer to the French coast. The argument was, as we know borne out by experience, because Plymouth had no air attack after April 30, 1944, which was more than a month before D-Day.

In effect, therefore, Plymouth was a raid-free port all through those interesting build-up days, and that freedom continued after the invasion.

And while we were interested and guessing spectators of this day-to-day scene in our historic harbour, we could not be blind to the fast-moving events ashore. All along the waterfront there were mysterious developments taking place, such as the construction of special concrete embarkation hards and slipways. We could only guess their purpose.

Then there came a time in April when these areas became strictly unauthorised ground. Specified and controlled areas they were called, and as such came under close military and police guard. Even people who worked or lived inside them had to have special identity permits. Security was severe.

Behind the walls of secrecy the incessant build-up went on. And through the streets of our city, particularly under the cloak of darkness; the great convoys rumbled to and from the embarkation points – lorries, guns, tanks, bulldozers, jeeps, equipment, and men.

Along our coasts, particularly up in the Slapton area of South Devon, where the coast, for a stretch of about seven miles and to an inland depth of about four miles, was completely evacuated of all civilians, for exclusive use by the United States' troops for seaborne invasion practice of the most realistic kind, there were astonishing scenes. Great fleets of landing craft would charge in from the sea with men and equipment, and practice with grim resolution the part which they would soon be playing on the other side of the Channel.

Yet the people who watched these preparations did not discuss them openly. It was as though they themselves were sharing in a great

Top, US troops in Devon, preparing for the great invasion. Bottom, the US base at St Budeaux, part of which was re-named Normandy Way soon after the war.

secret; as indeed they were. If ever they did talk among themselves it was with bated breath and a glance over the shoulder to see that there was no eavesdropper.

Huge convoys of landing craft packed with men and equipment could be seen from the cliffs tossing and manoeuvring out in the Channel in varying weather. These were indeed the guessing months of March, April, and May.

Then one day they went to sea - and did not come back. They went on and on through the darkness, and the dawn found them off a strange coast, where all their practice was put to its supreme test.

Now, I am afraid, my record must become a bit personal, but as I am a Plymothian and was representing Plymouth newspapers, chronicling as far as possible the achievements and experiences of Plymouth men and women during the invasion and the battles which followed, I make no apology.

Towards the end of May I knew that the invasion was imminent, but as to the actual day, my guess was anybody's guess. I was called three times to London. The first was to receive my credentials as one of the war correspondents to go overseas with the invasion force or as it afterwards was known, the British Liberation Army. The second was to attend a conference of war correspondents at St. Paul's School, Fulham, addressed by Field-Marshal (then General) Sir Bernard Montgomery the Commander-in-Chief of the Allied Invasion Army. The third was a Conference at S.H.A.E.F. – initials standing for Supreme Headquarters Allied Expeditionary Force – when we were addressed behind locked doors by General Dwight Eisenhower, the supreme Commander, and his Chief of Staff.

You can well imagine how completely absorbing those talks by the two great leaders were. We were told a lot, but as to the all important things, when and where the invasion would take place, we were still left guessing.

All the same, from then on I was "on my toes" with half my kit already "somewhere in England" but where, I did not know. How people used to ask me "When do you think it will start?" A foolish question, for even had I known, nothing would have induced me to say. But I simply did not know. Then I received a telephone call, wrapped in the most vague and mysterious language. It warned me to get a bit nearer, and "nearer" meant London. It also asked me to travel as inconspicuously as possible.

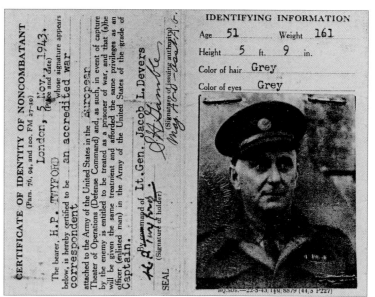

HP Twyford "accredited war correspondent" Certificate of identity of noncombatant, issued in London 5 Nov, 1943

So on Friday, June 2, I travelled to London in civilian clothes, my uniform in a suitcase, but I think my taxi-driver to North Road station – an old friend – guessed something of my mission, for he cocked a suspicious eye at my typewriter and murmured, "Ah, ah".

And the ticket collector on the train – another old friend of many journeys – said as he punched my ticket, "Only a single this time, sir?" I don't think my rather lame explanation of the possibility of coming back by road killed the thought that was in his mind.

I felt terribly alone on that journey. I kept wondering what the next few days would hold for me? I was not feeling very happy when the train pulled out through Laira and gathered speed at Plympton. It seemed as though everything that was familiar and dear was slipping away. Have you ever noticed how you can fit words to the rhythm of train wheels? On this journey they seemed to be saying, "You're going away", "You're going away", and then it changed to "Will you come back?", "Will you come back?".

Saturday and Sunday in London did not bring any solution of the immediate outlook, and among the few colleagues I contacted in Fleet Street the situation seemed just as vague.

135

Then, on Monday morning, about 7-30, the telephone at my bedside in the hotel suddenly startled me from sleep. It was a voice I instantly recognised, but there was no mention as to who was speaking. It simply said: "You know who this is speaking. Please meet Major at the Duke of York Barracks at three o'clock this afternoon".

That was all, but I knew that the next stage in the impending drama was set. I put on my uniform, looked to all my equipment, and packed up my civilian clothes and posted them home.

I kept that rendezvous with about twenty other war correspondents, many of them household names that you know so well. We were at once transported to Wentworth Golf Club, which had been set up as the headquarters of the war correspondents' unit to which I was attached.

That night we were given further instructions, including our overseas visa, and were forbidden to leave the grounds. We knew we were getting to the edge of things.

Still, however, we were completely ignorant as to the exact day or hour of the invasion. We were quite comfortable at Dormy House the millionaires' club-house I believe it was called in peace-time. I well recall how in the darkness of that first night, as we lay in our blankets on the hard boards, we discussed the project that lay ahead. How soon, we still did not know . what our exact part in the world's greatest drama would be, we did not know.

Many times since I have wondered what our reactions would have been had we known that while we were still sleeping on those hard boards the invasion fleet was actually closing in to the Normandy beaches; that from out of the black night our airborne troops were actually dropping in their thousands on those surprised German defences.

But we did not know, and we just slept as comfortably, or uncomfortably, as our new conditions would permit.

I should explain that a certain number of correspondents, whom we had not seen but who had been with various units of the invasion force for a week or more, landed with the assault forces, some by sea and some by air. Our party of front-line correspondents was to have followed across in the course of a few days. As events turned out; largely due to the unfortunate weather which seriously hampered the beach landings at one stage, our crossing was delayed for two or three weeks.

Meanwhile we operated from 21st Army Group, which was similarly on this side of the Channel.

The next morning, Tuesday, June 6, 1944 – a date which I venture to think will go down in history with all the familiarity of 1066 – was, of course, D-Day.

That morning we came down to our first breakfast still with no knowledge of the great event. In fact, quite a number of the correspondents had been planning a pleasant round of golf to fill in the day in those delightful surroundings.

Then Colonel the Hon. Harry Tufton, who was in charge of our outfit, came in and sat down. He started his porridge. After about the third spoonful, he remarked, in the most matter-of-fact way, "Airborne troops landed in France this morning".

No one took much notice, let alone appreciated the significance. So much so, that one correspondent sitting next to me mumbled, between his porridge, "One of Churchill's feints, I suppose?"

Again there was no comment for a few moments. Everyone was busy eating.

Then Colonel Tufton, with another spoonful of porridge poised in mid-air, said, quite undramatically, "Oh no. This is D-Day".

There was a dead silence. Time seemed to stand still with all of us. Suddenly it was broken. Some way down the table a chair went back violently, and a correspondent yelled, "What the hell are we doing here?"

Very few finished their breakfast. Our job had started. It seemed only minutes before we were haring away in our jeeps towards Southampton and the other embarkation ports, where we knew that for the next few days our story would lie.

That started a period of campaigning for me which, for months, was to be daily packed with intense battle drama and thrills.

In due course I landed on one of those beaches over which our troops – including many from Plymouth – had stormed their way into Hitler's fortress. The fanatical Nazi leader had boasted that any attempt at invasion would be thrown out in nine hours. But we know how our men went in and stayed, and how from those beaches they went on to the liberation of Europe.

Slapton provides the practice arena for the Normandy landings.

In those following months I was to be the eyewitness of every one of the grim battles in Normandy, from Caen to St. Lo. I was to see the door at last crashed back by fighting as dour as anything in military history. I was to be with the first British correspondents to enter Chartres, Paris, Amiens, Arras, Brussels, and Antwerp, to mention only the principal places which were liberated. I was to step over the border into Holland, and look across the frontier of Germany itself before I saw Plymouth again.

During those momentous days of invasion Plymouth watched the comings and goings through her historic gateway. Gradually she saw the war moving away from her door. Plymouth Hoe from Mount Batten - April 1944.

Then the strain began to tell, accentuated a bit when a 27-ton tank crashed into the car in which I was driving to Brussels, and left it a rather crumpled mass on the roadside. I had to come home for overhaul and rest.

I flew back to London from Brussels on Sunday, September 17 the anniversary of the Battle of Britain, and passed on the way home that gigantic airborne force which was outward bound to Holland for memorable landings, including the epic of Arnhem.

It was, too, the date on which the lights went up again over the greater part of England after five years of blackout.

I had been away nearly four months. It seemed four years. Into that period had been packed a lifetime of experiences, adventures, thrills, and drama. Yet it was an experience I would not have missed.

In the war of 1914-18 I went to France with a gun with the men of my generation; in the war of 1944 I went with a typewriter in the grand company of another generation.

My old comrades of the last war often ask me whether there was any comparison between the two wars. They were totally different in every way as regards the fighting, but they were the same in fighting spirit and in glorious comradeship.

This, however, is not a book about my experiences or even the liberation fighting on the Continent. Plymouth was a long way off. Yet there were many links which provide the excuse for this chapter.

It was always such a mutual joy to meet lads from Plymouth. I was constantly running across them-up in the grim, dusty, stinking, nerve-breaking forward areas where the fighting was fierce; in the congested back areas, straining and sweating to keep the communications and supplies flowing in ever-growing volume; in the cafes and estaminets; grandly bearing themselves with all their natural friendliness in those hysterical, unforgettable liberation scenes. Yes, I met them everywhere. And they were worthy sons of Plymouth.

There were times, too, when I slipped aside from the turmoil and stood silent by a mound of brown Normandy earth, with a little wooden cross at its head bearing the name of some Plymouth lad who had nobly given his life in the cause of freedom. Sometimes it was in or alongside the cornfields, where the scarlet poppies bent their heads over the graves as they did in Flanders a quarter of a century before for their fathers; sometimes it was in the quiet corner of an orchard which the war had passed and left in peace; sometimes it was by the

rough roadside, with its everlasting thunder of war traffic; sometimes it was in the ever-growing military cemeteries, so neat and orderly, where one day all the glorious dead of this war will sleep in spots "for ever England". There were some spots that to me were "for ever Plymouth".

Weep not, Mother Plymouth, for those sons who have not come home, for as was once written of one who fell in the last war:
"And you will speed us onward with a cheer,
And wave beyond the stars that all is well"

And what of Plymouth itself during the invasion months? I can write only from the records of the four months I was away.

The liberation of France meant the liberation of Plymouth from the fear of raids. Plymouth, with her hand on the pulse of the Services, which are her tradition, watched events with close personal interest. Each phase of the great drama unfolding itself on the sea or land or in the air had a close association with the city.

Over there I had visited several of the aerodromes from which the Germans used to launch their savage air attacks on Plymouth. It gave one a peculiar sense of satisfaction to walk on them and to see our own aircraft operating from the runways, chasing the Hun out of the very skies they had once dominated with such senseless hate.

It was the same with the ports along the Channel coast. I remember when I was flying home we crossed the recently captured little port of Fecamp. In its tiny harbour there were two vessels. But from their stern there flew the White Ensign of the Royal Navy. What a tingle it sent through the pulse.

During those momentous days of invasion Plymouth watched the comings and goings through her historic gateway. Gradually she saw the war moving away from her door. Yet she knew that right to the closing chapter of the world drama she would have a part to play. And she went on playing that part to the end.

When I came home I think I realised more than ever before just how tired the old country was. Yet, could you expect anything else? There had been five years of unsurpassing strain.

People on the Continent often used to ask me, "What is England like?", and I always answered, "Very tired".

They seemed to understand that answer, and they would murmur with a sympathetic appreciation, "Yes", adding, "But you have been so wonderful".

THE WORST BLITZED CITY

Before giving a description of the raids on Plymouth in their chronological order, a summary of the city's experiences between July, 1940, when the first bombs were dropped, and April, 1944, when the last attack was made, provides a revealing and grim picture.

Altogether Plymouth had 602 "alerts", and on 59 raids bombs were dropped.

The official Figures covering all the raids reveal:

Civilians killed	1,172
Civilians seriously injured	1,092
Civilians slightly injured	2,177
Missing, believed killed	7
Total civilian casualties	4,448

It will be noted that these figures relate only to the casualties among the civil population. But, in addition, there was a very considerable number of casualties, killed and injured, among the three Services, but these figures, for reasons of security, were not revealed.

Another point is that the figures relating to seriously injured civilians are rather indeterminate, for the reason that a number were sent to hospitals in various parts of the country, and it is known that some of these had injuries which proved fatal. So that it is quite reasonable to assume that the actual number who died as the result of raid injuries was in the region of 1,300.

The heaviest death rolls were, of course, caused during the intense raids in March and April, 1941. In March the two blitzes on successive nights resulted in 336 people being killed, and during the five nights in April the outright deaths totalled 590.

The extent of the damage to property is revealed in the following figures. Houses totally destroyed, or damaged so extensively that demolition was necessary, 3,754; houses seriously damaged but capable of repair, 18,398; houses slightly damaged (those with just broken windows not included), 49,950.

This meant that altogether the housing casualties totalled 72,102. An interesting reflection on this total is that it is considerably in excess of the total number of houses existing before the war. The explanation, of course, is that many houses were damaged on two or three occasions.

Left, the Municipal Building is gutted. Right, fires light up the night-time sky.

RAIDS

June 30 1940
Plymouth's first "alert". Lasted one hour; no incidents.

July 6 1940
First enemy bombs on Plymouth. These were dropped shortly before noon on a block of eight houses at the Corporation Housing Estate, Swilly Road, Devonport. Three houses were demolished, two wrecked beyond repair, and three others damaged. Blast also damaged other houses in the vicinity. One woman, one man, and one boy were killed, six other persons injured, four being taken to hospital. In all, three bombs were dropped. Raider was challenged by gunfire from anti-aircraft defences, but made off without being hit. Was flying very high.

July 7 1940
Plymouth had its second serious attack. This was Sunday and the time about 5-30 in the afternoon. Most people had either just finished, or were about to sit down to, their tea when the "alert" sounded. A German bomber came low over the east end of the city from the direction of Laira. The machine was so low that a man on duty at the gasworks opened fire on it with a shot-gun. A ship in the Cattewater also opened fire. The gasworks with its big holders, was obviously the target. The stick of bombs missed their objective, and crashed on the houses at the junction of South Milton Street and Home Sweet Home Terrace. Fortunately, most people on the sounding of the alarm had rushed for their shelters. This saved many lives. Houses came crashing down. Five people were killed, including a policeman and a soldier; four people were injured. The policeman and soldier were on duty in the street, and were killed by blast. Among the houses wrecked was the post office at the corner of the street. Many people were rendered homeless as the result of this savage attack on a peaceful Sunday afternoon. Police, fire brigades, wardens, and casualty services, in their first big test, worked efficiently. The emergency tested all their training; they did well. This second raid in two days, with their direct attacks on civil population, was a serious warning to Plymouth.

Top and middle, 09.07.40 Incident No1. Bottom, 07.07.40 South Milton Street.

July 8 1940

Another serious raid; this time early morning at Devonport. Four bombs were dropped in the vicinity of Morice Square and Marlborough Street. There was one death, Mr. Slee, butcher, who was killed in his shop when the building was demolished by direct hit. Three other persons were seriously injured and seven slightly injured. These bombs dropped within a few yards of the Royal Albert Hospital, but the building sustained little damage. One bomb penetrated the Royal Sailors' Club, Morice Square, from roof to basement, exploding in the kitchen, and wrecking the dining-room above, which half an hour before had been crowded with sailors having breakfast before reporting to their ships. There were no casualties in this building. Another of these bombs wrecked a dwelling-house, but the only casualty was a woman, who was dug out of the debris and taken to hospital. There was extensive damage from blast in Marlborough Street.

There was now no longer any question in anyone's mind as to the vulnerability or remoteness of Plymouth as far as air attack was concerned. Plymouth was bang in the front line.

July 10 1940

Another early-morning raid. This time bombs dropped in the Exeter Street and Hoe district. Five persons were killed and seven injured. Considerable damage was done to shop property in the Exeter Street area, where three of the bombs fell. There were two deaths here, and three in the Hoe district, where the damage was to big residential properties in the Leigham Terrace and Carlisle Avenue sections. On this occasion the enemy gave another taste of their terror tactics against civilians, for as people were running for shelter they were machine-gunned, but no one was hit.

July 12 1940

Three small raids. In the first – the most serious when the "alert" lasted from midnight for one hour, several bombs dropped in the residential areas of Alma Road, St. Levan Road, Swilly, Salisbury Villas, Greatlands Place, and Torpoint. It was random bombing, and while there was considerable damage to property there were no casualties.

Top, 12.07.40 Austin Avenue. Middle left, 07.08.40 Slee's butcher shop, rear. Middle right, 12.07.40 Unexploded bomb hole, Cookworthy Road. Bottom Leigham Terrace.

July 15 1940

Bombs were dropped on the R.A.F. Station at Mount Batten during a raid which lasted from 5 p.m. to 5-20 p.m. Four hits were made on the Station, causing damage to the new N.A.A.F.I. canteen, the sergeants' mess, and one of the slipways. One bomb failed to explode. There was considerable damage to the roof and glass of one of the hangars. This was caused by blast. The only casualty was a boatman at the Barbican, on the opposite side of the harbour, who was thrown out of his boat by the force of the explosions, and injured his spine.

On this day bombs were also reported to have dropped in open country in the Plympton and Ivybridge districts. They did no damage. It was also reported that five Heinkels attacked a merchant ship off Plymouth today. They were, however, successfully engaged by a Sunderland flying-boat from the Mount Batten Air Station. One was damaged; the others made off.

July 20 1940

Between 11-50 p.m. and 2-10 a.m., "alert", six bombs were dropped in the Cattedown and other east end areas. One person was killed and another injured, both soldiers. Anti-aircraft guns and searchlights were in action, and machine-gunning was heard.

Some pheasants were the only victims when bombs were dropped at random in the country outside Plymouth.

20.07.40, from the top; Cattedown; adjacent to Shell Mex, derailed trucks; and bottom, the bombed premises of British Oxygen.

July 21 1940

North Road station, completely missed, was obviously the target during a series of five raids, which were spread over the twenty-four hours from midnight. The chief incident was at the top of York Street. After the first "Raiders passed" at 2-15 a.m., there was an interval of only fifteen minutes before the next raid. In this heavy calibre bombs were dropped. One fell in the cul-de-sac of York Place a sort of vast courtyard surrounded by houses – a most congested spot. This bomb did extensive damage, and it was here that an elderly woman and a boy were killed. The death of the boy was particularly pathetic. In the earlier raid he had been taken to a shelter, and at the end was taken back to bed as he was suffering from influenza. When the second raid came it was decided he should remain in bed.

Another bomb struck the corner of Albany Ope, completely wrecking the premises of Edmund Walker, ball-bearing specialists. So extensive was the debris flung about from these bombs, that it was impossible to drive a car farther along Cobourg Street than the Education Offices. Big stones crashed through the roof of Christ Church, and stained-glass windows were broken. The shelter at the top of York Street was crowded with people when these bombs fell fifty yards away. Several families were rendered homeless.

August 12 1940

Frequent raids, but without incident until last night, when, during a series of "alerts", bombs were dropped in the Rectory district of Devonport, killing a woman who was walking along by the Brickfields and two sailors. Some houses were demolished, and a fire started.

August 14 1940

In the early hours of this morning bombs were dropped at Stonehouse and Keyham. At Stonehouse a girl, who was living with her parents in the Corporation flats, was killed by bomb fragments, while at Keyham two sailors, who were walking along the main road, were killed when bombs fell in Avondale Terrace. There was considerable damage to property, particularly to windows, and there was also one fire, which was soon under control. Several families were rendered homeless.

21.07.40; Top and bottom. "So extensive was the debris flung about from these bombs, that it was impossible to drive a car along Cobourg Street furtther than the education offices. Middle, York Cottages.

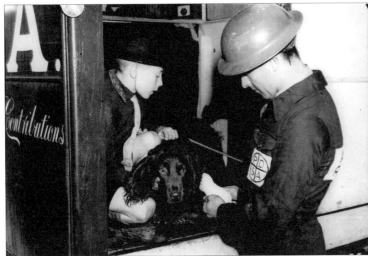

August 26 1940

In a raid about 9-30 last night five people were killed, three seriously injured, and a number slightly injured, when bombs dropped in the Keyham district. The dead were three civilians, whose bodies were recovered from the debris of their homes, and two sailors. Chief streets sustaining damage were Hamilton Street, Barton Avenue, Warleigh Lane, and Avondale Terrace. There were several miraculous escapes.

August 27 1940

Plymouth had its longest "alert" during last night, when relays of German bombers were droning over the city on their way to targets in the North. There were, however, a number of the machines which dropped their bombs over a scattered area of the city. Bombs fell in many districts, including Millbay, Crownhill, and Ford. The worst incident was at the last-named place, where bombs struck Ford House, the Public Assistance Institution. Great damage was done, and there was the heaviest loss of life to date. Thirteen women inmates were killed, and a number of others injured. Wonderful courage was shown by both inmates and staff when a heavy bomb penetrated the stone-built passage where the inmates were sheltering. Those women who were not injured walked quite calmly to another part of the building. A nine-year-old son of one of the officials was saved by a nurse, who flung herself on him and shielded him with her own body. She was rendered unconscious.

At Hartley Vale 150 people had to be evacuated from their homes when an unexploded bomb was found in the vicinity. Over 100 incendiary bombs dropped at Downderry, Whitsands, where a bungalow was destroyed by fire and others damaged. These raiders dropped a trail of bombs across the fields at Higher St. Budeaux, missing in a most amazing way the new reservoir, the ancient parish church in which Sir Francis Drake was married, and many houses. Budshead Farm, down in the valley, had a remarkable escape.

A cottage and part of the farmhouse were destroyed, but although there was so much wreckage, there were no casualties. One woman and her daughter were rescued after twelve hours from the ruins of the cottage and two evacuee Bristol children in the farmhouse were

It was not just humans who were rendered homeless.

saved, completely uninjured, when the roof collapsed on to the soft bed in which they were sleeping.

The raid lasted practically all night. It started during a performance at the Palace Theatre. The audience was invited to stay on. Singing until they were tired out, they then slept in their seats or on the floor. During this wait over six guineas was collected for the Spitfire Fund.

August 28 1940

During last night six bombs and a few incendiaries were dropped in the country between Higher St. Budeaux and Crownhill. Incendiaries which threatened the woodlands were quickly dealt with by the Auxiliary Fire Service. The high explosive bombs did no damage of any serious consequence.

September 5 1940

There were bombs in the countryside around Plymouth last night, and the electricity supply to Bigbury, Ringmore, Aveton Gifford, and Kingston was cut off. There were no casualties beyond a bullock which was killed on a farm at Shaugh Prior. Bombs at Wotter broke windows.

September 12 1940

Just after ten o'clock last night 13 people, 8 of whom were civilians and the rest Royal Marines, were killed by a bomb which exploded at the junction of Chapel Street and Emma Place, Stonehouse. Five other people were seriously injured and 10 slightly injured. The bomb dropped just in front of a fish and chip shop, which was crowded at the time. Most of those who were killed and injured were standing at the street corner. Several were young women talking to Royal Marines just before the latter were due to return to the nearby barracks. The damage was extensive to surrounding property but, bearing in mind the number of people about at the time, the casualty list might well have been bigger. Splendid rescue work was performed. There was slight damage to the ancient St. George's Church, about one hundred yards away.

September 25 1940

A day of "alerts" for Plymouth. There were six between 8-57 a.m. and 10-55 p.m. There was some damage to houses at Higher St.

Was anywhere safe?

Budeaux when bombs dropped above Higher Ernesettle Farm, but there were no casualties. Another bomb dropped in Agaton Fort, slightly wounding two soldiers. Two sailors walking up Prison Hill, Mutley, had a narrow escape when what was believed to be an anti-aircraft shell burst in a garden at the corner. They received only slight wounds. During these raids bombs missing their targets dropped harmlessly into the sea.

One woman was killed and several other people were injured when a stick of bombs presumably intended for the Dockyard, just over the wall on the other side of the road, demolished five houses in Goschen Street, Keyham, and damaged a number of others. This was during the afternoon. The street was completely blocked by the debris. Several houses were also damaged by a bomb in Hamilton Street, but there were no casualties. Most of the residents had gone to their shelters.

In these daylight raids on this day some of the bombers dived out of the clouds to the east of the city and, sweeping low over Staddon Heights, attacked the warships and merchant ships in Plymouth Sound. But not one of these bombs found a target. Altogether about a dozen bombs fell in the Sound, but every one went harmlessly into the sea, throwing up fountains of water, but doing no damage.

Ships and land batteries flung their anti-aircraft shells into the clear sky until it was absolutely peppered with the "cotton-wool" bursts. This heavy barrage made some of the raiders turn from their objectives, and drop their bombs quite aimlessly. There were numerous dog-fights between raiders and our fighters. This was the most thrilling and spectacular daylight scrap Plymouth had seen. Everywhere shells seemed to be bursting in the sky, and shrapnel and pieces of shell-casing were "zinging" down. People stood watching the afternoon fights. It was surprising that no one was injured by the flying splinters.

October 10 1940

A mother and daughter were killed, and a husband and wife injured, when bombs dropped on the Railway Housing Estate at Peverell last evening soon after dark. Two or three houses were wrecked, and gas and water mains fractured. The fractured end of the gas main, sticking out of the ground, was blazing like a beacon light for some time. The mother and daughter were killed in their Anderson shelter, some distance down the garden from the house. The shelter received a direct hit. By the irony of fate the house they had just left was hardly damaged. The whistle of these bombs falling was heard all over the city.

October 11 1940

In another raid last night Torr Home for the Blind was struck and two inmates slightly injured. The general body of inmates, however, had a remarkable escape. As the shelter in the grounds was very wet the matron had kept the blind people in the Home during the raid. The shelter was struck.

October 17 1940

In the 120th "alert" last night high explosives and incendiaries were dropped over a wide area - from Pennycomequick to Pennycross. Six planes were engaged in the attack, which lasted about an hour from 9-15. Only three people were injured. Bombs fell near the postal depot at Pennycomequick, at Pennycross Stadium, and Peverell. Bombs fell in the Old Cemetery, and vaults were damaged. Water and gas mains were fractured in Tavistock Road, Peverell, and Farley's Biscuit Factory at Torr Lane was struck. At this last-named place there was another amazing instance of escape. In an earlier "alert" local people had crowded, as usual, into the factory shelter. They had barely got home when the second and serious "alert" sounded. Hurrying back to the shelter, they were unable to get in. It was locked, and the care-

Farley's Biscuit factory at Torr Lane is struck

taker was not available. Rather angrily but, as it turned out, luckily, they dashed back to their homes. A few minutes later a bomb burst on the shelter. A corner house at Inverdene, Peverell, was wrecked, and eighty-two-year-old Mrs. Marshall, who was in the house alone, had a remarkable escape. She was found to be uninjured in the wrecked house. Houses in Holdsworth Street, Pennycomequick, were damaged, and here again there were some astonishing escapes. One bomb came through the roof and out through the window of a room in which a woman was sleeping. Smothered with the debris, she was got out unhurt, and was soon busy helping to clear up the damage. Among other places damaged in this widespread raid was the ancient Pennycross Church, where a bomb dropped at the base of the tower. But the old building withstood the shock.

October 23 1940

A single German raider swooped low over Victoria Park, Plymouth, last evening, with a sharp burst of machine-gun fire. This raider then carried on and dropped four high-explosive bombs between Moor Lane and St. Budeaux. No casualties; only slight damage.

November 2 1940

Watchers during an "alert" last night were spectators of an exciting incident. An enemy raider was fairly held in the concentrated beams of several searchlights. Anti-aircraft guns of every calibre seemed to fling everything they had at the intruder as the machine swooped low over Millbrook direction to beat the searchlights. There was strong conviction that it was brought down by this heavy fire. It was a thrilling spectacle, but, alas for the hopes, the morning brought no confirmation of the success. This incident occurred in the last of five "alerts" yesterday. There were incendiary bombs in the district, but no damage.

November 7 1940

Seven people were killed and several injured in a raid on the city last night – one of six "alerts" for the day. High explosives and incendiaries were dropped in considerable numbers. The enemy planes were clearly heard flying over the city, and bombs were dropped before the sirens sounded. Considerable criticism was aroused over this. Between thirty and forty incendiaries were dropped in the vicinity of North Road station, but small fires were soon extinguished, and did little damage. The most serious incident was at the junction of Gifford Terrace and Trelawney Road, where two houses on the corner were demolished and several others damaged. So extensive was the blast that windows of 150 houses were broken, some of them a quarter of a mile away. At this incident 5 people were killed, 3 men and 2 women. The males included two youths who were caught in the street without shelter. The injured included a six-month-old baby. A second bomb fell in the Hebrew cemetery on the opposite side of the road, disturbing a number of the graves.

Two other people – a woman and a sailor – were killed by a bomb which exploded near Kings Road, Devonport. The woman was returning from a visit to her mother at the Rectory, and had not taken cover. Other bombs fell on the Brickfields and in Victoria Park. At the latter place the crash was almost adjoining the Bowling Club Pavilion, where the annual meeting of members was in progress. They were flung about by the explosion, but not seriously hurt.

During this raid also between fifteen and twenty high-explosive bombs were dropped in fields adjoining the main railway between Hemerdon and Plympton.

November 18 1940

About three o'clock this morning 9 people were killed, 4 seriously injured, and 6 slightly injured when a raider dropped a stick of bombs which straddled Lipson Vale. They were obviously intended for the railway but missed, and struck private dwellings. A former boys' school, Hillsborough, fortunately empty, was demolished, also houses in Connaught Avenue, Pearson Terrace, and Alexandra Road. The killed were 5 women, a fifteen year-old-girl, a fifteen-month-old baby and 2 men. In addition, many incendiaries were dropped, but these did little damage, and were speedily dealt with.

18.11.40 Top, Tavy Place. Above, Alexandra Road and right, Connaught Avenue.

November 25 1940
Three German raiders were brought down in Devon and Cornwall during the weekend. Following the heavy raid on Bristol last night a Dornier "Flying Pencil" believed to have been hit, was returning over Plymouth when it struck the cable of a balloon near Torpoint. The machine crashed in flames on Rame Head. The crew baled out and were captured. One was rescued from the sea at Cawsand by local people, who put out in a boat. Another gave himself up at Millbrook. He attracted attention at a cottage by firing his revolver.

November 28 1940
Intermittent raids during about eight hours of last night resulted in Plymouth having its first big air raid fire – the oil tanks at Mount Batten. The fire lasted five days. The trouble started about 7-30 last evening, when an enemy machine, flying through heavy barrage, swept low over the city and dropped four flares. These were slightly to the west of Mount Batten. Almost immediately one of the big hangars at Mount Batten was set blazing by a high explosive. This made the Air Station the target for the night. Within a few minutes another bomber, screaming down on this target, got a direct hit on one of the oil tanks. Immediately there was started a conflagration which was to keep Plymouth very uneasy for the next few days. The city and surrounding district were illuminated in the lurid glare from this fire, which, looked down on from the surrounding heights, was like a Dante's Inferno. It was so light from this fire at night that people on the Barbican and on the Hoe could easily read their watches.
This blaze naturally attracted further attacks, and many more bombs were plastered on the district. Oreston, Turnchapel, Plymstock, the Cattewater, the Barbican, even as far away as Peverell and Crownhill, all came into the attack.
One Sunderland flying-boat at its moorings caught fire and was burnt out. Ten people were killed at Oreston, where four houses were demolished. All that was left of two families were the two husbands, both of whom were injured and taken to hospital. In Plymouth two men were killed and two seriously injured. It was estimated that more than one hundred German aircraft were engaged in this raid. It was also considered that about one hundred tons of bombs and thou-

Left and right, The city and surrounding district were illuminated in the lurid glare from this fire, which, looked down on from the surrounding heights, was like a Dante's inferno.

sands of incendiaries were dropped. The incendiaries came down in such showers that Staddon Heights looked at from a distance was like a fairyland. What with these, the shriek and crash of high explosives, the shattering fire of the anti-aircraft guns from ships and land batteries, the searchlights and the lurid glare of the oil tanks fire, this night was the most fantastic and fearsome that Plymouth had yet experienced. The blaze at the tanks continued and extended during the next day, when, in fighting this fire battle, two Plymouth members of the Auxiliary Fire Service lost their lives and four others were injured. The volume of smoke hung like a gigantic pall over the city. For four nights the lurid illumination from the inferno could be seen for miles. Everyone feared further attacks on the illuminated target. The fire spread from tank to tank, despite a gallant fight. Special "foam" appliances were sent down from London. Everyone felt relieved when this fire finally died down.

Top left, Sunderland flying boat RB F buring in the Cattewater. Right, RB A hanger ablaze and middle, the morning after. Bottom left, the Turnchapel oil tanks buckled by the heat. Below the burnt out fire-boat.

December 29 1940
We had a respite from raids during Christmas, but last evening, Saturday, in the 242nd "alert", the city met with its worst raid experience so far. According to an official statement, there were fourteen high-explosive bombs and about a thousand incendiaries dropped in the city area. At least a dozen of the high explosives missed the city centre and dropped in the Sound. There were a number of fires.

The casualties were 11 people killed and 12 seriously injured. Seventeen houses were demolished and 300 badly damaged. Some of the bombs were 500-pounders – the biggest Plymouth had so far experienced.

28.12.40, Police Incident No.25

The attack was quite early in the evening, from 6-40 to 7-55, and it was believed that about twenty-five raiders took part in the attack. The fires were all under control by midnight, but half a dozen were still smouldering at dawn, when begrimed, hollow-eyed firemen and police were still on the job.

Both the City Hospital, where three people were wounded, and the Prince of Wales's Hospital, Greenbank, were hit. York Street, Cobourg Street, Sherwell Arcade, Mutley Plain, Notte Street, and the Barbican were the areas chiefly concerned. About 230 inmates of Ford House had to be evacuated when the building was largely destroyed by fire.

28.12.40, Clockwise - above: Wilton Street; Boon's Place; Victoria Park; two more views of Wilton Street and Ricketts rag store.

January 10 1941

There was a lone raider in the moonlight over Devonport in the city's 247th "alert" last night, shortly after ten o'clock. One large bomb was dropped. Obviously intended for the Dockyard, it fell about three hundred yards away on the edge of Devonport Park, in front of Portland Place. Two people were killed, 9 injured, 20 houses seriously damaged, and about 300 slightly damaged.

January 11 1941

The Wolsdon Street bomb - the biggest yet dropped in the city – which has been there since the raid of December 28, was removed by the Bomb Disposal Squad this weekend. This bomb, which weighed one ton one hundredweight, was 9 feet long, with fins another 2 feet – a terrifying object. We felt relieved that this was a "dud". The devastation in the crowded district where it fell would otherwise have been appalling.

The story of its discovery – probably exaggerated – was that the bomb originally came down through the house while the people were out in the shelter. It made a hole down through the house, and in the kitchen there was a slight crater filled with rubble. It was at first assumed that an anti-aircraft shell had done the damage. At any rate, the people slept there for several nights, and one story was that one family used to pull the bed over the hole in their floor to prevent the kiddies falling through. Then there were complaints that the wet was coming in badly, and when the officials came they were suspicious of the crater in the kitchen. So they called in the bomb disposal officer who happened to be in Plymouth. He came and poked about the rubble, and located the fin. That decided the matter. The district was evacuated forthwith, and eventually the bomb was safely removed.

Let me here diverge for a moment to salute these gallant officers and men of the Bomb Disposal Squad. It was my lot to meet a number of them, to be in close association with some of their work. For sheer cool courage and an utter disregard for the danger in which they lived every moment of their handling of these unexploded bombs, I know no equal. In the course of the war they removed hundreds of unexploded bombs in Plymouth; a debt we could never sufficiently repay. They tackled these bombs with a grim jest on their lips and a

"For sheer cool courage and an utter disregard for the danger in which they lived every moment of their handling of these unexploded bombs, I know no equal."

13.01.40 Above, Verna Road, and a crater in which a house could have been lost and the surviving Anderson shelter. Below, Bulmer Road.railway bridge.

nerveless courage. To them it was just a part of their day's work. A few of these splendid men lost their lives in Plymouth, when even their courage was not equal to the sinister devilish ingenuity of the bomb-makers. Do not let us forget them. They gave their lives for our safety. The Wolsdon Street bomb, after it had been satisfactorily dealt with by the experts, was handed back to Plymouth City Police as one of the most interesting, certainly, the most formidable, "exhibit" in their war museum.

January 12 1941
During one of four attacks yesterday it was reported that one raider was shot down into the sea by a coastal battery. The crew was seen to bale out. Search parties could, however, find no trace of any survivors.

January 13 1941
Last evening, Sunday during the 254th "alert", three women were killed when three houses in Verna Road, St. Budeaux, were complete-ly demolished by direct hits. Not a brick was left standing on another where these houses had been; in fact, there was a crater in which a house could have been lost. Yet an Anderson shelter ten yards from the edge of the crater was undamaged, and the occupants, belong-ing to one of the demolished houses, were safe inside. St. Budeaux First Aid Post, in one of the houses backing on to the demolished site, was damaged.

January 14 1941

Plymouth has now had several nasty raids, but last night's, during the 256th "alert", was a nightmare. Many people were killed or injured, hundreds were rendered homeless, and for the first time damage seriously deprived large areas of the city of gas and electricity. Twelve people were killed, 55 seriously injured, and 62 slightly injured. The worst incident was a direct hit on a shelter in Madeira Road, opposite Phoenix Wharf, where a number of people were trapped. The raid lasted from 6-30 p.m. to 9-30 p.m.

The official report stated that 25 aircraft were reported to have taken part, and 56 high-explosive bombs were reported, also several unexploded bombs. These high explosives were preceded by showers of incendiaries. The attack was developed chiefly over the eastern end of the city. There were 82 fires – 9 large and 73 medium. Three of them were still burning next day.

Top, Leggo Wilson's Laundry. Above, Huxhams, Commercial Road. Below, Victoria Wharf. Right, top, Cattedown Road. Below, Embankment Road.

It was in this raid that Plymouth had its first church seriously damaged. This was Sherwell Congregational Church. The roof was destroyed by fire, and the building rendered unfit for worship. Services were afterwards held in the adjoining church hall. An interesting commentary was the fact that in September the minister had deprecated air raid reprisals on Berlin.

Plymouth and Stonehouse Gas Company's works at Cattedown were badly damaged, and Plymouth Corporation Electricity Power House was also put out of action. Neither commodity was available to the public from these sources. The electricity was restored through the grid system the next afternoon, but gas was still "off" and likely to be for an indefinite period. The loss of the gas affected only the Plymouth end of the city, as Devonport came under the undamaged Corporation supply from the Devonport works.

Railway services between Friary and Devonport and Turnchapel were interrupted. Buses provided alternative transport.

Damaged property included the City Hospital, where the casualties were four patients, one of whom was killed. Two wards were damaged, and sixty beds put temporarily out of action. Splendid heroism was shown by the doctors and nurses and rescue workers in extricating victims. The patients showed wonderful courage. The one killed was a young woman who was buried under a collapsed ceiling. At the Prince of Wales's Hospital, Greenbank, two wards were damaged, two members of the staff were injured, and here again sixty beds were temporarily out of action. Many of the patients of the two hospitals were evacuated to different parts of Devon and Cornwall.

Damage was also done to public buildings, wharves, schools, a tar distillery, and hundreds of private houses. About 175 people had to be given food and shelter. Among the old buildings damaged was "Island House" on the Barbican.

There were fires in many parts of the city, and fire brigades were rushed to Plymouth from all parts of the Westcountry.

An amazing incident was when a bomb hit the French ship Nivernais at the North Quay. It went down through the hatchway but was never found, so it was concluded that it passed right through the ship and buried itself in the mud. Bombs fell in the Cattewater and Sutton Pool "ten a penny".

13.1 40 From top, South Devon Hospital, Nurses Home, City Hospital bed. Right, back entrance to the Western Morning News Offices, in Frankfort Street.

When the supply of gas and electricity broke down, it was apparent that The Western Morning News could not be published at the Plymouth headquarters that night. The preparations for the first edition were well advanced when the raid cut off the supplies. Alternative plans were quickly made. The paper could not be published at Plymouth; then it should be brought out at Exeter and distributed from there.

Arrangements were forthwith made to publish the paper at the Express and Echo Office, Exeter. Members of that mechanical staff were collected by taxis, and meanwhile a skeleton staff of The Western Morning News, with "copy" and type so far set, were rushed by car from Plymouth to Exeter. The decision to publish at Exeter was made just before eleven o'clock; by midnight the Plymouth key men were in Exeter. The Express and Echo staff at Exeter had got their plant going. And so The Western Morning News was published. It was hardly as usual. It was a bit strange in appearance, and there was only one edition. But The Western Morning News was faithful to its traditions, and was "on the breakfast table". Few readers, however were aware of the dire state of emergency in which it was produced. The loss of the gas and electricity meant that for several weeks both The Western Morning News and The Western Evening Herald had to be printed and published at Exeter. The loss of the gas was the determining factor, because of the fact that the heat for the melting-pots of the linotype machines and the stereotype plant for the casting of the pages was from this source. Eventually they were converted from gas to electricity, but that took time.

As a consequence of the damage caused in this raid, city cinema performances had to be suspended, and the general lack of facilities for heating was a serious handicap in the cold weather which was at that time prevailing.

Emergency feeding arrangements had to be organised without delay. Private bakeries arranged to cook dinners during the weekend. Army boilers and kitchens were brought into use, and for several days hundreds of hot meals were provided. "Whatever is necessary will be done", said the Emergency Committee.

It was amazing, however, the way in which people, deprived of the "tap-turning" and "switch" facilities, adapted themselves. Primus stoves, oil cookers, and lamps were pressed into service with wonderful ingenuity.

The electricity was restored this afternoon, and that solved the problem for many people. Many a meal was patiently cooked on an inverted electric fire.

But the resumption of the gas supply was to be a much longer job than was expected. When, after a couple of weeks, an effort was made to resume the supply there were violent explosions, caused by water in the mains, and in many thoroughfares where joints in the mains gave out the streets simply pancaked into mounds several yards across.

Some of the outer parts of the area, like Peverell and Mannamead, were gradually linked up with the Devonport Corporation gas supply, but the centre of the city, the Hoe district, and Stonehouse were to go months before the domestic supply was restored.

January 16 1941

Amended figures relative to the recent heavy raid were given in a statement by the Lord Mayor today. These show: Killed, 26; houses demolished, 60; houses seriously damaged, 400; houses slightly damaged, 2,000. High explosives which fell in the city totalled 106; 3 being of delayed action.

The Emergency Committee issued thanks to the heads of departments and staffs, and gallantry at the City Hospital was commented.

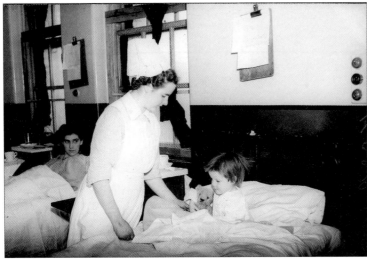

Life goes on the in the City Hospital.

January 19 1941

In connection with the lack of cooking facilities occasioned by the raid, hundreds of people sat down to a hot meal in Plymouth Guildhall today, Sunday. The meal was served between 1 o'clock and 2-30 p.m., and was, in the words of Mr. John Ainsworth, Food Control Officer, a "complete success", and provided valuable experience for the future.

January 27 1941

There was a terrific explosion at Plymouth Gasworks today when an attempt was made to renew the gas supply through the mains for domestic use. Three men were killed and five were injured at the works. It was on this day that the ominous "bulges" occurred in a number of the main thoroughfares, caused by the bursting of the gas mains underneath. The places thus "pancaked" were in the main thoroughfares of Sutton Road, Notte Street, Exeter Street, Bedford Street, and Union Street. This meant that there would be another long delay before the gas could be restored to the areas concerned.

February 13 1941

Plymouth will come to regard the 13th as an unlucky day. Early this morning, in the 272nd "alert" which lasted from 3-40 to 4-20, raiders returning from attacks on Cardiff and Liverpool unloaded a number of bombs on the city. The tragic feature was that this again happened before the sirens were sounded, so that the people were caught in their beds.

The worst of three incidents was at Alfred Road, Ford, where three houses were demolished, and eleven people who were trapped were killed. Three other people were injured and taken to hospital. Their salvation was due to quick and effective work on the part of rescue squads, but for the other victims there was no chance. They were caught in their beds and buried under tons of debris. There were again some amazing escapes, as in the instance of the man who was in bed when the whole side of the house fell away. He was uninjured.

During this raid two bombs fell in the grounds of the Royal Eye Infirmary, adjoining the railway at Mutley but they did not explode. Patients and a number of nearby residents were evacuated until the bombs were removed.

Above, Albert Road, Keyham. Right, the end of a Plymouth raider. Officials examine the wreckage of a German plane.

A paramine floated down and exploded close to the old St. Aubyn Cemetery near the Milehouse bus depot. It caused a tremendous amount of damage to neighbouring property, and one bungalow was completely destroyed.

There was considerable criticism over the fact that bombs had fallen before the sirens sounded, but it was subsequently explained officially that some seventy planes were believed to have approached the south-west over a line from Start Point to St. Eval on their way to Cardiff and Liverpool, in flights of six. When they were over Plymouth on their return, it was presumed that they had unloaded their bombs, and as the city was asleep and "under cover" the "alert" was not sounded.

February 16 1941

A German Heinkel III, which had been attacked and hit farther up the coast by our fighters, crashed and burnt out in a field at Higher Luscombe, Harbertonford, near Totnes, last night. When it made the forced landing a solid Devon hedge proved too big an obstacle. The crew members were burned to death, and their remains were subsequently buried in Totnes Cemetery.

February 19 1941

During the city's 278th "alert" this evening, between 7-15 and 10-50 when a strong force of German bombers, numbering between fifty and seventy-five, were on their way to South Wales, about a dozen high-explosive bombs were dropped in the areas of Valletort Road, Stoke, and Stonehouse Town Hall. There was some damage to property, and one person subsequently died from injuries, while three others had to receive treatment. In two later raids there were no incidents.

March 15 1941

During three raids between 8-30 last evening and 12-37 this morning, 5 people were killed, 5 seriously injured, and 17 slightly injured. Six bombs fell in Royal Navy Avenue and the surrounding district. Seven houses were demolished, 50 seriously damaged, and 300 slightly damaged. Six bombs also fell in Central Park area, two near the Southern Railway, Devonport, five at Beaumont Terrace, and odd ones in other parts of the Stoke area. In addition, about 1,000 incendiary bombs were scattered over the area, starting 27 fires, 2 of which were major blazes. All fires were out by 2-15 a.m.

Other bombs fell in the areas of Plymstock, Hooe, Newton Ferrers, Plympton, Saltash, Crownhill, and Torpoint. At St. Budeaux a fractured gas main meant that an area was without the Corporation supply until the next day, when repairs were completed.

March 20 1941

Their Majesties the King and Queen, paying their first visit to Plymouth, had left the city only two hours when it was subjected to the most devastating raid yet experienced. The King and Queen were having tea with Lord and Lady Astor at Elliot Terrace previous to their departure, when there was a comparatively brief "alert". As was customary with the daylight "alerts" by that time, no special significance was attached to it, beyond the fact that it coincided with the presence

of the Royal visitors. No machine was visible to the naked eye, but events justified the view that it was on reconnaissance as a prelude to two nights of horror which were to follow, involving a total death roll of no fewer than 336 men, women, and children of the civil population. These included 14 babies and 3 nurses at the City Hospital. The King and Queen, who had toured the city and seen the damage done in the earlier raids, left with the message of an air raid warden still fresh in their minds – "We are keeping our chins up". Little did they or the people know of the awful experience which was to be theirs within a few hours. The Queen had replied to that warden's words by saying: "Well done. It is only by keeping our chins up, as we are doing, that we shall win the war".

Left, their majesties arrive in Guildhall Square. Top, the King with Women Wardens. Above, the Queen talks to sailors. Right, the Royal inspect local cadets.

Above, Frankfort Street, taken when the Western Evening Herald office was evacuated. Right, George Street, taken from Bedford Street. Overleaf, fire around Derry's Clock

It was at 8-39 that evening that the inferno was let loose on the eastern (Plymouth) end of the city, and this devastating attack went on without any weakening for about four hours. It was well after midnight that the attack died out.

The attack started with the dropping of thousands of incendiary bombs and a "circus" of flare-dropping "pathfinders". They were followed by wave after wave of heavy bombers dropping high explosives. The heart of the city, from Stonehouse to Cattedown, from the Hoe to Mutley, was the target.

Fortunately, the businesses had been closed for the day, otherwise the casualties inevitably would have been fearful. It was obviously the attackers intention to destroy the business centre, and it was with unmistakable ferocity and grim deliberation that they set about their task. Plymouth's heart was torn out and mauled.

There were fearsome major fires raging in many quarters, and into this blazing furnace the high-explosive bombs were poured by bombers which, coming in at a high altitude, swept down in terrifying dives to release their devastating loads. The smoke and dust rising in the lurid glare were well-nigh choking.

The first big fire was at Messrs. Spooners, whose imposing stores facing St. Andrew's Cross had for years been a feature of the shopping centre. The fate of this imposing block was soon apparent. It was a furnace, with the entire shop and vast showrooms blazing from roof to floor. The whole island site was doomed; the efforts of the fire brigade were as unavailing as they were gallant.

Shortly afterwards the second of that night's big fires gutted the entire Royal Hotel, and only stopped short at the adjoining new Royal Cinema, which a year or two before had been rebuilt on the site of the old Theatre Royal. But the entire block, as far as the hotel, palm court, long bar, and assembly rooms were concerned, was burnt out.

There were many other fires, and the regular and auxiliary fire brigades, augmented by many others which were rushed to Plymouth, the police, wardens, and thousands of the Civil Defence services, together with officers and men of the Navy, Army, and Air Force, were well-nigh overwhelmed by the fury of this attack.

Throughout the four hours the noise of crackling fire, the terrifying rush of aircraft and falling bombs, the crash of explosives, the bark of anti-aircraft guns, the crack of bursting shells was incessant, and through it all thousands of men and women worked heroically to save their beloved city. Tired, begrimed, and soaked, they toiled on. They were beyond fear. It was a grim desperation which carried them on.

If one wondered at all in those fearful hours, it was as to whether anything would be left standing when the dawn came, and whether the casualties would not be a fearful roll.

When the grey dawn did come, the revelation was painful. How had Plymouth lived at all through that hail of death and destruction? Hollow-eyed for want of sleep, grimly silent, and with vengeance and hatred raging in their hearts against the vile perpetrators of total war, they gazed on the seared heart of their beloved city. Many places, so long familiar, had gone in a night; nothing left but a shambles, smouldering ruins, blackened walls, and twisted steelwork.

One of the first places I visited was St. Andrew's Church. The building so loved, mellow with so many cherished memories, dear to the hearts of Plymouth people all over the world for centuries, was mauled, but not beyond repair. The main building had been saved, but it was not easy to get inside, because a bomb had burst between the north door and St. Andrew's Cross, causing fairly extensive damage.

But it was a sad, forlorn spectacle to gaze across those once bright and colourful gardens to Spooners' Corner. Some of the municipal offices were badly damaged, but the Guildhall stood four-square, to all intents undamaged. At the other end of the Square, however, there was a scene of destruction, for the new Post Office, the County Court offices, and other buildings were completely destroyed. Everywhere one looked there was the evidence of insatiable hate wreaked on a civil population.

Plymouth had indeed tasted the full blast of the Luftwaffe.

March 21 1941

The attack was repeated on an almost identical plan. It began at approximately the same time, with the Nazi "circus" dropping their flares and thousands of incendiaries, followed by another terrifying pounding by high explosives. Under that weight of attack surely the already bleeding heart of Plymouth would be utterly destroyed. It was again hell let loose, and the Civil Defence forces, already without sleep for twenty-four hours, worked feverishly but the task was gigantic and beyond their single capacity.

The same area was engulfed. The next morning (Saturday) told how devastatingly the attack had been driven home on the same mauled target. From Dingles' Corner at the junction of Bedford Street and Cornwall Street to the already destroyed Spooners' Corner, the popular shopping thoroughfare of Bedford Street was a heap of ruins. Only the walls, wrecked and grotesque, remained of the beloved St. Andrew's. This second assault had been too much for the mother church. It was burnt out from end to end, roofless, windowless, only the tower standing solid and symbolic at the west end. The Abbey Hall was badly damaged; the lovely Guildhall was just a burnt-out shell. The municipal offices flanking the entire length of the north side of the Square, housing the Town Clerk's department, the Council Chamber, the Lord Mayor's Parlour, the Committee Rooms, had been gutted by fire.

The only building standing intact in Bedford Street was the comparatively new Westminster Bank.

Frankfort Street had suffered a like fate. Destroyed beyond repair, gutted from top to bottom, was that magnificent pile of buildings housing the Plymouth Co-operative Society; and Messrs. Costers' premises were just a pile of smouldering ruins. In this street the only building of any note left standing intact was Leicester Harmsworth House, the headquarters of The Western Morning News and Western Evening Herald. With everything down all around it, this building undoubtedly owed its survival to blast and fire to the fact that it was only two years old, and built in the most modern style, with fire-resisting materials, which provided no food for incendiaries. There was also the fact that while high-explosive bombs literally ringed it, the building sustained no direct hit and was strong enough to withstand the heavy blast from those which burst near by. This block, running right through from

Left, Old Town Street, Lascelles on right and Woolworths on the left.

Frankfort Street to Frankfort Lane, housing the administrative, commercial, editorial, and mechanical departments, was intact, save for the photographic and process sections at the rear which caught fire when the Company's store on the opposite side of Frankfort Lane was burnt out. Thousands of photographic records, negatives, and prints were lost.

Parts of Union Street were blasted and burnt into ruins, and there was one period when it seemed that the entire Octagon was ringed with fire which engulfed Service & Co.'s premises and Jay's Furnishing Stores. Hotels which were destroyed that night included the Westminster and Hackers, situated in the Crescent.

Havoc was widespread. Almost whole streets of old and imposing houses in the Hoe district, many churches, schools, clubs, revered public buildings, and business premises whose firms had for years been household names, were swallowed in that welter of senseless destruction. In sad truth, it could now be said that Plymouth's shopping centre had been wiped out in two nights of veritable hell.

But Plymouth's heart, bleeding and torn, was still beating. The splendid spirit of the people remained. In those two nights of death-raining blows the first aid and rescue services did magnificent work. At some of the first aid posts hundreds of casualties were treated. Every section of the Civil Defence organisation was called into action.

How was Plymouth to recover from what seemed an almost paralysing blow? Stunned, but with spirit unbroken, she grimly set about the task of recovery. The clearing-up and the re-establishment of the life of the city was promptly tackled. Many thoroughfares, blocked by debris or by bomb craters, were closed to traffic. Miles of fire-hose twined, snake-like, everywhere. Plymouth had taken a succession of hard knocks, but she was not done. Brushing the sweat and tiredness from their eyes, the people set about meeting the emergency.

The business centre was smashed out of existence, but, with amazing spirit of recovery and enterprise, firms searched out new quarters, mostly in the Mutley Plain and Mannamead districts, where they opened new branches in small shops, private houses - in fact, anywhere they could find.

Mutley Plain, never regarded as a very prosperous business thoroughfare, became the main shopping centre, at least, for the Plymouth end of the city.

As yet, the Devonport end of the city was still intact.

As the clearing-up proceeded there came to the ears all day long heavy detonations as demolition squads brought down the dangerous shells of burnt-out buildings. Not the least of these awesome spectacles was when the tower of the Co-operative Society's premises in Frankfort Street was demolished.

All over the area bomb disposal squads were at their work, coolly, efficiently, and with complete disregard for danger, dealing with the many unexploded bombs. There were one or two tragic incidents in connection with this work. At Osborne Place, the Hoe, the squad had removed one heavy bomb, and were on the point of driving it away on a lorry when it exploded. The lorry was blown to pieces, and all five men killed. There was also one civilian casualty, a man being killed in an adjoining street as he was about to enter his car. He was struck by a granite set.

A rough estimate of Plymouth's damage in these two raids was placed at not less than £100,000,000. On the first night alone some 150 planes were plotted as taking part in the attack, and the weight last night was on a very similar scale.

Altogether some 20,000 properties were either destroyed or damaged. Many building operatives were rushed to Plymouth to help deal with the housing emergency.

There was no doubt but that fire was the chief factor in this destruction of Plymouth's shopping centre. Many of the brigades which were rushed to the city were helpless because their equipment would not fit the hydrants.

While many of the big stores which supplied the bulk of food and clothing were utterly destroyed, supplies were rushed to the city in ample quantities to meet requirements.

Plymouth continued under the full control of the municipal authorities.

Messages of sympathy in the heavy blow inflicted on the city and expressing admiration for the courage shown by the citizens poured in from all parts of the Empire. One from New Plymouth, New Zealand, was characteristic: "Citizens of New Plymouth, with sympathy and admiration, salute the superb courage, unbreakable spirit, and confidence of the citizens of old Plymouth, in face of wanton German air raids. Thumbs up!"

Meanwhile, thousands of homeless Plymothians were showing that "superb courage". There was a grim smile, with the set determination

Old Town Street and Drake Circus

that one day the debt would be repaid. Plymouth would certainly not forget.

All places of entertainment in Plymouth and Stonehouse – the area affected by these two raids - were closed for the time being.

With the destruction of the Town Clerk's Department in the municipal offices, new quarters were found in the commodious Pounds House, Central Park, and here also the Central Control for A.R.P. services was established, to take the place of the one burnt out under the Guildhall, from which the staff had managed to get away just in time.

The City Treasury and the City Engineer's Department at the east end and the back of the Guildhall respectively were not seriously damaged, and continued to function. The Old Guildhall in Whimple Street, which accommodated the Stores Department, was burnt out with all the records, and this department had to be re-housed in scattered accommodation.

The General Post Office found new accommodation at Spears Corner, Tavistock Road, the County Court offices moved to Elliot Street, and later to St. Lawrence Road, and the Western National bus terminus was temporarily moved to Sherwell Arcade.

With so many thousands of damaged houses, hundreds of tons of furniture was in need of storage. The bulk of this was taken for temporary accommodation, at all events, to the spacious grandstands at Home Park. Included in this was between fifty and one hundred pianos. This proved a tragic move. The furniture remained there safely for about a month, and then, in another series of heavy raids, was completely destroyed by fire.

Among the well-known Plymouth churches destroyed in these two nights were St. Andrew's, Charles, St. James-the-Less, King Street Wesleyan, Courtenay Street Congregational, and George Street Baptist. Other notable buildings which were completely destroyed included the Athenaeum, Ballard Institute, Millbay Drill Hall, Promenade Pier, Hoe Cafe, Plymouth Club, Plymouth Conservative Club, Plymouth Masonic Club, Notte Street Balfour Hall, Devon and Cornwall Female Orphanage, Hoe Grammar School, several elementary schools, Y.W.C.A., Central Y.M.C.A., Lockyer Street Y.M.C.A. Hostel, Nurses' residence, Lockyer Street Prince of Wales's Hospital, Proprietary Library and Public Library. Cinemas destroyed included the Palladium, Ebrington Street; Cinedrome, Ebrington Street; Criterion, Cornwall Street; New Empire, Union Street; and Grand, Stonehouse.

Above, Westwell Street. Far right, top, the Crescent, middle, Old Town Street, bottom Union Street. Near right, top Union Street, bottom Old Town Street.

Many well-known public-houses were wiped out, including the Posada, Noah's Ark, Golden Lion, Post Office, Newmarket, Fountain, Prince of Wales's, West Hoe, and Westwell Street Vaults. The destroyed hotels included the Royal, Westminster, Hackers, Waverley, and Farley. Banks, insurance offices, solicitors' offices, accountants' offices, and complete terraces of private houses went out of existence in the holocaust.

Yet, in the midst of all this wreck and ruin, Derry's Clock Tower, one of the best-known landmarks in Plymouth, remained solid. But while the tower remained, the four-faced clock no longer gave Greenwich time. The faces were smashed by flying debris; the delicate mechanism could not stand the violent concussions.

Above, Guildhall Square. Far page, top left, Cornwall Street, right, Old Town Street. Far right middle, Union Street, bottom, Millbay Station, near right bottom, Courtenay Street.

April 2 1941

The Hun has given Plymouth a respite. But the city was still staggering a bit from its fearful battering. Day after day there were the shaking detonations, as the demolition squads brought down to rubble and dust all those towering, ragged walls which were a danger. There were definite indications that life was reviving and steadying; the harassed, haggard looks going. People were, however asking the question "Will Devonport experience the same awful fate?" By comparison that end of the city, at least, the business part, was almost unscathed. We had been told that "Haw-Haw", the renegade William Joyce, who was well remembered in Plymouth as one of Mosley's Blackshirts, had declared over the German radio that Devonport's turn was to come.

Opposite page, top, Plymouth Pier. Bottom left, Princess Square, middle, Barbican, right, Russell Street. Above, the nightly trek into the countryside begins.

One of the most tragic scenes had been the nightly trek into the country of thousands of citizens – those who had managed to secure accommodation in the neighbouring towns and villages, and those who just went out "anywhere", to make sure of being away from such frightfulness as they had experienced. Let it be remembered that a large number of these people had had their homes destroyed; had seen their relatives and friends killed and injured. They trekked out by car, bus, lorry, tradesman's van, bicycles, walking – all equipped for a night "somewhere" or "anywhere" in the country. It was, indeed, a pathetic sight. War was a cursed thing.

Nevertheless, the grim desire for some sort of vengeance received a little solace on this day when it was announced that of the six raiders brought down in the past twenty-four hours two plunged to their end in the sea off the south-west – a Heinkel III off Budleigh Salterton, and a Dornier 214 off Cornwall.

179

April 8 1941

Another unpleasant night. Between 9-30 p.m. and 3-35 a.m. there were three "alerts". The first two were without incident, save for aircraft being heard, but hundreds of incendiaries were dropped during the third "alert" in the Hartley, Mannamead, Mutley, Lipson, Beaumont Road, and Friary areas. There were, however, few high-explosive bombs. About thirty fires were started, but so prompt was the action of the police, wardens, and civilians in tackling the incendiaries – some were of the explosive type – that the fires were not able to gain serious hold. The few high-explosive bombs that were dropped fell mostly on the Swilly Housing Estate, where four houses were wrecked, and four people were injured.

April 15 1941

Last night practically the whole of England came under the "red" warning, so widespread were the German raids. In Plymouth the "alert" lasted from 9-50 p.m. until 4-45 a.m., and during that time bombs were dropped at St. Budeaux, Hartley, Stonehouse, and Mount Wise. Little serious damage was, however, sustained, and the casualties comprised one person seriously injured and one slightly injured. One of the raiders was brought down at Holcomb Burnell, near Newton Abbot. One of the crew was killed and two were taken prisoner.

April 22 1941

Last night there commenced another series of appalling raids, and until the end of the month the city was to pass through yet another terrible ordeal which was to test the spirit, the endurance, and the courage of its citizens to the limit. These new raids caused all the greater apprehension, because we still had the all too vivid memory of the events last month, when 336 citizens – civilians – were killed, and so much wanton destruction to public and private property had been caused in the eastern half of the city. It now seemed that the Nazis were determined to finish their fiendish work. Their March attacks had left the city with its heart bleeding, business premises which had been household words in the Westcountry heaps of smouldering ruins, lovely public buildings and churches mere blackened shells and fire-scorched husks, hundreds of once happy homes piles of blasted plaster, stone and timber strewn with grim relics of the home comforts,

The scene of devastation from the Guildhall tower.

and an awful trail of dead and injured. Yet Plymouth had emerged from that with courage still high, and was beginning to heal her gaping wounds when these next blows were hammered on her broken body.

It was about 9-30 last night when the sirens wailed their warning, and from then until 3-30 this morning it was, in very truth, "hell let loose". Death and destruction rained down once again from the starlit heavens. We knew the stars were there, but we could not see them for the dust and the smoke. The flashes from guns and bursting bombs, and the lurid glare of the terrible fires blotted them out of vision. The beast was again loose to pour out his total warfare on a civil population.

The raiders' tactics were very much the same as those employed a month before – a vanguard of planes dropping thousands of flares and incendiaries, which turned night into day and set the beacon fires to illuminate a target area into which successive waves of bombers dived and released their loads of destruction. I was told that the majority of these bombers came in at a height of about 20,000 feet, and then dived to about 5,000 feet to release their bombs. At that height and in that glare their targets must have been easy. The din was terrific. The glare from the fires could be seen from all parts of the Westcountry. People outside the city, on the faraway hill-tops, in the distant towns and villages, watched that fearful glare, fascinated and horrified. Poor Plymouth!

The heavy detonations of the bombs, following the nerve-wrecking dive of the bombers, and the shriek of the falling missile, the crackle of fire, the choking dust and smoke, the crash of the anti-aircraft guns, as they did their best to put a barrage against those waves of raiders, the sinister whine of shell splinters, the falling of destroyed buildings – those were the elements which dominated during those five hours of hell.

Fires raged over a wide area – from Cattedown to the top of Devonport Harbour and Saltash. The worst conflagration was, however, again in the centre of the city where premises which had escaped the desolation of the March "blitz" became just raging furnaces. Embraced within this inferno were the north side of Cornwall Street, both sides of Russell Street, parts of King Street, the north side of Frankfort Street, and the "island" area bounded by Willow Plot, Frankfort Street, Mill Street, and Cornwall Street – areas which had escaped the previous attack.

A little farther afield there was the beacon light of blazing St. Peter's Church, one of the city's loveliest edifices, with its rich ornaments and distinctive architecture and stately tower. The Notre Dame Girls' School was also blazing from floor to roof. Other large fires raged over a very wide area of the city, including Devonport, where the General Post Office at the top of Fore Street was among the early buildings to be gutted.

Then there was the widespread destruction from the high-explosive bombs. Public buildings, business premises, private houses, were brought down to heaps of rubble and timber, twisted steel, and clouds of choking dust. Several streets were blocked by yawning craters.

An amazing escape was the railway bridge spanning Pennycomequick Hill and providing the railway link with Cornwall. One bomb missed it by a few feet and left a huge crater in the road below. As a matter of fact, one of the most remarkable features of the whole of these intensive raids was the escape of the railways running through the city, the railway bridges, and the several viaducts. It would seem inevitable that they should receive material damage. In point of fact, it was negligible. At Wingfield, Stoke, the track was torn up a bit, but the dislocation could not be regarded as serious.

High explosives close to the Royal Albert Hospital, Devonport, necessitated the patients and staff being evacuated.

Another unlucky western-end target was the Corporation Gasworks at Keyham, which received several direct hits and where fires were started. It resulted in the undertaking being put out of action for some time, as far as the provision of gas for public consumption was concerned.

Among the military objectives where damage was done were the Royal Marine Barracks, the Royal William Victualling Yard, the Royal Naval Hospital, the Royal Dockyard, Mount Wise, Raglan Barracks, Granby Barracks, and the Royal Naval Barracks. The full extent of the damage to the Services' establishments, and the casualties among Services' personnel in the port and garrison, was not revealed for security reasons, but the most tragic of their incidents was at the Royal Naval Barracks, where there was a direct hit on the petty officers' block. The killed were stated to number about eighty.

Among the civil population the casualties were heavy, the most terrible single incident being at the Portland Square underground shelter. This was hit by a bomb of heavy calibre, and seventy-two of the occupants of the shelter were killed. There were many tragic stories of entire families being wiped out.

The wisdom of Plymouth's decision after the March raids to close places of entertainment at 8-30 was well justified. Thus it was that most people were in their homes when the raid started, and this, combined with the fact that the centre of the city was comparatively quiet, undoubtedly lessened the casualties.

With the stories of stark tragedy which swept so many homes there were also the stories of amazing escapes and wonderful courage. For example, as I subsequently wandered amid the shambles that was once Plymouth, I frequently came across the Union Flag bravely and proudly stretching in the breeze from a ragged, blackened wall or a pile of rubble. It seemed symbolic of the city's grim purpose and still high courage.

Once again Plymouth had to muster all her resources to deal with the grave emergency. Fire brigades had again been rushed to the city from all parts, and these joined with the local brigades in a disregard of danger and an almost frantic desire to help in every way, regardless of the cost.

The many other Civil Defence services added to their battle honours, and they were again aided fearlessly, courageously, and voluntarily by the men of the Services who could be spared from their own heavy duties. Again there were instances where officers, non-commissioned officers, and men paraded before their commanding officers for permission to "go into the city to help".

And outside the organised services, both civil and military, there were the hundreds of just ordinary citizens – Mr. and Mrs. John Citizen, hero and heroine.

Here let me also record a word for those staffs who carried on with their essential work. As one instance, The Western Morning News was on the reader's breakfast table as usual this morning. Only those who worked in Leicester Harmsworth House, the head offices where the paper is published in Frankfort Street, will remember how that was accomplished. Leicester Harmsworth House was the sole survivor of that street, and it probably owed its survival to untiring devotion on the part of employees and again to the fact that it was a modern building, mainly constructed of fire-resisting materials.

Only when the raid was at its worst spells did the workers seek the protection of the shelter in the basement, and even down there they

Left, top, Guildhall Square, bottom Western Morning News Offices survive in Frankfort Street, but the Co-op emporium is burnt out. Above looking up Frankfort Street.

carried on with as much work as possible. In the lulls they were back at their desks and machines.

In very truth, the issue of The Western Morning News for April 22, 1941, was memorable. It was produced, six pages of up-to-date news, in a building encircled by fire, with bombs crashing down all around, and yet itself miraculously escaping. Some of the glass in the windows was broken by blast and heat, and when the fire brigades played cooling jets on the front the clouds of steam which came away gave the appearance of the building being on fire. For the second time Leicester Harmsworth House withstood the shock of blast and fire, and it was to survive many more furious onslaughts.

But after night always comes the dawn. Those of us who went through the Plymouth raids will not forget those dawns – and the grim pictures which the stricken city presented. On this morning tragedy stalked with heavy feet. Old wounds were gashed anew; new gaping wounds were opened.

Let me add a tailpiece to this rambling story of the night's horror. The B.B.C. news service this morning described the raid as "short and sharp". That was amended later in the day – and with good reason.

183

April 23 1941

Yet another nightmare; practically a repetition of the previous night's raid. Again the raid started about 9-30, and went on with devilish intensity for six hours. It would seem that the Hun was determined not to leave anything of Plymouth standing.

The procedure was much the same – showers of incendiaries, followed by wave after wave of bombers diving down on the flaming city. If anything the raid was heavier than on the previous night, and hardly a section of the city escaped the widespread destruction caused by fires and high explosives. The chief centres of destruction, and where the fires raged at their highest, included both sides of Old Town Street, from the Co-operative Society's large stores at the corner of Drake Circus down to and including Treville Street, Ebrington Street, Market Avenue, Russell Street, Mill Street, Fore Street, and other adjacent streets at Devonport, many terraces and avenues of large houses in the Hoe district, and whole streets of private houses at Devonport, were among the major scenes; and among well-known buildings which went down in this holocaust were the Royal Western Yacht Club, St. George's Church, Stonehouse, the Garrison Church, and the two stands at Home Park, which were packed with thousands of pounds' worth of furniture rescued from the bomb damaged houses after the March raids. These were among the major fires. Fanned by a stiff breeze, and with the fire-fighting services utterly unable to cope with such a major task, the flames spread with terrible fury, devouring everything in their course.

Left, Old Town Street, Spooner's Corner. Right, Home Park, Plymouth Argyle's stand.
Above, Bedford Street and Basket Street.

And while the fires raged the ceaseless bombing gave the already weary citizens another night of terror. Violent death and injury again laid heavy hand on the civil population.

On this night the enemy raiders certainly fulfilled the threat of "Haw Haw" that "Devonport's turn is to come". Devonport and Stonehouse did, I think, receive the worst of the mauling. The whole of Fore Street, the shopping centre of the western end of the city, was laid in ruins, with one or two small exceptions. The adjacent areas of Catherine Street, Tavistock Street, Marlborough Street, High Street, and Queen Street were all embraced in the welter of destruction. Famous buildings like the Royal Sailors' Rest, known the world over, the Welcome, the Central Hall, Electric Theatre, Alhambra Theatre, the Belisha Hall, the Hippodrome, and others, were totally destroyed.

Another dawn came today, revealing an even more agonising picture. There seemed to be a seething rage and hatred in the breast of every citizen. Haggard, begrimed, weary to the point of dropping, they were still gritting their teeth, and their one earnest appeal seemed to be summed up in the phrase "Let them have it back for this". It was utterly impossible not to feel and express the spirit of revenge for this wholesale destruction of life and property.

On this day there was yet another pitiful addition to the homeless, the bereaved, and the distraught, and it was at once apparent that gigantic organisation would be needed to deal with the emergency problems of shelter, feeding, and general welfare.

In my diary for this night I see I made this comment: "Again the already tired-out and heavily-pressed Civil Defence services worked heroically. There will be 'inquests' and criticisms. But let us take the big view. There was splendid courage".

I feel I must record that in the midst of all this nightmare of destruction The Western Morning News offices in Frankfort Street again stood four-square to the blast, and when there were lulls in the fury of the raid, editorial and mechanical staffs succeeded in maintaining production. The Western Morning News was, as usual, on the breakfast table.

Above and left, Fore Street, Devonport.

April 24 1941

This morning I asked myself, as hundreds of citizens must have asked, "When will this hideous attack on Plymouth cease?" For the third night in succession the whole business of fire, blast, death, and destruction has been visited on the city. The features were much the same, but they brought only more misery, more ruin, more hatred. This time – the raid was of similar duration, worked almost to a time-table – the greatest weight of the attack was in the Devonport, Stonehouse, Saltash, and Torpoint areas. Casualties were again very high. The official report, rather scanty this morning, stated that there were a large number of fires, and among the wrecked buildings were four churches.

On this day, without any question, I think, Plymouth stood as the worst blitzed city in the country.

Last night it became no longer possible to make the night publication of The Western Morning News at the Frankfort Street offices. Every effort was made to do so until round about midnight, and then the position was so hopeless that it was decided to once more make an emergency publication at the Exeter offices of the Express and Echo. That meant another night dash by car to Exeter with key editorial and mechanical staffs.

The fearful picture of Plymouth as we left the inferno behind us, was one I shall never forget. I was driving, but all the way to Exeter, especially when we got to the top of Haldon, colleagues sitting in the car with me were looking back, watching that terrible glow in the sky which marked the burning city.

Anyhow, we again got to Exeter on a vital mission, and with the unhesitating assistance of the staff of the Express and Echo - their ever-ready co-operation was one of the things which made this "emergency publication a memory worth retaining - The Western Morning News was able to maintain its unbroken publication.

Not until October, 1944 - three and a half years later - was The Western Morning News again published at Plymouth. It continued to be published at Exeter until the duplicate offices at Tavistock were ready, and from then onwards the nightly production was completed at Tavistock without interruption, and the early morning distribution was made from there.

The Western Evening Herald, however, involving only day work, continued to be printed and published from the Frankfort Street offices.

The Western Independent, the Plymouth Sunday paper, was less for-

Left and above, Marlborough Street, Devonport.

tunate with its head offices and works in Russell Street. These were completely destroyed, but, here again, publication was maintained. Fresh offices were opened at Alton Terrace for the editorial and commercial departments, and printing and publication were carried out at alternative works which had been organised at Ivybridge to meet such an emergency.

April 29 1941

For five nights Plymouth was given respite from trial bombardment, but we had by no means seen the end of Hitler's expense of fury on the city. Last night waves of German bombers again drenched parts of the city with incendiaries and high explosives in a raid which lasted from 10 p.m. to 1 a.m. St. Budeaux, Swilly, Stoke, Bull Point, and other parts of Devonport were the areas which took the heaviest blows. A first aid post was among the places damaged. Gas, water, and electricity were affected in parts. There were many fires. The night sky was again a lurid glow which could be seen for miles. As far away as Exeter they watched the glow anxiously. "Poor old Plymouth is getting it again" was passed from mouth to mouth.

At Torpoint and Saltash there was also extensive damage. A train was derailed between St. Germans and Menheniot, but there were no casualties. A signal-box at St. Budeaux was smashed by a direct hit. Scores of private houses in the most thickly-populated parts of Devonport were added to the scene of destruction, and casualties were again heavy among the civil population.

Left, Catherine Street, Devonport. Top, St Budeaux Station upside, right, downside.

April 30 1941

Yet another vicious night attack. One begins to wonder how much longer the mental and physical strain can last? Surely we have reached the limit. What courage there is in some people! What did they call us – a decadent race? Well, if this is a decadent spirit, then I am proud to have been associated with it. I see my diary for this morning says, "Plymouth has again taken it right on the chin, but with what courage". While many people had perforce left the city because there was no longer habitation for them, or because the ordeal was too much, there were still thousands left to carry on the fight. And what a grand lot they were! I met one of the thousands of voluntary wardens this morning; a man with four young children, who might well have been excused for taking his family away from the inferno. All through these nights of agony he had been out "doing his stuff", and the wife and little children had huddled in the garden shelter. But he would not budge. When I said to him "Why don't you take the family away?" he replied: "This is my home, and all I've got. My job is here". Then, as if by way of an afterthought, he quietly remarked: "Besides, this is Plymouth's finest hour. I should hate to miss it!"

And that was the magnificent, quiet, efficient and determined spirit of Plymouth expressed in thousands of incidents.

Anyhow, last night Plymouth was hammered again. The raid was quite characteristic of the previous heavy attacks – the opening shower of incendiaries and then the high explosives. Again the toll in life and property was heavy. Fires blazed everywhere. Among the places damaged were two hospitals, several shelters, St. Joseph's Home for the Aged – here the nuns in charge showed a marvellous courage and self-sacrifice in protecting the old people; there were instances where they flung themselves across them and were badly injured in so doing – a school used as a feeding centre, and wardens' posts. The smoke and dust-laden air must have made the picking out of objectives well-nigh impossible, and all the raiders seemed to do was to pour their bombs into the fiery cauldron.

It was reported this morning that seven of the raiders were brought down-three by night fighters and four by gunfire. That was the best single night "bag" for the intensive raids period. The Navy played a big part in this heavier barrage. Last night's special targets included the Corporation Bus depot at Milehouse, Swilly Isolation Hospital, the Royal Eye Infirmary, and Johnston Terrace School. The London-Penzance express was partly derailed at Keyham, where the main line was damaged. The main street at Saltash also received heavy damage by fire and blast.

Thus in March and April Plymouth and Devonport were destroyed during seven nights of merciless bombardment. No fewer than 750 enemy aircraft were reported to have taken part in the April raids on the city.

During the raids on the two nights March 20 and March 21 there were 336 civilians killed; during the raids on April 21, 22, 23, 28 and 29 the number of civilians killed was 590. In addition, of course, there were thousands injured. Many civilians were reported missing, and no trace has been found of them. They were simply buried under the tons of debris or blown to pieces.

By this time the heart of Plymouth had been gutted, and Devonport had been similarly treated. It was a fearful sight. The main shopping streets of Old Town Street, Bedford Street, George Street, Frankfort Street, Cornwall Street, Treville Street, a considerable portion of Union Street, Courtenay Street, Fore Street, Devonport, Marlborough Street, Tavistock Street, Catherine Street, St. Aubyn Street, and many other side and back streets adjacent to them, were virtually wiped out of existence, and there were scores of other places like Princess Square, Westwell Street, Lockyer Street, Athenaeum Street, Millbay Road, and whole areas of private houses in the Hoe district, at Keyham, Ford, Swilly, Beacon Park, and other parts of the city completely destroyed.

It was a devastation beyond anything ever dreamed of in the earlier days of the war. There was not a single part of the city which escaped, either business or residential, and there was scarcely a house in the entire area which did not sustain some damage, either serious or minor.

Far left, top Aggie Weston's, bottom, Chapel Street, near left and above, Fore Street

At the May meeting of the City Council the Chairman of the War Emergency Committee (Alderman L.R. Dunstan) gave some striking facts regarding the five nights of heavy raids in April. These five attacks, collectively, he said, covered 23 hours 16 minutes of continuous bombardment, and there were dropped approximately 1,140 high-explosive bombs, 17 paramines, and many thousands of incendiaries. At that stage he reported the casualties as: dead, 494 identified and 75 unidentified (later it was reported that the total killed in the five raids was 590); while the injured were 427 detained in hospital, 190 out-patients, and 527 treated at first aid posts. It was estimated that 1,500 dwellings were demolished or damaged beyond repair, and altogether 16,500 damaged.

The city police received reinforcements to the extent of 68 from Devon County, and 45 from Cornwall County police forces. During the first three nights 139 reinforcing pumps were sent into Plymouth to help the city fire service.

On the night of April 21 there were 68 fires, covering Keyham, Beacon Park, Mount Wise and H.M. Dockyard, involving four churches, one convent, two homes, two schools, post office, and the Corporation gasworks. Fire appliances used were: Plymouth, 87 pumps, one fire float, one T.T. ladder, 52,650 feet of hose; Reinforcements, 71 pumps, one fire float, and 90,000 feet of hose.

On the night of April 22 there were 47 fires, covering Fore Street, King Street, Morice Street, Marlborough Street, St. Catherine's Street, Chapel Street, Home Park grandstand, Millbay Docks, and flour mills. The reinforcements of equipment for this night was 78 pumps, two T.T. ladders, and 103,000 feet of hose.

On the night of April 23 there were 56 fires, covering Millbay Docks, Victoria Wharves, Cattedown, Torpoint oil depot, etc. Water dams containing 5,000 gallons of water each were erected at nine points. Reinforcement of equipment for this night comprised 20 pumps and 32,000 feet of hose.

On April 24-25 the water supply for fire emergency was augmented by the laying of 6-inch steel piping between Mutton Cove and Fore Street, Sutton Harbour and the city centre, Millbay Docks and Drake's Reservoir and Mutley Plain.

On the night of April 28 the attack was largely centred on the North Yard, Devonport, Bull Point, St. Budeaux, and Camels Head areas within the city, and Saltash and Torpoint. There were 42 fires, but the

damage was not so extensive as on the previous nights. There were 88 pumps and 92,000 feet of hose in use.

On the night of April 29 the attack was again mainly in the Devonport area, and fires included the one at the Milehouse Corporation bus depot and the St. Levan's Road gasometer. On this night the fire equipment used comprised 108 pumps and 102,650 feet of hose.

The fires referred to so far in this report by Alderman Dunstan were, of course, of major importance. But there were hundreds of others which were tackled so promptly and efficiently by anybody and everybody that they were almost immediately under control. For example, on the nights April 21, 22, and 23 there were no fewer than 17,550 incendiary bombs dropped in the area, causing 1,378 fires, of which 1,155 were brought under immediate control. On the nights of April 28 and 29 the incendiaries started 932 fires, of which 740 were brought under immediate control.

During the five nights 165 water mains were fractured, and the Corporation buses destroyed or damaged numbered 64.

The A.R.P. Control H.Q. underneath Devonport Market and 4 wardens' posts were demolished. Nine first aid posts were functioning, and these employed 33 to 37 first aid parties, 33 to 37 ambulances, and 8 to 12 casualty cars. The personnel employed in these services totalled 429. There were also many ambulances and parties rushed into the city from the neighbourhood. Altogether 225 "incidents" were attended by the ambulance and first aid parties during these raids.

Between April 24 and May 8 no fewer than 65,000 meals were served in the British Restaurants in the city. W.V.S. canteens toured the fire centres, and the mobile kitchens did valuable work.

Of the wardens' service there were 127 posts in action, manned by 330 full-time and 1,406 part-time wardens. Casualties among the Civil Defence services during these five April nights were: police, 7 killed, 27 injured; fire service, 17 killed, 43 injured; wardens, 7 killed, 20 injured; rescue service, 1 killed, 1 injured. These were the figures given by Alderman Dunstan, but later it was stated that the casualties in the whole of the Civil Defence services were 40 killed and 121 injured. I give this report and these figures by Alderman Dunstan because, while they might not be completely accurate in the light of subsequent checking, they do reveal something of the picture of what Plymouth went through in those five April nights. The extent of the damage caused to Service establishments in the heavy raids of

March and April, 1941, and the loss of personnel, was, for obvious reasons, not made public. Nevertheless, both in loss of life and in material damage to establishments, it was known to be extensive.

Some time later I had the opportunity of writing the story of the raid experiences at the Royal Naval Hospital, Stonehouse. This was a really "hot" centre, and I think this hospital can, without any challenge, lay claim to being the most heavily "blitzed" hospital in the country. Over twenty high-explosive bombs, and scores of incendiaries, fell on the hospital buildings or in the grounds, but, in the words of one of the senior officials, "they were very lucky".

Half of one of the big wards was demolished; it was the reception half, and was empty. But two people were killed by this bomb, a staff man and a patient who were nearby. The mental ward was struck, and one patient killed. Another block was blown up by a delayed-action bomb; it had been evacuated in time. Two residences were demolished, and the chaplain's house half wrecked. There were no casualties here, although most of the occupants were sheltering either in the basements or ground-floor rooms.

With the normal service of electricity and gas cut off – fortunately there was a reserve electric lighting for the operating theatre – windows blown out, and other serious material damage, the hospital improvised and carried on in true Royal Naval spirit, taking in not only Service casualties from the establishments outside the hospital, but civilians from the neighbourhood as well. Altogether, something like 1,400 casualties were treated, of which 200 proved fatal cases. One ward was given over to half a dozen mothers and newly-born babies, evacuated from a neighbouring blitzed maternity home.

Other Service establishments which sustained extensive damage included the Royal Naval Barracks, an ammunition ship off Bull Point, the Raglan Barracks, Granby Barracks, hutment's on the Brickfields, the North and South Dockyard, including the drawing office, the ancient Ropery, and the official residences, the Royal Marine Barracks, while at Mount Wise the temporary operational rooms and offices in huts on the parade ground were gutted by fire.

I have already indicated the main areas of the city which were affected by these heavy raids of March and April, but it is of interest to recall some of the prominent and familiar features of the city which by this time were blasted or burnt, suffering either total destruction or serious damage. These included:

Left, Ambulances from the Commonwealth. Top left, Mount Gold first aid post, with Sister Winifred Twyford. Top right, Men at Milehouse Bus Station, every ready with a stretcher Above the bombed City Hospital Maternity Ward.

Public Buildings

Guildhall, Municipal Offices, Council Chamber, Council Committee Rooms, Lord Mayor's Parlour, Lady Mayoress's Parlour, Western Law Courts, General Post Office, Devonport General Post Office, County Court Offices, Old Guildhall, Promenade Pier, Public Library (with 80,000 volumes), Stonehouse Town Hall, Hoe Cafe, Millbay Drill Hall, Proprietary Library, Plymouth Chambers, Plymouth Argyle grandstands, Devonport Belisha Hall, The Athenaeum, the Abbey Hall.

Clockwise from top left; Stonehouse Town Hall, the Athenaeum, Plymouth Library, the old Guildhall in Whimple Street and the Promenade Pier.

Churches

St. Andrew's, Charles, St. Saviour's, St. James-the-Less, St. Peter's, All Saints, St. George's, St. Aubyn, St. James-the-Great, St. Thomas, St. Stephen's, St. Michael's, St. Paul's, St. Augustine's (destroyed in subsequent raid), the Garrison Church. Devonport Synagogue. Plymouth Unitarian. Salvation Army Congress Hall, Plymouth; Salvation Army Hall, Devonport. Holy Redeemer Catholic Church, Keyham.

Top, Salisbury Road Baptist Church. Above, George Street Baptist. Right, a service in the ruins of St Peter's Church.

Schools

Hoe Grammar School, Notre Dame Girls' School, Cattedown Road Senior Girls, Cattedown Road Junior Mixed, High Street Senior Girls, Hyde Park Boys, Johnston Terrace Senior Boys, Johnston Terrace Junior Mixed and Infants, Keyham College Road Infants, King Street Senior Girls, Montpelier Mixed and Infants, Morice Town Junior Mixed, Morice Town Infants, Palace Court Senior Girls, Palace Court Junior Mixed and Infants, Paradise Road Junior Mixed and Infants, St. James-the-Less Junior Mixed and Infants, St. Stephens Junior Girls and Infants, Union Street Junior Mixed and Infants, Stoke Senior Boys, Tamar Central Boys, Salisbury Road Special Boys, Salisbury Road Special Mixed, Montpelier Girls' Secondary.

The Director of Education reported that this represented a total loss in school places of 7,646, out of a total of 16,808 children attending. A few of these schools were subsequently found repairable, and after a year or two were again in use.

Clubs

Plymouth Club, Lockyer Street; Royal Western Yacht Club, The Hoe; Plymouth Conservative Club, Princess Square; Plymouth Masonic Club, Princess Square; Plymouth Liberal Club, Russell Street; Devonport Conservative Club, Fore Street; Devonport Liberal Club, Chapel Street; Minima Yacht Club, Promenade Pier; Devon County Billiard Club, George Street; Jokers' Club, Athenaeum Lane; and Devon Barbarians Club.

Left, Princess Square, pre-war home of the Conservative Club. - 20 March 1941.
Above, York Street School - 2 March 1942.

Cinemas
Palladium, Ebrington Street; Cinedrome, Ebrington Street; Criterion, Cornwall Street; Electric, Fore Street; Devonport Hippodrome; Forum, Fore Street (afterwards repaired); Savoy, Union Street; New Empire, Union Street; Tivoli, Fore Street; Grand, Union Street.

Theatre
Alhambra, Devonport.

Institutions
Royal Sailors' Rest, Fore Street; Welcome, Fore Street; Plymouth Central Y.M.C.A., Old Town Street; Ballard Institute, Millbay; Devon and Cornwall Female Orphanage, Lockyer Street; Y.W C.A., Lockyer Street; North Hill Blind Institution (partial); St. Joseph's Home, Hartley (partial); Dockyard Orphanage, Stoke (partial); Ford Public Institution.

Hotels
Royal, Plymouth; Westminster, The Crescent; Waverley Millbay Road; Hackers, The Crescent; Farley's, Union Street; Royal, Devonport; Lockyer, Plymouth (partial).

Above, the burnt out shell of the Royal Hotel. Right, Palladium Cinema, Ebrington Street.

Prominent Businesses

Messrs. Pophams, E. Dingle & Co., Spooner & Co., John Yeo & Co. (drapers and outfitters), J.C. Tozer & Co. (drapers and outfitters), Costers Ltd. (drapers and outfitters), Garratts, Plymouth and Devonport (drapers and outfitters), Goodbodys, George Street and Bedford Street (confectioners and catering), Plymouth Co-operative Society (shops and offices) in Frankfort Street, Drake Circus and Fore Street, Woolworths, Marks & Spencers (Plymouth and Devonport), Boots Ltd. (Plymouth and Devonport), Timothy Whites & Taylors, Harris & Sons (decorators and furnishers), Bowdens (jewellers), Page, Keen & Page (jewellers), Lawleys (glass and china), Perkins Bros. (outfitters), Prynn Bros., Plymouth and Devonport (outfitters), Winnicott Bros. (merchants), S. Ball & Co. (wholesale warehousemen), Snells Motors, Pikes Motors, Army & Navy Stores, Moon & Sons (pianos, music and furniture), Parker & Smith (music), Turner & Phillips (music), Underhills Ltd. (printers and stationers), Plymouth and Stonehouse Gas Company (showrooms and offices), Mikado Cafe, Butland & Treloar (tailors), W.H. Smith & Sons (books and stationers), Sellicks (books and stationers), Wm. Brendon & Son (printers and publishers), Tucketts Ltd. (confectioners, shops and factory), London Furnishing Co., Mumfords Motor Showrooms, Balkwill (chemist), Rundle, Rogers & Brook (warehousemen), Dunn & Co. (hats), Hepworths (outfitters), Liptons (food), Maypole (food), Willsons (gowns), Whitbread (ladies' outfitter), Samuel Edgcumbe (jeweller), Bateman (optician), Randalls (footwear), True Form (footwear), Saxone (footwear), Dolcis (footwear), Red Line (footwear), Austin Reed (outfitters), Jays (furnishing), Harding (furnishing), Thomas Cook & Sons (travel agents), Service & Co. (builders' merchants), Wrights (hairdressers), Cousins (hairdressers), Snell & Co. (tobacconists), Samuel Gluckstein & Co. (tobacconists), Limpennys (sports), Wakeling (umbrellas, and sports), Skewes (outfitters), Sun Buildings (offices), Plymouth Chambers (offices and public rooms), Old Town Chambers (offices), Corporation Electricity Showrooms, Singers Sewing Machines (Plymouth and Devonport), Edwards (outfitters), Barbers (outfitters), Gieves (outfitters), Fifty Shilling Tailors, Montague Burton (tailors), Williams (cafe and florist), Breeze's (Plymouth) Ltd. (druggists), Andrews Motor Showrooms, and numerous others so familiar to every shopper in Plymouth.

20-21 March 1941. Pophams (top) is a smouldering ruin, so too is Dingles.

Over one hundred public-houses were completely destroyed, and among the well known of these were Noah's Ark, Westwell Street Vaults, The Post Office, Golden Lion, Newmarket, Fountain, Prince of Wales, Posada, Corn Exchange, West Hoe, Thomas's Wine Vaults (Devonport), Two Trees, and others.

There was hardly a hospital in the city which escaped damage. The Prince of Wales's sections at Greenbank Lockyer Street and Devonport (Royal Albert); the Royal Naval Hospital, Stonehouse; City Hospital, Greenbank; Isolation Hospital, Swilly; Royal Eye Infirmary, Mutley; and Stoke Military Hospital all suffered.

Of the public services, there was damage to the Corporation Electricity Works at Cattedown; Plymouth and Stonehouse Gas Company's Works, Coxside; Plymouth Corporation Gas Works, Devonport; Corporation Transport Depot, Milehouse; Western National Bus Depot, Prince Rock. Many gas and water mains were put out of action.

Most of the leading banks had their premises in the centre of the city destroyed, including the Midland (Bedford Street and Union Street); Barclays (Princess Square); Lloyds and National Provincial (Bedford Street).

There was also wholesale destruction of offices of solicitors, accountants, auctioneers, doctors, dentists, and others.

Above, Bedford Street banks. Right, Union Street with the burnt out Posada.

Above and right, Winston Churchill visits Plymouth. Above, clearing up.

May 1 1941

My diary notes for this day tell their own picture:
"A raid-free night - and blessed sleep. Was that sleep good! We were a bit concerned about five o'clock last evening when the 'alert' again sounded, and wondered whether it was reconnaissance for another night raid. But, happily, it did not materialise, and we spent the whole night in bed without interruption. Everyone looks and feels the better equipped for a renewal of the fight. Plymouth is striving gallantly to gather up the broken threads. How the poor city has been battered. It is a ghastly picture. Now the weather has turned wet. The dust has become black mud. What a state the thoroughfares are in — many of them still completely blocked. Arrangements are now being made for the evacuation of the children. It is like closing the stable-door after the horse has bolted. The Ministry would not heed Plymouth's plea months ago to be made an evacuation area; now, when the city has become the worst blitzed place in the country when the children have known those nights of horror, murder, and devastation, the authorities are frantic to get them away."

May 2 1941

The Prime Minister, Mr. Winston Churchill, came this day and saw for himself the tragedy that had swept the city. He toured the devastated areas; it took him a long time. He was deeply moved by the scenes, but enormously heartened by the wonderful spirit of the people. It was a typical Churchillian visit. His presence had an enormous effect on the morale of the people, and the way in which they everywhere flocked around and greeted him, and his response with characteristic mannerisms and gestures, were all features which helped to rekindle the flame of hope and grim resolution in the hearts of the citizens.
The Prime Minister was told in detail how the situation was being tackled. I see that my notes say: "Food and other necessities are being rushed to Plymouth. There is no shortage".

May 6 1941

Another raid last night, but it was light in comparison to recent experiences. There were only three or four high-explosive bombs. One of these struck the houses in Percy Terrace, Lipson. In the demolished house three people were killed. Incendiaries were dropped in the Compton district, but there was no fire damage.

May 7 1941

Night raiders were again over the district, when the Westcountry as far up as Taunton was subjected to scattered attacks. Residents in the Pomphlett district had a narrow escape when a bomb demolished three houses and damaged fifteen others. There were, however, three killed, including Rev. W. Spencer, a well-known Methodist minister, a Plymouth business man, and a naval man. In Plymouth itself bombs were dropped in the areas of Thorn Park, Mannamead, Millbay, and Stoke, but there were no serious casualties.

May 8 1941

Plymouth again received the raiders' attention, when they were over various parts of the Westcountry last night. Three bombs and a para-mine fell in Central Park, but in this "wide-open space" they did little or no damage. Plymstock, however, did not escape so lightly. Here, two people were killed and three injured.

May 9 1941

These scattered raids were continued over the Westcountry last night, but the nearest points at which bombs were dropped were Saltash, Torpoint, and Staddon Heights. Two people were injured at Saltash.

May 12 1941

Again the same sort of tactics were adopted by raiders last night, when their attacks seemed to cover various parts of the Westcountry. The Plymouth "alert" was round about midnight, and at 12-50 a.m. six bombs fell in the Cobourg Street area. A house in the main street was demolished, killing one person and injuring three. People were trapped in an adjoining house, but these were all rescued after some fine work by the rescue parties. Some bombs also fell in the Beaumont Road and St. Judes district, and while there was some damage to houses, there were no additions to the casualty list.

May 13 1941

Again these scattered raids, and, as far as Plymouth was concerned, there were bombs on the official residences adjoining the R.N.E. College at Keyham, where one person was killed and two injured.

Right; Bomb incident at Laira.

May 17 1941

There were tip-and-run raids last night. The first one came soon after 1 a.m., and we had two more before 5 o'clock. During the first attack a bomb fell in Lyndhurst Road, seriously damaging the nearby Montpelier Elementary School. During the second there was a bomb at Mount Wise. The third attack was more prolonged, and bombs dropped in Albert Road, while a land-mine in Pentamar Terrace caused great destruction in two streets. There were no casualties. On this night, from the high ground around Plymouth, the glow of a great conflagration illuminated the western sky. The Germans claimed to have bombed the St. Eval aerodrome.

June 13 1941

Details were made available on this day revealing how two Plymouth fishermen were killed when their hooker, Pansy, was attacked by German aircraft out on the fishing grounds. The boat was swept by a hail of bullets. The two men had no protection, and were subsequently found dead in their drifting boat.

July 5 1941

The respite which Plymouth had from serious raids since May 17 was too good to last, and last night, during a sharp attack, there was widespread damage and a number of casualties. The clear moonlight aided the raiders, which were in considerable force. High-explosive bombs were dropped in the Hoe, Hartley, Keyham, Crownhill, Laira, Beacon Park, St. Budeaux, and Devonport Park areas. From that list it will be seen that again the residential areas were the chief sufferers. Altogether there were 18 people killed and 14 injured. There were a number of fires from the incendiary bombs, including one at the Mount Gold Hospital, but they were not serious, and were soon under control. In the Hoe district there was one particularly bad incident, when the Windsor Arms and adjacent houses received direct hits. Here, two families were completely wiped out. Such was the violence of the explosion that one man's body was hurled over the tops of the trees, and was found three hundred yards away on the Hoe. At Keyham the Corporation gas supply was again temporarily affected over an area, and at Laira an oil bomb fell on a railway truck. At Pomphlett a timber yard was set ablaze, and at Cornwood the woods were on fire.

July 9 1941

Plymouth was again the target last night during an "alert" which lasted from 12-30 a.m. to 4 a.m., but the attack was not heavy. Bombs were dropped in the Devonport area. Two policemen - one had just arrived to relieve the other – were killed by blast as they were sheltering in one of the very few remaining doorways in the badly devastated Fore Street. Seven other people were injured; eight who were trapped under a demolished house were safely extricated. Bombs also fell on the railway near Bere Alston, putting the main Southern Railway line out of action for a few hours.

17 August 1941, Millbay goods shed, the Duke of Cornwall Hotel to the left and the shell of the Ballard Institute on the right.

August 18 1941

Bearing in mind that the weather was extremely rough, it was rather surprising to get an "alert" early last night. It was blowing hard, and there was drenching rain. But those who did venture into the streets were witnesses of a thrilling spectacle. The single enemy bomber which was making the raid was hit by anti-aircraft fire – the Royal Marines claimed the honour – and crashed in flames at Gawton Woods, near Bere Alston, and a short distance from the Tavistock-Launceston main road. The four members of the crew were all killed, blown to pieces, when the machine crashed into this woodland and exploded. It was a gruesome spectacle which daylight revealed. The trees had been blasted away for about one hundred yards, the bomber was blown to pieces.

Top left, Millbay Goods Yard, 17 August 1941, opposite the Greyhound. Above a bomb falls on the Torr Estate.

November 22 1941

There were numerous "alerts" in the intervening period since the last attack, but no incidents. Last night, for instance, one raider which attempted to come over the city met with such a hot reception from the greatly intensified barrage that it made off with all speed in an easterly direction and unloaded its bombs at Ugborough, where a bungalow was destroyed, killing a Plymouth evacuee woman and injuring eight other people.

November 24 1941

Plymouth had a tremendous thrill last night, when a raider was brought down by a Polish night fighter directly over the city. I was a spectator to the whole incident as I stood with wardens at the junction of Glenhurst Road and Abbot's Road. The raider seemed to be rather lower than usual, and we were straining our eyes to try and pick out the machine against the black sky. Suddenly, there appeared almost directly overhead a glow of fire. It was moving and growing in size. From the crowd there was a concerted yell, "He's hit!". The glow spread, until the machine looked like a flaming cigar racing through the night sky. The machine continued in an almost complete encirclement of the city, and then, in a northerly direction, suddenly crashed, a fiery mass, to earth. For a moment the whole countryside was illuminated as the machine blew up. The four occupants baled out successfully – one of them, who was wounded, was pushed out by the others and landed at Plympton, and the others were captured in the Bickleigh district. The machine itself crashed in a field near the Roborough-Tamerton road, and this morning when I went out to see the wreckage I found it scattered over two fields. The force of the explosion, on hitting the ground, had been terrific.

December 6 1941

The raids were now of a very sporadic type. For the first time for several weeks there were two "alerts" today. They each lasted only about five minutes, but the first was noteworthy as the raider was successfully attacked by our fighters over the Whitsands and crashed into the sea. Sightseers saw the bomber emerge from the clouds with the fighters streaking after it. There was no escape. They gave it a final burst, and the intruder's fate was sealed.

Above, this page and opposite, a bomb falls opposite the Continental Hotel.

January 26 1943

When the "alert" sounded this afternoon, Plymouth was not the target. It was the little centuries-old village of Aveton Gifford, in the picturesque South Hams. Hit-and-run raiders, of which there were many round about this time, swooped in low over the coast and unloaded their bombs on this peaceful village. There was hardly a house which was not damaged; in fact, one third of the village was rendered uninhabitable. The beautiful thirteenth-century church was destroyed. The casualties included one fatal – a child.

February 14 1943

About ten enemy planes took part in an attack last night – the first night attack for nearly eighteen months. The "alert" lasted eighty minutes, and the casualties included six people killed, nine seriously injured, and eleven slightly injured. The most serious incident was at Palmerston Street, Stoke, where a bomb of heavy calibre completely demolished two houses and seriously damaged about fifty others in the immediate vicinity. The crater left here was one of the biggest seen in the city.

Other bombs fell in the vicinity of Millbay, one in the roadway immediately outside the Continental Hotel, where a largely attended dance had been in full swing. There was considerable damage by blast to the hotel, but the casualties fortunately were only a few people injured.

June 14 1943

The very sharp raid which Plymouth and Plympton experienced in the early hours of this morning, and which came after a long respite from air attack, was a grim reminder of the danger which still threatened and the necessity for all the air raid services to be on the top line of efficiency.

The "alert" sounded at 12-15 a.m., just as most citizens were deep in their first sleep. If there was any reluctance at turning out, the activity which so quickly materialized had an immediate effect. From the raiders' point of view operations commenced when the "pathfinder" – a single flare-dropping machine flying very fast and low some minutes in advance of the bombers – tore across the city. The flares were dropped in the region of the Central Park, and in their glare there was again that awful feeling of being stripped of every bit of protection.

The main activity of the raid lasted about half an hour. It was one of the liveliest half-hour's Plymouth citizens spent. In the glare of the flares, which had slowly drifted back over the residential part – Mannamead and Mutley areas in particular – the bombers dived at terrific speed, and with terrifying noise, to release their bombs at low level. They were met by the fiercest barrage Plymouth had yet experienced, including the full power of the new rocket defences.

The sky was alive with tracers and exploding shells, and, in "the sure and certain knowledge" that "what goes up has got to come down", the air seemed to be full of fragments, whining and zipping in every direction.

It was a damaging raid while it lasted, but by comparison the casualties were, I think, light. In the city itself between seventy and eighty high explosives were dropped. They were of mixed calibre, from the 1000 kg. down to the 250 kg. The most amazing feature was the number of unexploded bombs – something like fifty per cent. For many days afterwards the gallant bomb disposal squads were busy removing these potential dangers. The fact that so many failed to explode undoubtedly saved a heavy casualty list and much greater damage.

It was in this raid that the main police headquarters at Greenbank had an amazing escape. In previous raids it had experienced quite a number of "near misses", but this escape was providential. One of the heaviest calibre bombs, 1000 kg., crashed through the roof in the centre of the main building, bringing something like 140 tons of masonry down with it, and then lay unexploded on the first landing outside the police court and magistrate's rooms, and immediately over the cells, in which there were a number of prisoners, and the control room, where full "action" staffs were at work. A considerable force of police was also in the building at the time. Another bomb, 500 kg., crashed into the adjoining building, the Corporation Laundry and this also went unexploded.

Police headquarters had to be evacuated, and the reserve headquarters and control at Widey Grange, Crownhill, was brought into operation for several days until the unexploded bombs were safely removed. Another 1000 kg. fell in Freedom Park Villas, went through a house, and came to rest leaning out of the window on to the garden. This, too, was unexploded. There were quite a number of these remarkable incidents.

In this raid 13 people were killed and a considerable number injured. Some 3,000 houses were entirely destroyed or damaged.

Plympton shared this raid with Plymouth, and had their worst experience of the war to date. Thirteen high explosives and 4,380 incendiaries, 40 fire-pots, and 38 phosphorus bombs were dropped in this area. Five people were killed, and of the 600 houses damaged, 11 were totally destroyed.

This raid had another noteworthy feature. The attacking force was estimated at about twenty and four of these were brought down. One, a Junkers 88, crashed in the garden of a house at Stoke which was being used as a hostel for the W.R.N.S.; a second crashed at Stokenham near Kingsbridge; and the other two came down in the sea. This was the first occasion that an enemy aircraft crashed actually within the city. The crew of this machine were burnt to death, and their charred remains were subsequently buried at Weston Mill Cemetery with the customary Air Force honours.

Three members of the crew of another machine which was hit baled out over the city. Two of them were captured unhurt – one in the garden of a house in Alexandra Road and the other in Lisson Grove. They were taken to Greenbank Police Station, and later, when that place had to be evacuated, to Plympton Police Station, where the Services took charge of them for interrogation. The third member, badly injured, was picked up between Plympton and Crownhill and taken to hospital.

This raid was the first big test for the reorganised National Fire Service, and it was the first time that the Canadian fire-fighters, stationed in the city, had seen action. They were given one of the biggest fires, namely, that which gutted – but was restricted to – the premises of Messrs. Timothy White on Mutley Plain. The work of these Canadians generally evoked praise. There were about thirty fires altogether, one of the biggest being the huge pile of timber from blitzed houses which had been accumulated at the Lipson tip. There was again some splendid work by the Civil Defence services, both full-time and voluntary, but the work of the National Fire Service was criticised.

August 12 1943

During last night Plymouth had one of the worst raids from the civil population point of view since the heavy blitzes of 1941. About nine o'clock there was a brief "alert" but in actual point of fact this was occasioned by two unidentified aircraft in the region of the Start; they were afterwards identified as two of our Spitfires. But the public went to bed just a little nervous.

It was about 12-30, when everyone was well settled in sleep, that the sirens sounded again. There was a prompt turn out of all the various services, but the "alert" lasted only ten minutes, and although there had been no activity the distant sound of aircraft was not very reassuring. Most people, however, turned into bed again, under the impression that they were our own aircraft.

But they had not got comfortable before a machine came roaring across the city at a very low altitude. It dropped flares. Within a few moments the sinister whistle of falling bombs was heard.

This machine had been the "pathfinder" to light the target for the following bombers.

It was only then that the sirens again wailed. By this time bombers were diving on to the city, releasing their loads on the residential areas. There was a wild scramble for shelter, but it was too late. The deadly damage of catching people in their homes before they could regain their shelters had taken its toll.

What was the explanation for the belated sounding of the sirens, and for the fact that during the ensuing sharp raid the defence barrage seemed so half-hearted? That was the rather furious question on everyone's lips.

At this distance of time I can safely give the explanation. In the brief "alert" which had preceded the raid there were enemy aircraft in the area, and when they passed out the "raiders passed" was sounded in the ordinary way.

Then the enemy aircraft employed the clever intruder tactics so skilfully exploited by our own airmen. They mixed up with a much stronger force of British bombers which were returning, and came in over the coast with them.

They came in well to the east of Plymouth, and then, suddenly turning south-west, crossed the city from the direction of Plympton to Devonport. The "pathfinder" streaked across the city at only 500 feet – most of the balloons were down in order to allow our bombers a safe crossing – and the German bombers, after crossing the coast at heights varying from 6,000 to 19,000 feet, dived on to the city.

In the clear moonlight, and aided by the flares, the city lay almost "naked" below them. Their bombs were a mixture of high explosive and incendiary, the latter including some of the phosphorus type.

The extent of the raid can be best gathered from the facts of casualties and damage. It was again the civil population which carried the load. In all, 41 men, women, and children were killed, about 90 seriously injured, and a further 70 slightly injured.

Heavier casualties and more damage was averted by the fact that again – as on the last heavy raid – a very high percentage of the bombs failed to explode. For the best part of a week the gallant bomb disposal squads were busy removing some forty or fifty of these. Many were of the delayed-action type; others had just failed to explode. They were all dealt with.

The lads who handle these unexploded bombs must be devoid of nerves. It gave one quite a thrill to see the bomb disposal lorry dashing full speed through the streets of the city on its way out to the moor,

Far left, St Augustine's Church. Above, Mutley takes a direct hit.

where they were safely exploded. The lorry was always preceded by a police patrol car bearing a red flag and equipped with loudspeaker.

"Clear the way! Unexploded bomb!" was the message of this pilot car. Then came the lorry with its "danger red" paintwork, and if you looked at it from the rear you would see the ugly snout of a bomb sticking out over the tailboard – and a couple of grinning bomb disposal men calmly sitting alongside it.

The damage in this raid was scattered from Laira to Devonport. The worst incidents were in James Street, Hotspur Terrace, Welbeck Avenue, Ryder Road (Ford), Queens Gate (Victoria Park), Union Street, Craigmore Avenue, and Portland Square.

Once again the central police headquarters at Greenbank and the nearby City Hospital had an amazing escape. One bomb exploded in the Corporation laundry, which adjoins the police station, with only a stout wall separating it from the cells in which there were a few prisoners, and the police control room, where the members of the Women's Auxiliary Police Corps, flinging themselves on the floor, escaped with nothing more serious than being smothered in dust.

An unexploded bomb fell in the roadway outside the City Hospital main gate, close to the nurses' home, and another in the grounds. The

wing of a ward in the City Hospital was burnt out, but there was only one patient in occupation, and she was removed safely.

There were a number of fires, and the N.F.S. did a splendid job of work in getting these under control or out before five o'clock in the morning. The main fires were at the City Hospital, Portland Square, Union Street, and at Millbridge.

No fewer than seven of the unexploded bombs fell in Central Park, adjacent to the anti-aircraft gun site, mostly in the Corporation cabbage patch. There were other "unexplodeds" at Laira and Embankment Road.

One fire-bomb container fell intact close to the Canadian fire station at Hartley. A phosphorus bomb made a direct hit on the isolated Westminster Bank – the only remaining building in Bedford Street, and did damage to the two upper floors before being dealt with. The Midland Bank at the corner of Union Street and Phoenix Street, and the adjoining garage, were demolished by a direct hit, and blast damage to the Palace Theatre was such, that entertainment for the rest of the week was suspended.

Civil Defence services again did a grand night's work. Most of the casualties were dealt with at the North Hill first aid post. Rest centres and emergency feeding centres were opened in various parts of the town.

American troops stationed at Crownhill were sent into the city to help with the work. For most of them it was a raid "baptism".

Afterwards one of them said to me: "I guess we know now what was meant by, 'Plymouth can take it'. The people were grand".

This raid was carried out simultaneously with one on Bournemouth. Only one of the raiders was brought down.

The "intruder" tactics succeeded at Plymouth to an alarming degree. The barrage, in which so much confidence had been felt, could not get going against the mix-up of our returning bombers and the enemy aircraft. Only one parting salvo went up from the rocket barrage, and the guns barked off some 3,000 rounds without success.

November 16 1943

It was at exactly four minutes past five this morning that the sirens wailed the warning that enemy aircraft were in the vicinity, and within a quarter of an hour a sharp attack had developed, resulting in considerable damage to residential property in various parts of the city, and a casualty list including 18 people killed and about 60 injured. They were all civilians. The B.B.C. described this raid as "slight" – they said there was slight enemy activity over the south-west – while the Germans claimed "a successful attack on the port of Plymouth". In point of fact, it was neither. It was a sharp attack on the residential areas.

The enemy adopted the tactics of their last raid, when, it will be remembered, they came in and launched their attack after the sirens had sounded the "raiders passed". This time the authorities were not caught with that trick. In point of fact, the raiders - the total force was stated to be about fifteen – were "playing about" for a time outside. Then they suddenly concentrated, swept in via their old route to the east, and launched their attack on the outward run from north-east to south-west.

Although the "alert" lasted for nearly an hour and a half, the attack was concentrated into about half an hour. During that time high ex-

Left, A blaze is tackled in Union Street. Right, the American troops get stuck in.

plosives, oil and phosphorus bombs, flares, and many hundreds of incendiaries were dropped. The Saltram bank of the River Plym, opposite Laira, and the Central Park, in Plymouth, were drenched with incendiaries, but these did comparatively little damage.

Most of the damage was caused by high explosives, and there were many fewer unexploded bombs than on previous raids this year. Altogether there were five major incidents, and at four of them there were fatal casualties. The worst of these was when a cluster of four bombs dropped within twenty-five yards of each other in the area around Camilla Terrace, Pennycross, closely adjoining the Greyhound Stadium, and the new popular hostelry The Cherry Tree. Well over a hundred houses were either completely destroyed or seriously damaged in this area, and the casualties included eight people killed. Among them were a Home Guard lieutenant and a special constable, both of whom had gone into the street soon after the "alert" sounded.

Another serious incident was at Lonsdale Villas, Mutley where a large house at the end of the terrace, and occupied in three flats, was completely demolished by direct hit, and the victims were five people, who were trapped. It was three days before the last of these bodies was recovered by the rescue squads, who worked in relays almost day and night in the forlorn hope that they might get to the trapped people in time.

Haddington Road, Stoke, was once again a target for the Nazi bombs, and here, too, there were fatal casualties. It was at this incident that several people sheltering in an Anderson shelter in one of the gardens had an amazing escape. The edge of the huge crater left by the bomb, which wrecked all the houses around, was only about six feet from the shelter. The occupants were uninjured.

A fourth incident with fatal consequences was in Duke Street, one of the congested parts of old Devonport, where several houses were wrecked, and the victims included a man and a woman as well as others injured.

The fifth big incident was in Seymour Road, Mannamead, where two bombs of heavy calibre fell, one bang in the centre of the wide tree-lined thoroughfare, and the other in the grounds of Abbotsfield, a Salvation Army hostel. These bombs did a lot of damage to the big houses in the immediate district – some of the biggest houses in residential Plymouth – but there were no casualties.

How fortunate the district was in this respect can be gathered from the fact that the bomb in the road was within a few yards of a hostel accommodating about one hundred members of the W.R.N.S. The windows and doors were blown out, the roof was almost lifted off, rooms were wrecked, but the W.R.N.S. were true to Navy traditions, and stood fast. Within a short time they were tidying up, gathering up their scattered belongings for transfer to new accommodation and breakfast was served as usual. A well-known citizen, Mr. W.J. Law, had a remarkable escape, for he was standing on fire guard in the road within twenty yards of the bomb, but the blast and debris went right over him, and he was unscratched. The staff and inmates of the Salvation Army hostel likewise escaped, although the bomb there virtually burst on the doorstep.

Altogether in this raid no fewer than 2,500 houses were found to be in need of repair to a greater or lesser degree. Some 40 were completely destroyed, and 600 were badly damaged.

This night produced some fine work by the Civil Defence forces, and one of the features was that by daylight the first aid repairers were tackling the house damage. American troops helped in the removal of furniture from damaged homes.

Above, opposite page and overleaf, Plymstock is hit in the last raid of the war.

April 30 1944

After a respite of nearly six months, the Hun gave Plymouth a sharp reminder in the early hours of this morning that it is still very much a front-line city. The "alert" sounded at 3-15, and lasted about seventy minutes, during which time the attack was made by between thirty and thirty-five aircraft. They were heavily challenged by the guns and rockets of the anti-aircraft defences, and night fighters of the Royal Air Force were ready to strike with deadly effect as the raiders approached and left their target. In all four of the raiders were destroyed, two by a Canadian fighter pilot within a few minutes of each other. The destroyed aircraft came down in the sea, but from at least one of the raiders most of the crew escaped by parachute, and members of the Home Guard patrolling the adjoining Cornish foreshore in the vicinity of the Whitsands, collected some of them and made them prisoners as they came ashore in their rubber dinghies.

The main weight of the attack was concentrated on the waterfront, with the heaviest incident in the vicinity of Oreston. It was at this village, so close to the Sutton Harbour and the Cattewater, that the civilian population was tragically hit, with a death roll of 18 – 4 men, 11 women, and 3 girls – and 7 injured seriously. The heaviest toll of life here was taken when an Anderson shelter received a direct hit and 6 people were killed, while in a public shelter which was also hit, 9 people were killed. Among the victims were the wife of a merchant sailor serving at Alexandria and her two daughters, aged twelve and four.

In Plymouth itself there was a death roll of 9, including 3 fire-watchers at the Western National Omnibus Company's bus depot at Prince Rock, and 16 people were seriously injured. The bus depot received a direct hit. There was heavy damage, and a few of the buses were destroyed by fire. The second most serious incident within the city was in the Milehouse region, where bombs fell in Browning Road, Fisher Road, and Beaumont Street, claiming victims and causing widespread havoc among residential property in the district.

One of the targets for the enemy was obviously the railway sidings at Laira, for a number of bombs fell in this district, but without causing any very serious damage or inconvenience. One fell near the Rising Sun Inn at Crabtree, another fell right in the centre of the Gas Company's recreation ground, it simply left a huge crater, without causing any damage to the tremendous collection of vehicles and other war materials assembled around the fringe of the ground.

Bombs were also dropped in Lucas Terrace and the Tothill recreation ground.

THE CLOSING SCENES

It was to my lasting regret that I was not able to be with the Army of Liberation for the European 'kill'. As I indicate in an earlier chapter, I had had to come home just when we were within striking distance of Germany. The grim dramatic trail from the Normandy beachhead through Northern France into Belgium and Holland had been milestoned by the liberation of many famous places – Chartres, Paris, Amiens, then the onward dash through territory I knew so well in the 1914-18 war, for the freeing of Brussels, Antwerp and a dozen other places.

Then an unlucky encounter with a tank ended that most colourful and hectic period of my life. Under medical orders I had to come home. By the time I was fit again for active service the historic unconditional surrender had been signed. How I envied those of my colleagues who were still carrying on into Germany and the graphic stories they were able to send from the occupation scenes and incidents!

I had, however, been reserved for one more memorable episode in the closing chapter of the war – the liberation of the Channel Islands. These oldest possessions of the British Empire had not been forgotten in the wild excitement and events of the Second Front leading on to the German surrender. True, they had been isolated from the time we had occupied the northern coast of France. Thus cut off from the French occupied mainland, things became very grim for the islanders and the strong German occupying force. From a land of comparative plenty it was speedily reduced to a land of acute shortage. The position of the inhabitants became so bad that two Red Cross ships had to be sent with food parcels. The situation was such that it became almost impossible to purchase any goods: the whole system of existence was one of barter.

To within a week or two of the end of hostilities in North-West Europe it had been anticipated that the Channel Islands would have to be taken by assault. Accordingly, a sufficiently strong task force was organized. It was intended that the War Correspondents should go in with the assault in the same way as they had gone into Normandy. Happily, that assault was not necessary. The Germans in the islands, realizing the hopeless nature of their position as an isolated force, were agreeable to surrender and so it was with a much smaller occupying force, instead of an assault force, that one evening we steamed out of Plymouth Sound.

It was a 'hush-hush' departure, but early in the evening when the Correspondents were assembled at the Grand Hotel – I remember how we were taken out of the hotel to the seclusion of a corner on the grass in font of the raid-ruined Royal Western Yacht Club to receive our briefing – I think there were a fair number of the public there who sensed the significance of our gathering.

Plymouth had, of course, been the temporary home of a great many Channel Islanders since they had fled from their homes on the German occupation in 1940. In fact, they had formed their own Society, and it was astonishing how they used to get information through. I had made friends with some of them. I longed to be able to tell them where I was going, but that would have been a serious breach of confidence.

When we went ashore at St. Peter Port, Guernsey, and saw the defences which the Germans had prepared over the years, I was mighty glad that the islands had not had to be taken by assault. I had been through the touching, throat-catching liberation scenes at many places. This was something even more grim, save, of course, that it was a surrender and not an occupation by force – a very different thing.

The scenes when we went ashore were almost indescribable. I think it was the knowledge that at last there was relief from the gnawing pangs of hunger which made so many people break down and cry. They had had six months of increasing shortage. It would be impossible to find anywhere so utterly destitute of the things that matter – food and clothing - as those Channel Islands. I met one of the most distinguished ladies in the islands. She was smoking a foul cigarette made from some vegetable matter that had little of no resemblance to tobacco. I gave her a packet of 'Player's'. The emotion she showed at that gift was almost overwhelming.

But things were soon organized. The food boats and the clothing ships were on the way. The Germans were under control, and being sent back to England as prisoners of war with all speed. I remember standing down near the harbour and seeing a bunch of Germans driving a herd of cattle. In the dire shortage they had commandeered them. Now they were being made to drive them back to their rightful owners.

I remained in the islands nearly a week and that included crossing with a small military force to receive the surrender of the heavily fortified island of Alderney. It gave one a sense of elation to be steaming in under those guns, occasionally wondering whether behind them there might even now be someone with a light trigger-finger.

With the reporting of the surrender of the Channel Islands my active participation in the war as a War Correspondent finished. Soon again I was back in 'civvies' gathering up the threads of the Plymouth war story.

But I must retrace my steps a bit to those days of great expectation leading up to the unconditional surrender which brought with it the end of hostilities in Europe – 'VE' Day. The writing was plainly on the wall for some time. Germany was in her death agonies. What grim and dramatic news poured out of Germany in those fateful days of the Third Reich; how the whole fabric came down, bringing with it those who had been responsible for this challenge to civilization!

Then came the final news – the unconditional surrender had been signed. We looked at each other – could it really be true that the nightmare was over, that the tension of five years had ended, that we could tear down the blackout with its evil memories, that we could light up the streets, that the horror of war with all its blasting of civil populations and its wholesale destruction of life and property was coming with the dawn! Could we be sure that we should not be wakened by the siren to find it was all a dream; that the dark heavens over Plymouth would not again be stabbed by the gun flashes, that the pencils of concentrated searchlight beams would not weave their fantastic patterns against the backcloth of night, that there would be no more fearful crashing of bombs, with all the agony and misery of their effect?

Yes it was true. We cheered; for a short spell we were a little hysterical. There was a touch of 'Mafeking' about life. But there were also moments of reaction. There were premature bonfires, which was rather a breach of regulations. You will remember that, even after the German surrender had been signed, Plymouth was one of the places where the blackout was still imposed for the time. This was due to the uncertainty that some of the German submarines, still in the Channel, might have been out of wireless touch with their authorities, and be inclined to take a little late revenge if tempted by the coastal lights of a place like Plymouth. But, as the days went, these submarines were all rounded up. One by one they were brought into the ports, until the last of them had been accounted for.

The memorable dates to remember here are that on May 2, 1945, came the first dramatic news of the end of the war – the unconditional surrender of the German forces in Italy. The wedge, fatal to Germany, was now being driven in with relentless blows. Events followed in rapid succession. Three days later Montgomery accepted the unconditional surrender of the forces opposing the British in North-West Europe. This German force alone was estimated to number a million men. The rot had now thoroughly set in; every day brought more visible signs that the end was little more than a matter of hours.

The fact was that the German military machine was completely disintegrated. Control from the top had disappeared. Elements of the Army, large and small, were out of touch.

At 2.41 am, on Monday May 7, came the complete and final collapse when the German representatives attended the Little Red School House in Rheims, Eisenhower's headquarters, and signed the nation's unconditional surrender. So the mightiest military machine that the world had ever known was broken, the fires of war which had once again ravaged Europe at the lighting by Germany were extinguished, leaving behind the devastation and the scars, a war-weary world, thousands of little mounds as memorials to undeviating sacrifice, and a gigantic task for those who survived.

Above and right Lord Mayor Mason announces Victory in Europe at the Guildhall.

Above, The Lord Mayor attends impromtu VE Day parties on the Hoe. Far right - One of the many street parties held around the battered city.

Tuesday, May 8, will be marked in future history books as 'VE' Day – meaning Victory-Europe Day. That day and the next were officially designated as public holidays, observed in Plymouth, as elsewhere, with an abandon which released like a flood all the pent-up emotion and longings of six long weary years. The official declaration of the end of hostilities was made at 3 o'clock on that historic day.

Quite frankly, the memory of events in Plymouth on that day are something of a dream. Newspaper offices, of course, never sleep. But, except for essential services, the employees of which all had subsequent days of victory relaxation in compensation, everything was at a standstill. So marked was the interruption to the unbroken activities of the war years that many people hardly knew what to do. And I think, too, at the back of our minds, was the knowledge that, while we had survived the European struggle, there was still the enemy in the Far East, Japan, to be overcome.

We had no doubts about the issue of that struggle, but one could not enjoy the complete celebration of peace knowing that on the other side of the world the fighting was still racing to its climax, that lives were being lost, that our men were still languishing in the horrible conditions of the Japanese prison camps.

But the end, even out there, was in sight. The Japanese resistance had now become fanatical rather than impudently confident and assertive. Still we know that it was only a matter of time before 'VE' Day would be succeeded by 'VJ' Day.

Nevertheless, the weeks went into months, and it was not until August 14, three months after the cessation of the European hostilities, that Japan surrendered unconditionally, just as Germany had been forced to do. Our minds go back to the remembrance of how the atom bombs brought the Far East war to a dramatic end, and at the same time threw into the war machine a new and terrifying weapon.

Now World War II was over! Do you remember the words of the Prime Minster on that memorable night. I can hear them now – 'Japan has today surrendered. The last of our enemies is laid low.'

That was August 14, and it was announced that the next day, August 15, would be celebrated as 'VJ'Day. Now it was really ended. But the public could not wait until next day to celebrate. The war was over. Why wait? Despite the late hour at which the declaration was made, Plymouth aroused itself to a few hours of revelry. I decided to go down to the centre of the city from Mannamead to see what was happening. Halfway along the 'Mead I got mixed up with a bunch of wildly excited Wrens who had tumbled out of their nearby hostels en masse.

It was curious how everyone seemed to be drawn towards the Hoe. Yet not so strange, for that has been the case all through history. Whenever there has been a big event the Hoe seems to have been the magnetic point for the public. Perhaps it is that the Hoe is the shrine to Plymouth's greatness; that at that spot there is a mingling of spirits past and present!

All the way down to the city centre the numbers of people increased. By the time I got to the Hoe the crowd had really taken charge. Predominating was the Service personnel. On the Hoe a mighty bonfire had been prepared by the Corporation for the next day's official celebrations. The temptation was much too great. Within a very short time it was a mountain of fire – a beacon light as of old, sending its message to the far-distant hill-tops of Devon and Cornwall. In the blackout of that night it seemed almost garish. When the fire began to die out the wooden seats of the Hoe were thrown on as added fuel by a few of the irresponsible and excited youngsters. It seemed too, that the premature lighting of the Hoe bonfire was something of a signal to Devonport, for within a few minutes the flames of victory were leaping into the darkness from the bonfire which had also been built there for the official celebrations. At other distant places the pinpoints of light indicated that there were others who could not wait until the morrow.

It was in the early hours of the morning that the last of these tired and jubilant citizens tumbled into the beds to snatch a few hours' sleep before the official celebrations started the next day. Of course, 'VJ' Day was another public holiday. This was really the end of the war.

Undaunted by the premature lighting of the bonfires on the Hoe and at Devonport Park, fresh ones were built by the authorities. The day's celebrations began, as was befitting, with a service of thanksgiving attended by the civic heads and chiefs of the Royal Navy, Army and Royal Air Force, with contingents of those forces also attending. Warships were 'dressed', giving a touch of colour and gaiety to our harbours for the first time for six years.

It was, however, at nightfall that the scenes became most animated. It was reckoned that there were fully thirty thousand people on the Hoe that evening. The bands played; there was al fresco dancing on

the promenade. How that dancing recalled other days – those evenings during the raids when the folk gathered there to dance away the anxious hours of waiting for the enemy bombers.

But now joy had replace anxiety in their minds. They danced not to maintain their morale but to give wild expression to their feelings of relief that the war was over.

As darkness fell over Plymouth the scene took on a new animation. Form the warships in the Sound and harbour sprang thousands of tiny lights as the illuminations were switched on. There was no need for extra illuminations on the Hoe. The huge bonfire provided all that was required. Against its glare the Drake, Armada and Naval War Memorials were thrown into sharp silhouette – milestones of history marking those other great occasions when Plymouth played its part in shaping the destiny of the world and this island home in particular. Fireworks from the warships added to the peace night spectacle from historic Plymouth Hoe.

Far into the night the celebrations continued. They were carried through with good temper; the little extra boisterousness of the oc-

casion could be readily forgiven. And then, with the passing of the night, there was the dawn of peace coming over the eastern hills.

It was shortly after this that Plymouth was the setting for one of the most historic events of those immediate post-war days – the meeting between His Majesty King George VI and President Truman of the United States. President Truman had been on a visit to Germany for the Potsdam meeting of the Big Three. On his return trip he flew from the Continent to the Harrowbeer (Yelverton) Aerodrome, then drove into Plymouth, where he boarded the United States cruiser Augusta, which was lying in the Sound ready to take him back across the Atlantic. This historic date was August 2, 1945.

In the meantime the King had travelled down from London by special train, which took him right into Millbay Docks, where the barge of the Commander-in-Chief, with brass gleaming and in a spick-and-span coat of fresh green enamel, was waiting to take him out to the famous battle-cruiser Renown, lying also in the Sound under the shelter of Staddon Heights. The Lord Mayor of the City (Alderman H.G. Mason) was at the Docks to welcome His Majesty on behalf of Plymouth, but this was an international occasion, not a Plymouth civic occasion, and so the meeting was quite formal. The King and The Lord Mayor chatted for a few minutes, and then the King embarked in the barge.

Here once more it was my good fortune to attend and report a memorable event in my professional capacity. The way in which President Truman was hustled though the city on his journey from Yelverton to the waterside was an acute disappointment to the people who had hoped to mark this rare visit with a demonstration of goodwill, especially remembering that Plymouth had been such an important base for the United States operations in connection with the European war and had so many historic links with America. It was understood that the President would be escorted from Yelverton to Millbay Docks by the main thoroughfares. The entire route was thickly lined with citizens eager to give him a Plymouth welcome at the docks, where distinguished officers also awaited the President.

But those in charge of the arrangements made a last-minute change, and citizens who were lining that long section of the route from Mutley Plain to the Docks were disappointed. The President, with his powerful escort of United Stated military police, came as far as the top of Alexandra Road and then the cavalcade, instead of proceeding by way of North Hill and Tavistock Road, swept up Prison Hill, down Greenbank and by way of Friary to the United States naval base embarkation point in the Cattewater.

It was not action on the past of the British authorities that make this sudden change in route. In fact, they were caught on the hop. The City Police were manning the main road route and there were important officials waiting at Millbay for the President. Why the sudden change was made, I never heard. But I do know that there were may people who felt just a little bit hurt that they were deprived of the opportunity of seeing the President and according him a greeting. There seemed no apparent reason for the sudden change of route. However, our in the Sound, important events were taking place. This was a most historic meeting. The King, aboard Renown, received the President; the President, aboard Augusta, received the King. On the quarter-decks and in the wardrooms they chatted with extreme cordiality. There was about the visits to the two warships the formal naval ceremonial befitting the occasion. With the memorable meeting over, the Augusta steamed out of Plymouth Sound and soon disappeared into the haze of the Channel as she shaped her course for America through waters which were no longer hostile. The King came ashore by barge, landed at Millbay Docks, where the Lord Mayor again extended the official courtesies. They chatted for a few moments before the King entered the Royal train for his return to London.

Another post-war event of outstanding importance was, of course, the General Election, which took place in July 1945. It was sandwiched between the end of the European hostilities and the final surrender of Japan.

As far as Plymouth was concerned the election had two significant features. It was the first time for thirty-five years that the Astors were not represented in the contest. Shortly before the General Election, Lady Astor, who had represented the Sutton Division continuously since 1920 – before that Lord Astor, until he succeeded to the family title, had represented the same division continuously for ten years – indicated that she would not be seeking re-election. This, of course, was a big break, for whatever political view people held there was a general regard for the services which both Lord Astor and Lady Astor had rendered to the city in public live and in particular in Parliament.

Far left, A group of youngsters pose in front of the Armada Memorial on VE Day. Above, the King greets the American President on board HMS Renown.

Lady Astor's place as the Conservative candidate for the Sutton Division was taken by a soldier, Brigadier Grand, who came very much as a stranger. In the Devonpost Division Mr Leslie Hore-Belisha defended his seat as a Liberal-National with the support of the Conservatives, and in Drake Division Colonel Henry Guest defended his Conservative seat.

History records how this General Election swung with an over-whelming majority in favour of the Labour Party. It was an election landslide and the three Plymouth seats went down with it. By big unmistakable marjorities three Labour candidates were returned for Plymouth – Mr HM Medland for Drake, Mr Michael Foot (son of Mr Isaac Foot, the well-known Liberal) for Devonport, and Mrs Lucy Middleton for Sutton. Only once before had a Plymouth constituency been represented by a Labour member and that was when the late Mr J.J.H. Moses won the Drake seat for one Parliament 'life'. It was a big change in the political life of the city.

In Plymouth's post-war public life it should be recorded that the Lord Mayoralty was occupied by Alderman H.G. Mason (1944-45), Mr Isaac Foot (1945-46), Mr W. Harry Taylor (1946-47), Alderman H.J. Perry (1947-49) and Alderman Frank Leatherby (1949-50). Under the new Local Government legislation, Council elections were changed from November to May. Similarly mayoral elections. That accounts for Alderman Perry occupying the office from November 1947 to May 1949.

Far left, a Victory Parade through the City. The new players in the post-war political representation of Plymouth, including a young Michael Foot, whose father, Isaac (pictured above), succeeded Mason as Mayor for 1945/46. Top right, a march past on VJ Day. Right, Celebrations as our Prisoners of War start arriving home.

RECONSTRUCTION

PEACE! The tumult and the shouting of victory had died down. Our minds became sobered. What now? We had won the war. Democracy and civilization had been saved. Or would it be better to say that democracy and civilization now had to be salvaged from the shambles left by the war. Could we win the peace? Were we not too exhausted to tackle the almost frightening problems of victory? The price of six years of war had been frightful. What would be the price of peace? Our allies were going home, Plymouth belonged to Plymouth once more.

These thoughts tumbled in confused fashion in the minds of all sober-thinking people. We looked around. Where was the first thread to be picked out of the tangled skein? One could almost be forgiven for shrinking from the ordeal.

No one who possessed a glimmering of imagination could underestimate the colossal task which confronted Plymouth, with its vast areas of raid devastation, with business eager for rehabilitation, with between 15,000 and 20,000 new homes urgently required to make up the building leeway of the lost years and to make good the war destruction and with thousands of its citizens scattered like refugees over the countryside, all eager to return to the city.

But the task, monumental as it was, had to be faced boldly and urgently. Within a few months a new and interesting situation arose in Plymouth. The November municipal elections showed the same violent swing to Labour as had the General Election. For the first time, and by a substantial majority, Labour won control of the City Council. That meant they could direct policy in connection with local administration. Well, the Conservatives had enjoyed the monopoly for a great many years. The change, to say the least, would be interesting.

Alderman H.G. Mason, who had then completed his memorable victory year Lord Mayoralty, became the leader of the new dominant party in the City Council, and as was only to be expected, Labour took the chairmanships of most of the important committees, like Reconstruction (Alderman Mason), Finance (Alderman H. Wright), Housing (Alderman W.A. Miller), Education (Councillor Neil Bradley) and Transport (Alderman Louis Hodge).

Illustrations from the 1943 Plan for Plymouth.

PROPOSED CENTRAL LAYOUT
SHEWING PROPERTIES EXISTING 1943

REFERENCE

EXISTING PROPERTIES

SITES AVAILABLE FOR RECONSTRUCTION

PREVIOUSLY CLEARED SITES

PROPOSED CENTRAL LAYOUT SHOWN THUS

SCALE OF FEET

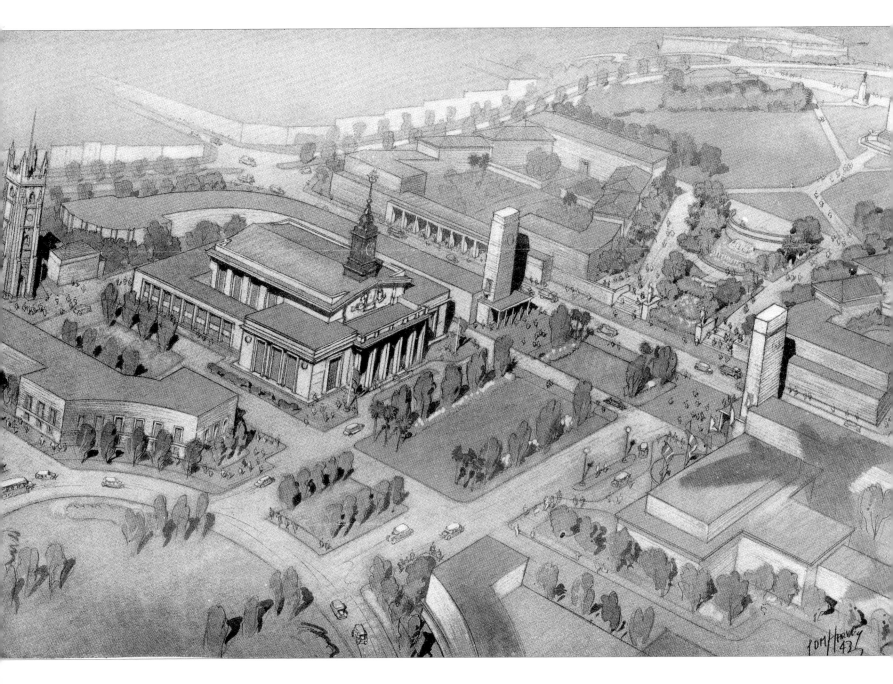

The City Council had already approved in principal 'The Plan for Plymouth' which had been prepared by the City Engineer (Mr J. Paton Watson) in collaboration with that eminent town planner Sir Patrick Abercrombie.

Now came the momentous time for the implementation of that plan for a new Plymouth. It was part and parcel of the plan that housing had an important place, and with the knowledge of the acute shortage of houses and the very long waiting list of tenants, it was right and proper that the provision of homes for the people should become a No. 1 priority, even over the important reconstruction of the city centre. No one disagreed with that in principle.

To the everlasting credit of Plymouth – and this applies to the responsible people of all parties – the task of laying out and developing new housing estates and the rehabilitation of the business life of the city by reconstruction of the devastated shopping centre was tackled with expedition and enthusiasm.

These public representatives were mindful of their responsibilities, and while there might be divergences of opinion on detailed lines of policy and action, I think it can be sincerely said that before the eyes of all of them there was the constant vision of the new Plymouth, the new Plymouth for which generations to come would either commend or admonish according to their verdict.

So they showed commendable action, and once a decision was made, there was from all sides a readiness to carry it out. While other blitzed towns and cities were still thinking, Plymouth was putting its plan into action.

Thus it was not surprising that Plymouth should win commendation from Whitehall when it was a long way ahead of other places in submitting its overall plans to the Ministry of Town and Country Planning.

And so, while priority was always given to housing, and while new estates on the outskirts of the city assumed mushroom growth, there was, moving side by side, the implementation of the plan as far as the reconstruction of the city centre was concerned.

I think perhaps I had better deal with the housing first. Let us see what has been accomplished in the four years. I do not intend to hazard myself into the dangers of party politics. In this book there are no politics. It is the record of Plymouth. Whether more could have been accomplished by other methods is not for me to argue here; whether

Left, Plans for the new Council House and route to the Hoe. Above, George Street.

Top left, L De Soissons -traditional house, right, Cornish unit, semi-detached. Middle, new school, Efford. Below, Efford Estate. Far right, Ernesettle, looking south.

less would have been done under other policies is for others to debate. All I want to set forth here is a picture of what has been done in the few years since the war. And, in assessing the accomplishment, let it not be forgotten that the post-war years were packed with difficulties – shortage of labour, shortage of materials, soaring costs and a hundred and one things which hampered and discouraged.

There were two contributory factors to Plymouth's serious housing shortage – blitz and blight. The blitz, of course, applied to the destruction of residential property by enemy action; blight referred to that property which was already in a serious state of dilapidation before the war and could now be written off as completely un-repairable.

By the middle of 1949 it was claimed that 18,900 persons, representing 5,730 families, had been housed in new properties. This accommodation was made up of temporary bungalows, 2,250; permanent bungalows, 64; British Iron and Steel Federation, 1,000; traditional brick housed, 1,500; Corporation rebuilt (cost of works), 170; private owners rebuilt (cost of works), 610; private enterprise, new houses 16.

These new houses, of course, have involved the layout and development of several extensive estates. Among these are;

EFFORD. The third largest estate developed by the Housing Committee, providing homes for approximately 3,000 people. This estate is laid out for 924 houses, and at the time of writing about 880 houses and flats have been completed.

ERNESETTLE. This estates lies on the side of the hill from Higher St Budeaux, almost down to the bank of the Tamar and bounded to the north-west by Tamerton creek. On this estate has been erected the magnificent new Bush Radio factory, which is already employing several hundreds of employees, and when in full production will be producing up to a set a minute. On this estate there is provision for 1,204 houses and flats, which will accommodate approximately 4,000 people. The building of the houses here is in operation at the time of writing and the first occupations have taken place.

HAM. This estate is situated to the north-west of the city, and occupies some of the most delightful scenery in the district, including the historic Ham Mansion, once the home of the Trelawny Ross family, which has been turned into a very active cultural centre and library for the estate. The Ham estate is to accommodate 530 houses, of which nearly 500 have been completed and occupied.

HONICKNOWLE AND WOODLAND. This widespread estate is situated on the south and north sides of the main road from Highest St. Budeaux to Crownhill. The sites have been laid out for 904 houses, of which nearly 800 are completed and occupied.

WHITLEIGH. At the present time this estate is being laid out. It lies between Crownhill and Tamerton Foliot and so is actually outside the present boundary. This will accommodate something like 1,870 houses and flats, and will be the largest of the city estates.

Thus it will be seen that Plymouth has accomplished a considerable amount of work in the matter of housing. With very few exceptions they are, of course, Corporation houses. It has been a costly programme, the more so because of difficulties encountered through the very uneven character of the terrain over which some of the estates are spread.

By the erection of all this property Plymouth Corporation has become one of the biggest landlords in the West Of England. Even now the weekly rent roll from the Corporation houses is in the region of £10,000.

Considerable attention has also been directed towards the rebuilding of the war-destroyed houses. It will be remembered that 3,754 houses were either totally destroyed or so badly damaged that they had to be demolished. These, of course, were entitled to be rebuilt under cost-of-works payment. A large number have been rebuilt. The ugly gaps that one encountered so frequently in the terraced houses are gradually being built up. The most striking example of this rebuilding is on the Keyham Barton estate, where whole streets of terraced houses, mostly occupied by the workers in the nearby Dockyard, were devastated. The majority of these houses have now been rebuilt.

But even with all this building of new houses and rebuilding of old ones, the deficiency is still serious. It is estimated that there is still a waiting list of some 15,000 requiring houses, and the situation is accentuated by the fact that in the course of reconstruction in the Plymouth city centre and the requirements at Devonport's most densely populated area by the Admiralty for Dockyard extension adds several thousand to the list of families who still require to be accommodated.

Top left, the Bush Radio factory, Ernesettle. Left, the Ham estate. Right, the widespread Honicknowle and Woodland estates. Bottom right, temporary school at Ham.

New housing estates also require the provision of the necessary public services and amenities for each 'neighbourhood' such as schools, community centres, shops, transport, recreation grounds and health centres. For the most part these are provided along with the general development of the estates.

Over 7,000 school places were destroyed in Plymouth by enemy action. Furthermore, in the five years from 1944 the school population grew from 19,858 to 26,305, an increase of approximately 6,500. But the Education Authority has manfully tackled its big task. Those schools which were not too far damaged have been repaired, schools on which building was suspended at the outbreak of war have been completed, and a very considerable programme of new school building has been undertaken. Plans for a further ten schools in a 1951-54 programme has been approved by the Education Committee. The schools being erected in connection with the new housing estates are the last word in design, general layout, and in equipment. Yet another problem which confronted the Education Authority was the provision of midday meals for the children. At the time of writing, one out of every three children attending the Plymouth schools is provided with a hot midday meal and the number of such meals served every week is between 40,000 and 50,000. New school kitchens have had to be built, and the whole organisation is one of considerable magnitude.

Some idea of the layout involved in Plymouth's post-war schemes can also be gathered from the fact that twenty-eight miles of new roads and fifty-five miles of sewers have been laid.

While on this question of Corporation property I might say that it has been found necessary to establish a Property Maintenance Department to deal with the 11,000 tenanted properties and over 1,000 other buildings like schools, libraries, etc. This department employs over 300 workmen, and they do about 30,000 repair and maintenance jobs a year.

Now let me pass on to the gigantic task of the reconstruction of Plymouth's city centre. This was where the great destruction by enemy action had been most concentrated, virtually laying waste all that area incorporating the top end of Union Street, George Street, Bedford Street, Westwell Street, Princess Square, Old Town Street, Cornwall Street, Frankfort Street, Courtenay Street and Russell Street with their many side streets, lanes and inter-sections.

Plymouth's plan was a completely new layout for this area. The old streets, which had served for generations, were gone for ever. They remain only in memory, and even at this short distance of time to come across pre-war pictures of the shopping centre is like turning back the pages of some old family book.

Work begins on the east–west axis of the new city centre.

It was decided to implement the Plan with every ounce of energy. The times were difficult. There were severe restrictions, labour and materials for the laying of new thoroughfares and the construction of buildings were in short supply. The needs for housing had to have prior claim.

And, of course, there were long drawn-out preliminaries attached to putting the work in hand. All that vast area had to be compulsorily acquired by the Corporation, for they were to be the future landlords of the city centre. They would complete the layout; then it would be for the developers to lease the sites on up to 99-year agreements and to build their own premises to approved plans.

It was well that Plymouth had had its plan prepared; it meant that as soon as the war was over they could get on with the implementation. So it was that in March 1946 the first big public enquiry was held for the compulsory acquisition by the Corporation of the area – No.1 Area it was officially called – required for the relaying and reconstruction of what has become more familiarly known as the City Centre, roughly comprising the area to which I have previously referred. There was, of course, very considerable opposition on the part of the private owners of properties and sites, but the powers of local authorities under the Town and Country Planning Legislation are today very considerable, and so it was that, in due course, the necessary orders were made and confirmed.

In years to come the figures '21-3-47' cut into one of the kerb granite setts of the gigantic roundabout at the western end of Royal Parade might be noticed by passers-by with a questioning thought for their reason.

I say 'might', because they are so inconspicuous that the casual passer-by would probably not see them. But in point of fact they mark a most notable date in Plymouth's history, and also a spot which has considerable significance.

It was at this spot near the top of the old Raleigh Street that the first stake was driven for the layout of the new city centre. That was the point at which work was started. I hope that one day there will be a better commemorative recording than just those obscure figures which to any stranger, or to future citizens, might mean anything or nothing.

But, nevertheless, that date is worth noting. From that point Plymouth fairly 'stepped on' the job. Soon there were many indications of the shape of things to come. Royal Parade, the main east-west axis of the future city centre, began to spread its broad ribbon over the devastated areas, cutting right across from the top of Union Street to where Spooner's Corner used to be in the old days. At each end there were to be great roundabouts.

The work progressed at such a rate that it was possible for Their Majesties King George VI and Queen Elizabeth to come to Plymouth in October 1947 and inaugurate the rebuilding of the city centre by officially naming Royal Parade and Armada Way and unveiling a commemorative tablet recording the significant occasion.

The visit of the King and Queen in the mayoralty of Mr W. Harry Taylor was a memorable occasion for Plymouth and one which was highly appreciated by the citizens. Their Majesties had come to Plymouth during the war, visits which had greatly encouraged and heartened the people in their grim battle. That they should now come back to inaugurate the rebirth of the blitzed city centre was singularly fitting and a gesture which won loyal gratitude. The King and Queen were obviously impressed by the way in which Plymouth was tackling its great post-war problems.

The work of relaying the thoroughfares of the new heart of Plymouth went on at a steady pace. It was not easy, and no one will ever know the volumes of work performed by certain of the Corporation departments like those of the Town Clerk, the City Engineer, The City Architect, the Treasury and the Estates and Valuation. The difficulties which they fought and overcame were amazing. Tardiness in the granting of ministerial approvals and sanctions, shortness of staffs, especially on the technical side, limitations in labour and material, innumerable little irritations and emergency problems – all these things were encountered. It was, at times, almost amazing that the will to accomplish did not break under them. Fortunately, the planners were imbued with Plymouth's fighting spirit. It was as if they always had before them the motto which hung in the Devonport Dockyard offices and workshops during the war – 'The difficult we can accomplish now; the impossible may take a little longer.'

And so the work went on and the layout of Plymouth's new city centre, especially the shopping centre, steadily took shape.

The fact that the Corporation now became landlord and the developers only leaseholders – a drastic change over from the old days of private owner-occupier of property – entailed a vast amount of work between the Corporation and traders. It was this which brought into being the comparatively new Estates and Valuation Department of the Corporation, with a new official in charge. Many difficulties arose between them but fortunately there has been, on the whole, a spirit of goodwill and co-operation. There were many conferences between the traders' organizations and the Corporation.

And so, at the close of the year 1949, just two years since the King and Queen inaugurated the rebuilding of Plymouth's blitzed city centre, the developers began to move in along the splendid new streets. As this book goes to publication the scaffolding of the first block – namely, that of the premises of Messrs. E. Dingle & Co., which occupy frontages on Royal Parade, Armada Way and New George Street – is being prepared. The plans we have seen for these and other premises on Royal Parade, Old Town Street and New George Street give a shopping centre vision of the future which must give an inspired and proud feeling to every Plymothian.

What will be the ultimate cost of the reconstruction of Plymouth's new city centre no one can foretell at this stage of the developments. Already in acquisition and the layout of streets so far developed over £2,000,000 has been spent. Many of the traders at this stage view with considerable apprehension the ever-soaring building costs. The small private traders are quite unable to face the financial obligations single-handed. At the present juncture there are two big insurance companies taking considerable sites. Their plans are to build on and then sub-let to individual traders on the ground floor and as offices on the floors above. For example, it is intended by one of these developers to build a block of fifty shops, taking the whole corner fronting Royal Parade, Old Town Street and New George Street.

Then again, a large number of the private traders formed themselves into an association. The suggestion emanating from here was to form a company to build a block of shops and sub-let them to small private traders at economic rentals.

But whatever policies are adopted the costs are, at the present time, frightening, and the general economic situation is only intensifying the outlook. In any case, the ultimate completion of the city centre must be one of long-term, patient plodding, not a little courage and, above all, a faith in Plymouth's future.

Their Majesties King George VI and Elizabeth come to Plymouth in October 1947 to inaugurate the rebuilding of the city centre by officially naming Royal Parade.

1948, February, a thick coating of white snow gives the blitzed city a new look. clockwise, St Andrew's, the Hoe and Plymouth Guildhall and Westwell Gardens.

While still on this part of Plymouth, let us look at some of the other features. First of all, the Mother Church of St. Andrew. As I write this chapter the work is actually in hand. The re-roofing has started, with the concrete Gothic inner ceiling already spanning the chancel. The complete ceiling covering for the church will, it is expected, be finished in the spring of 1950, but meanwhile, on October 22 1949, Princess Elizabeth, on her first official visit to Plymouth, unveiled a tablet at the south porch commemorating the rebuilding. As her Royal Highness performed that simple ceremony at the entrance in the presence of thousands of citizens, there were many eyes lifted to that challenging word 'Resurgam', which had remained over that porch since the morning when St. Andrew's lay smouldering in ruins after the night's devastation in 1941. In due course the inner ceiling of the church will be covered by a slated roof.

Let us pass to the Guildhall. It was the subject of considerable controversy for four years. Should it be demolished or preserved and rebuilt? In the original plans, demolition was the clear intention, but there was a growing volume of opposition to such drastic action. Both from the point of view of sentiment and from the usefulness to which the building might still be put there was a feeling that it should be retained. The position at the end of 1949 is that the City Council has decided to get expert opinion from eminent architects before making a final decision. With the demolition of the municipal buildings, which accommodated the Town Clerk's department, Council Chamber, Lord Mayor's Parlour and various Committee rooms, the vista of the Guildhall from Royal Parade has been thrown open. Framed between the St. Andrew's church tower and the tower of the public buildings, the 'lacy' outline of the Guildhall windows above the imposing façade with its allegorical figures, seems to make a fresh appeal, and quite frankly I shall not be surprised if ultimately we do not find something of the old Guildhall worked into the plan of the new public buildings. At the moment that is all that can be said.

While on the question of building, I might here interpolate by saying that restoration of several churches has been in hand for some time. The first of the damaged, but repairable, churches to be restored was Greenbank Methodist and that church has 'taken in' Ebrington Street Church, which was completely destroyed. In hand at the present time is the re-roofing of Sherwell Congregational Church, which was the first to be damaged by enemy action in the city.

Plans are now in hand for the reconstruction of the Public Library. This, it will be remembered, was completely burnt out with practically all of its magnificent stock of 80,000 books, many of them irreplaceable. The library is still accommodated in the Museum and Art Gallery with a great extension of branch libraries all over the city, especially on the new housing estates. It has a bigger stock and a wider range of books than ever before. The accommodation of the old destroyed library is badly needed. The plans have been approved for the rebuilding on a greatly improved layout.

A little earlier I mentioned the markets. Both the meat market and the pannier market will have to go. New George Street will have its track laid across the site of the meat market and, of course, the pannier market will find a new home somewhere down in the region of the destroyed King Street Methodist Church. The official original intention to make a pannier market to the north of Union Street adjoining the railway embankment has been abandoned. No site has yet been agreed upon for the wholesale meat market. That is wrapped up in the provision of a new abattoir.

One other thing to be recorded before we leave the reconstruction of the city centre is the fate of the old Westwell Street burial ground. Armada Way, from Royal Parade to the Hoe, cuts right through these grounds. The first section from Royal Parade and emerging into Princess Square has already been laid. All the human remains were removed from this burial ground and re-interred at the Efford Cemetery.

Before we leave Plymouth at the end of 1949 I should say that orders for the development of other areas have been made, but it will obviously be a long time before any reconstruction plans can be put into operation. The plate is already overflowing with work actually in hand, and one fears that with the country's economic position as it is, there is bound to be considerable slowing-down in development.

But orders are in existence for dealing with the Hoe district and for Stonehouse. The intention as far as the latter place is concerned is that Union Street will be the virtual dividing line between light industries to the south and residential areas to the north.

8 March 1949, Royal Parade.

And so to Devonport. The Plymouth Plan made provision for the Admiralty taking over a very considerable area of the residential and business part which adjoins the Dockyard, for extension purposes. It was not until the summer of 1949 that they gave any clear indication of their intentions. Their first bite into the old Devonport that we knew so well comprises just about 60 acres in the congested Fore Street area, and this is to be absorbed into Dockyard extension in stages. Plymouth Corporation obtained the necessary order for compulsory acquisition of this area and will transfer it to the Admiralty as required. The first cheque for £100,000 from the Admiralty has already been received by the Corporation, which seems to everyone to be a good augury that the Admiralty intentions are still good. If the plans are carried out as announced, all that congested area from Pembroke Street, near Mount Wise, to Morice Square goes out of existence as the pre-war generations remember it. It was, of course, terribly blitzed in the Fore Street area. Incidentally, those who remember the old Fore Street will be interested to know that 'Aggie Weston's' – the Royal Sailor's Rest – which went down in the blitz, has reopened in the magnificent building formerly occupied by the United Services Orphan Home for Girls at the top of Albert Road. The Orphanage, now a much smaller affair, was evacuated to Newquay and remains there.

What has happened at Plymouth in the way of new industries? Well, this is one of the most gratifying features of post-war development. At the present time, at least three new major industries have been started in entirely new buildings. They are all in production and add very materially to the employment of the district. These three are the new Bush Radio factory at Ernesettle, the new Tecalemit factory for motor accessories at Marsh Mills, and the Berkertex clothing factory in what was the Ministry of Labour vocational training centre on the main road from Crownhill to higher St. Budeaux. In addition, there are a number of smaller industries helping Plymouth's employment problem. The year 1949 closes with unemployed in the Plymouth district not much more that 2,000 and these comprise a considerable proportion of seasonal people and other whose employment will always be difficult. In the building trades and in the heavy industries there is no unemployment at this stage.

And now, lastly, can we take a peep at the future? First of all, the extension of the boundaries. Well, when Plymouth was asked to submit proposals after the war it went 'the whole hog'. It asked for an area bounded on the west by Downderry, on the east by Mothercombe, and back into the hinterland as far as Ivybridge and Yelverton, also to include on the Cornish side, Saltash, Torpoint and St. Germans.

Well, of course, that was rather asking for the moon. At the moment, Plymouth has got nothing. There have been two recommendations by the Local Government Boundary Commission set up by the Government. The first was that Plymouth should absorb the parishes of Tamerton Foliot and Bickleigh, which will take the Plymouth boundary line out on to Roborough Down where you turn in to Maristow. The second was to take in those parishes, but also with the townships of Plympton and Plymstock.

Now the Commission is to be wound up without anything definite taking place. But I think that, ultimately, Plymouth will get the two parishes of Bickleigh and Tamerton. They are already in Plymouth from a Parliamentary divisional point of view, Bickleigh being absorbed

Top left, Easi-Form house, three-bedroom type, top right, Old People's flats. Below, St Budeaux to Crownhill Road. Above, work begins on the new north-south axis.

by Sutton Division and Tamerton coming into Devonport. Having got nothing from the Boundary Commission, Plymouth quickly realized that urgent expansion would only be possible through the normal procedure of a Parliamentary Bill. This Bill, seeking to take in the parishes of Bickleigh and Tamerton Foliot, has now been laid before Parliament and the speed with which it is dealt with must largely depend on what objection is offered. Plympton Rural Council has adhered to its willingness to concede these parishes, but there have been hints of objections from the parishes and Devon County Council.

Here let me record that the Parliamentary Divisional Boundary Commission has decreed that, in future, Plymouth will have only two Divisions, Sutton and Devonport. The old Division of Drake, now represented by Mr H.M. Medland, will be absorbed by the other two constituencies.

Just one other fact which will be of interest to historians. Buckland Abbey, the home of Sir Francis Drake, about ten miles from Plymouth, has been acquired for the nation under the National Trust. Lord Astor played a notable part in this acquisition. It is being restored as a show-place and a Drake museum. The restoration has been made possible by a substantial grant from an American Trust. A few years ago the old Abbey was considerably damaged by fire, and the restoration is a substantial job.

Plymouth Corporation will be the caretakers for this very fine historic show-piece and it is hoped that it will be open to the public in 1950.

From these chapters I hope the reader has gathered something of the picture of the new Plymouth and will have appreciated the gigantic task which has been undertaken with such bold determination and with such faith.

When after the awful ordeal of 1941 it was obvious that vast reconstruction would be necessary, Plymouth was told, I think it was by Lord Reith, to 'play boldly'. It did so, and at the end of 1949 we can say that is has implemented that plan as boldly as the conditions of the time have permitted. The picture of the new Plymouth is now there for all to see. Bit by bit, the pieces of the gigantic jig-saw are being fitted. It may, indeed, it will, take a long time for the picture to be finished. Many of us may not see it, but let us hope that the verdict of posterity to all who took part in the reconstruction will be: 'You have left us a great and worthy heritage.'

21 September 1949, the new Plymouth City Centre starts to take shape.

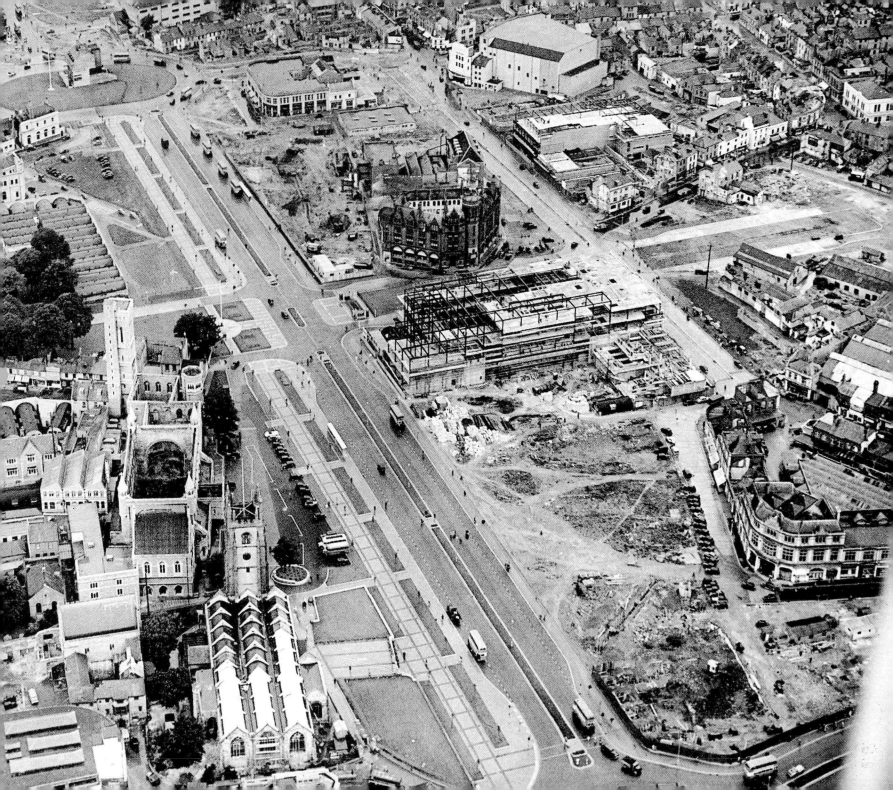

DOWN MEMORY AVENUE

As all old soldiers of any war will tell you, time does take away edges of experiences. It is as well that time is such a healer. Such awful experiences as Plymouth went through during those bombings left ghastly memories for a while, but in due course we were all able to talk over our adventures, our miraculous escapes, with a calmer recollection than was possible in the days immediately after the raids.

We could not forgive, but I think our rage had settled down; we could not forget, but our recollections were in quiet retrospect.

In those crowded hours there were events enough to fill a lifetime. When people used to ask me what I felt like during those heavy raids, I could only say that one had passed beyond the stage of fear, and I always found that the busier I was the less was the effect on the nerves. I remember having experienced that same peculiar feeling when I lay under a heavy bombardment in France, before I became a casualty. The inevitability of the occasion seemed to dominate everything.

At this distance of time, when the raw edges of the tragedies have been so softened, there is the recollection of incidents which illuminated, often with a touch of humour, the grim spectacles. Life seems to provide us with these little interludes even in the midst of such wanton destruction of life and property as we experienced.

Perhaps if I recall some, it will help the reader to pull out of memory some even more interesting personal experiences. Once you set the match to the train of "I remember", it never seems to end.

While on the subject of incendiaries, there was the first-class story concerning the young Cornish policeman who, in the height of the heaviest raids, when Plymouth was in the grip of terrifying fires, was one of a party doing duty at Drake Circus.

Down came a veritable drenching of incendiaries at that famous Plymouth crossing. The streets were littered with them.

"Come on", shouted the inspector in charge, and the lads in blue got among those fire bombs with grand vigour.

But the young Cornishman was not going back to his village and

70,000 Plymouth houses were destroyed or damaged in the 59 raids on the city.

quiet country patrol without a well-earned souvenir of the "battle of Plymouth". There was the light of battle in his eyes and in his pocket something bulky.

"What have you got?" asked the inspector, hearing that the lad had collected a souvenir.

"Here you are. Look!" said the constable, as he yanked a sinister-looking object from his pocket, an incendiary bomb.

"Fine!" said the officer. "But you'd better drop it quickly or it might go off. It's unexploded, and it's the explosive type!"

The young policeman dropped it like a hot cake.

The next moment a heavy piece of metal cracked down on his "tin hat" with a blow that nearly put him out of action.

"There's your souvenir", shouted the officer.

The constable grabbed at this "gift", but it was far too hot to hold, and he promptly dropped it with a grim "Oh, hell!".

At that moment came another shower of incendiaries, and with it the call to action.

But the souvenir-hunter was not to be denied the hot, jagged chunk of metal that had nearly put him out. He dribbled it along the street like a soccer player, then picked it up, thrust it into his pocket, and was on the job of putting out the incendiaries with the first man.

Somewhere in a policeman's house in Cornwall I expect that souvenir is cherished to this day. I should like to hear him telling the story.

Neither shall I ever forget the police officer and warden who dashed across some gardens to tackle incendiaries which were threatening the back of a big house. Two women inside were shouting for help. By the time they reached the back door leading to the scene they had fallen over some rose bushes, over a wire fence, and over a wall.

The back door presented them with a first-class chance to show their strength. They shouldered it, and they kicked it, but it was a particularly well-made back door, and held fast.

Then the police officer tried the obvious way of entry - the latch. And the two of them fell through in a heap.

"Here's the hose" said one of the women, thrusting the tubing into the officer's hands. He payed out and payed out until he got to the nozzle; there seemed to have been miles of that hose.

"O.K. Turn on!" he yelled, taking his stand to "drown" the two incendiaries, which by this time were blazing merrily. And, would you

What Hitler's "total war" meant to hundreds of Plymouth homes. Right, life goes on.

believe it, there was not a drop of water. It had been turned off at the main.

How the heroism flopped. In sheer disgust, he turned the dustbin over one incendiary and the cover of the dustbin over the other.

One or two colleagues and myself can look on the humorous side of another incident when Plymouth was burning. We were in the vicinity of Frankfort Street about three o'clock in the morning, when it was seen that Oliver's Corner was in danger of catching fire from an outbreak which was getting nicely set in the attics of the adjoining building in Russell Street. But how were we to reach those attics?

We solved it by forcing an entry through a butcher's shop and up a winding iron staircase. Inside the shop it was pitch-dark as I jumped from the window. I landed plump into a large container of swill. But there was no time to dwell on the niceties of the occasion.

We had to get on with the job. Stirrup pumps were of no avail; firemen were too busy on bigger jobs.

Eventually we commandeered two hoses, dragging one length from the bottom of York Street and the other from George Street.

Later, when things had calmed down and the excitement of the night gave way to a feeling of indescribable tiredness, and we were gathered indoors, the atmosphere was pervaded with an ominous odour.

I looked down at my trousers legs – and remembered the swilltub.

Another incident which comes to mind in the chapter of random memories is the experience of a colleague in regard to her small car, which she had left in the seclusion of Frankfort Lane before one of the heaviest raids took place.

In the small hours of the morning, when she went to collect the car, it had vanished.

Next day she informed the police that it was missing, but not for more than a week was it discovered. Then it was found on some waste ground off one of the back streets near the Octagon.

Actually, that little car had been doing noble work all through the blitz. Some of those splendid young officers from the Royal Naval Engineering College, Keyham, who had stormed into the city to give any help they could - and the memory of those helpers I shall never forget, as they participated in fire-fighting and rescue work where the danger was greatest – had promptly "commandeered" the car, and had used it throughout the night as an ambulance, and when they had finished, they just parked it at a convenient spot and went back to college.

The owner's loss was intensified by the fact that in that car when she left it in the lane was the produce of an afternoon's shopping - a shoulder of lamb, a bottle of whisky, a loaf of bread, and other viands.

And, believe it or not, but the fact remains, all these things were intact in the car when she recovered it, more than a week later. The meat had "turned", the bread was stale, but the bottle of whisky was unbroken.

She was rather proud of that car when she heard the full story of its work during the blitz. It carried the marks of battle, and the hood was open to the sky from an incendiary which had pitched on the roof – but "Daphne" was still full of "go".

It was the night of a heavy raid. The bomb crashed down on a public shelter in which a score of people were seeking protection. There were a number of casualties, among them being some who were trapped. Feverishly the police, rescue squad, and ambulance workers toiled to release the victims.

One man was pinned from the shoulders down by great slabs of concrete. But he was alive, conscious, and amazingly patient. All he could do was to move his head.

Eventually two policemen worked their way close enough to talk to him. "Keep your chin up, Jim; we'll soon get you out," they encouraged him.

"I'm O.K. Get on with the others," he answered, with a grim smile.

"What about a cup of tea?" enquired the constable.

"Cup of tea?" replied Jim. "Make it a pint of beer, and I'll stay here all night. Gosh, but couldn't I just do with a pint!"

The policemen looked at one another. It was two o'clock in the morning. Where could they get a pint at that hour?

Then one of the policemen remembered. "Well, I guess his need is greater than mine," he said. "I'll just slip up home. The missus is sure to have got a pint in for my supper. I certainly shan't want it for breakfast".

In a few minutes he was back. Gently he held the jug to Jim's lips, and Jim supped the pint to the last drop.

"Gosh, that's the best pint I've ever tasted; now you can go and leave me," he said as the policeman brushed the drips from his lips.

Four hours later they got Jim out and took him to hospital. There was never a squeak from him all that time. He just patiently waited.

But Jim did not forget that he had had the policeman's supper beer. He stood that round back the first time they met.

During the blitz of 1941 over 150 public-houses were put out of action. They provided some first-class stories.

Among the Plymouth publicans was an outstanding character well known to the Services, especially the Navy in which he served many years before becoming a pensioner and a publican.

His house was badly wrecked. Little more than the front seemed to be standing. Early in the morning, when the battle had died away, they discovered "mine host", cheerful as ever, sitting on a broken chair in front of his open door.

"We're open" he had chalked on the wall.

On one side of him he had a small barrel of beer, on the other a bottle of whisky. He was happily dispensing free drinks to any weary raid worker who came along.

But it was no indiscriminate liquor party. Each drink he carefully measured by Imperial measure before he passed it to the "customer".

The raid was over. The shattering noises had ended. Only the great fires crackled and the early morning wag still lit by the lurid glare. The throats of the workers were parched from the dust and smoke.

Police, watching for looting – after all, their primary job is the protection of life and property – were here, there, and everywhere.

A couple of them worked their way through the blown-out side door and passage of a public-house. Their boots crunched over broken glass, they groped by the light of their torches over timber and masonry. Eventually they reached the saloon bar. It was fairly intact, lit by a solitary candle.

The landlord was there. He had stuck there all through the raid.

February 1942 - Farmer's Arms … bar now open!

George Street, piled with debris and still obscured in smoke and dust after the raids which in 1941 destroyed the entire shopping centre.

But he had had enough. He looked at the two officers and grinned through the dirt that clogged his face.

But at once he reached up and took his coat and hat from a peg.

"Well, there you are, chaps!" he said, with a wave of his hand. "The whisky's up there, the bottle beer's down there, that kil' of mild is half full, and the glasses are over there. Help yourselves. I'm off."

And off he went, leaving the officers in complete possession, but his last remark as he went out of the door was "I've emptied the till!"

Not a hundred miles from the centre of the city a rescue party, led by a police officer, found another public-house "open after hours" by a German bomb.

The building looked pretty much of a shambles, hut the men worked their way through the debris-blocked dark passage to the bar.

Here, again, the only illumination was from a guttering candle stuck in a beer bottle.

They found the landlord seated on his bar stool, lustily singing a navy shanty – he was another old sailor – and polishing glasses. All around him the bar was confusion itself.

"Hello, boys!" he greeted them. "What'll you have?"

Well, there were twelve "boys" in that party, and they all had dry throats, so the first officer passed on the order for twelve pints. Laboriously the landlord completed the service.

"And that'll be thirteen and sixpence," he said as he planted the last pint on the dusty counter.

What is more, the officer had to pay!

It was something like five o'clock in the morning when one weary-eyed, heavy-footed and begrimed "special" reached the door of his home.

A crowd of men sheltering in the doorway of a nearby building shouted to him. "You can't go in there. There's an unexploded bomb about here somewhere" one of them said. "We heard it come down, and we're positive it's not gone off."

"Well, let's find it," said the special, and so the search in the darkness began. Automatically he was the leader, but his hair was a bit "on end".

At last, in the garden of a neighbouring house, they found the "crater". Carefully and closely the special searched the tell-tale signs with his torch. Yes, that was the bomb.

With the same, there came a female voice from the doorway. "Hey what are you doing in my garden?"

"You've got an unexploded bomb here. We've found the crater. You'll have to get out at once," said the special.

"Don't be daft. That's where the old man was digging for the drain this afternoon!" was the ironical reply.

The scene was Union Street, Stonehouse, and the time was the morning following one of the heavy raids.

Along the street came a police inspector and an officer of the Bomb Disposal Squad, and they were looking suspiciously at some of the buildings. Then they stopped, and the inspector pointed to some superficial damage to one or two premises.

"Don't like the look of that," he said. "There's an unexploded bomb here somewhere!"

They nosed about for some minutes.

"Here you are," he said at last, and pointed to a substantial "disturbance" where the wall joined the pavement.

Not five yards away a navvy was energetically working a pneumatic drill.

The officers looked at him. "Better stop that and get away," said the inspector to the worker.

"Why?" asked the man, and there was a half resentment in his voice at the interruption of his work.

"Oh, nothing. Except that there's an unexploded bomb just there!" replied the inspector.

"Blimey!" said the navvy and he cleared.

Men of the Royal Navy, the Army, and the Royal Air Force rendered yeoman service in helping the civilian population during the heavy raids. None were more gallant, almost reckless, in their work than the spirited young officers of the Royal Naval Engineering College.

Wherever there was a dangerous job to be done, they were among the willing volunteers. How often had I seen these fine young lads going all out on the Rugger field, cracking a ball to the boundary, or letting rip in a Rugger night "rag".

It was the same glorious spirit which animated them in the raids – adventurous, fearless.

In one of the hottest corners of the raids were two of these College midshipmen. They had just taken part in the salvaging of some cars from a blazing garage, and were on their way to find another job.

A bomb crashed down near by. One of them fell to the ground; the other was unhurt. We came upon them a few minutes after this tragedy.

The uninjured was looking down at his comrade, but he was beyond human aid. We covered him.

Then the other took a last look and turned to us. "Come on," he said. "He's gone; we can't do anything for him. Let's get on with the next job."

Gallant lads.

The raid during the night had produced an unusually high percentage of unexploded bombs – UXB, as they were described in the official records – and, as was customary these were immediately being plotted for the expert attention of the men of the Bomb Disposal Squad stationed in the district.

One such suspect was found perilously close to the Great Western Railway main line in the vicinity of Marsh Mills. There were all the evidences of an unexploded bomb under that characteristic crater.

Miraculously rail links to the city survived a number of very close calls.

It was examined and probed by police and military, and the view was taken that the bomb was probably slipping away into the soft earth of the tidal water of the Plym, over which the railway runs at this spot.

All precautions were immediately taken. Train services over this important stretch of main line were suspended, and a linking bus service between Plympton station and Plymouth was put into operation to meet the emergency while the bomb disposal men began a grim race against time and tide to reach the bomb before it completely slipped away into the soft underground.

Frantically they dug in relays for several hours, their perspiration being only matched by their language.

Their excavation had reached considerable depth when a railway ganger came along the track. He paused to watch the workers for a few minutes, and then, in as many words, asked "What's the big idea?"

They told him. He was silent for a few moments again, and then suddenly almost folded up with laughter.

The diggers couldn't see the joke, and told him so.

"But I can," he said. "That's no bomb crater; that's the hole we left when we moved a signal a couple of weeks ago."

Such was the fury of the fire which destroyed the Guildhall.

There was one absolutely priceless story going the rounds in Plymouth, but I must confess that I accepted the assurance that it really happened during a raid on the city with an unusually heavy pinch of salt. I think it more likely that it went the rounds of all blitzed places – with variations. Nevertheless, it is worth repeating.

The raid was at its height. Fires were raging, buildings were crashing down in volumes of smoke and dust.

Suddenly the police were amazed to see a sailor staggering about the street with a door handle firmly gripped in his fist. At the same time his raving and language against Hitler and the German Air Force in general would have turned any ordinary air blue.

At last the police got hold of him firmly, and sought to calm him.

"Everything's all right" they assured him.

"All right be buggered" he shouted. "The buggers blew the pub clean out of my hand."

More salt, please.

Service men manned the hoses with a parade-ground discipline which one could not help admiring.

George Street and Bedford Street were fiery furnaces. At the junction, in the centre of the street, four bluejackets, who had obviously had a glorious night out following pay-day, were jointly holding the brass nozzle of a hose. But the water was in a dying state, just gurgling out of the end for a few inches and splashing down in the street at their feet.

They were still holding on grimly and swaying unsteadily, when a huge building came crashing down not twenty-five yards away.

Surely they were gone, we thought, as we flung ourselves flat. When the dust, smoke and sparks had cleared, and we got to our feet, we looked back apprehensively to where those bluejackets had been standing.

There they were, still standing in the centre of the street, and still holding on to that nozzle, from which the water was still coming in merely a feeble dribble.

One of the most heart-throbbing scenes was that which followed the raid when so many lives were lost in the Portland Square shelter.

Among the victims were the wife and six children of a soldier.

He was serving away from Plymouth, and was the sole survivor of the family.

He came to Plymouth on special leave for the melancholy task of identifying his wife and children.

In the mortuary he stood for a few minutes looking at his sleeping family. But only for a few minutes. There was no scene; just a grim tightening of the lips. He was a soldier.

Suddenly he pulled himself upright, put on his cap, clicked his heels to attention – and saluted.

Then he about-turned. "Come on," he said to the attendant. " I've got a job to do."

He went back to his regiment, and forthwith asked to be sent to the battlefront.

Such stories as these could be told in their thousands – separate tragedies and countless little comedies, all playing themselves out to unexpected endings.

As I have said, time is a great healer; it has taken off the raw edges of a terrible ordeal. But whenever conversation turns, as it inevitably will do on occasions, to those nights of devastation and death, of amazing escapes and incidents grim even in their humour, there will be a wealth of stories to pull out of memory's vast storehouse.

FOR SERVICES RENDERED

Considerable as is the list of honours bestowed on Plymothians for gallantry in the "total warfare" attacks which were directed against the city by the enemy, it must by no means be regarded as the full measure of the spirit which wrote such a fine chapter of courage and endurance.

All honour to those whose deeds were recorded and officially recognised. But it was not the few who fought to save Plymouth during those terrible nights; it was the many. And they belonged to both sexes, all classes and all creeds; they came from the mansion and the back street. There was the heroism of the actual fighting against the overwhelming destruction which enveloped human beings and property; there was that amazing patience and endurance shown in the homes and in the shelters; there was that wonderful courage in the strain of the immediate aftermath.

That was why earlier in the book, I expressed the view that I should have liked to have seen some recognition for Plymouth as a city; something which could have been handed down as an inspiration to future generations.

But be that as it may - and I know it is a view shared by many - there were many well-earned individual honours, ranking from the George Medals awarded to eight people for outstanding gallantry in civil defence down to numerous commendations.

In the list of decorations to Plymothians which I give, and in the compilation of which I have to thank the Regional Commissioner, Plymouth City Police, and others for information from their records, I fear there may be one or two omissions. If there are, I apologise to the individuals concerned.

This list deals only with the civil side of Plymouth in the war, and where a Service man is mentioned it is for gallantry in helping the citizens, not for a Service deed. Neither does the list include those many decorations which were awarded for gallantry in the Dockyard and other Service establishments. There were also a number of decorations awarded to outsiders, especially fire-fighters, who came to Plymouth's help. I have, however, included as far as possible the names of those who received decorations in the Honours Lists, as apart from gallantry, for their valuable services.

Awards For Gallantry
George Medal
Police Constable R.J.S. Willis, City Police: Patrol Officer G.H. Wright: Leading Fireman C.G. Lidstone: Dr. A.J. McNairn: T. Yabsley: Mrs. Fitzgerald: C. Legg: Lieutenant J.A.R. Crews, R.N.

M.B.E.
Chief Superintendent J.P.W. Hingston, City Police: Superintendent A.B. Hawkins, City Police: Divisional Commandant C.C. Cooper, Special Constabulary: Superintendent R.J. Smith, National Fire Service: R.J.H. Clark, Engineer, Plymouth and Stonehouse Gas Company: A.R. Langford, Distribution Superintendent, Plymouth and Stonehouse Gas Company: A.G. Hartley, Deputy Engineer, Plymouth Corporation Gas Works: Captain N.W. Nicholson: S.F. Willey: Miss S.E. Hartshorne.

B.E.M.
Inspector C. Stroud: Inspector J.F.W. Lindsey: Inspector H.W.D. Beswick: PC A.W. Larson: PC A.J.T. Hill: PC W.T. Hill: PC W.C. Marshall: PC J.F.C. Peace: PC D. Crutchley: PC R.J.S. Eakers: PC T.A. O'Connor: PC F.S. Stanley: PC V.C. Cobley: PC G.H. Shapter; aforementioned all of Plymouth City Police Force Special Constable A.H. Dearing, Special Constabulary: A.V. Nicholls (Chief Foreman), E.A. Webb (Distribution Mains Foreman), and P.V. Tripp (Mains Layer), of the Plymouth and Stonehouse Gas Company: P. Fletcher: Nurse A.V. Clancy: Nicholas Mann: R.C. Moore: L.E.P. Stephens: Bertie Andrews: C.B. Smith: Mrs. A.W. Tribe: W.A. Edgcumbe: Miss B.M. Rendell: Peter Williams: Mrs. Janet Evans: J. Vale: L.A. Burley: W.C. Killburn: Miss M. Sheard: Mrs. D. Page.

Bar To B.E.M. (Military)
Inspector F.J. Cox, Special Constabulary.

Hon. B.E.M.
M. Jaskowski, United States Seaman.

Commendations
Sergeant W.J. Loram, City Police: Inspector G.H. Strathon, Special Constabulary: Special Constable F.J. Balsom, Mobile Section, and Special Constable P.T. Gollop, Special Constabulary: J. Rice, R.S. Bate, and A.J. Burley, Plymouth Corporation Gas Works: F.J. Pooley: W. Collister: E. Hill: B.N. Blyth-Palk: Mrs. Rosina Lloyd: Sister W.M. Yearling: Nurse K.M. Giles: Nurse G.J. Edwards: Midshipman R.L. Lane, R.N.E. College: Midshipman L.J. Rees-Spaling, R.N.E. College: Midshipman Penhaligan, R.N.E. College: Miss G.M. Burn: Miss Mabel Stanton: W.J. Coppola: W.N.A. Downs: P.W.L. Waldron: D.C. Pallett: E.H. Tookey: Chas. Palmer: Alan Webber: Richard Miller: E.T. Vosper: A. Spencer: A. Shillabeer: J. Gerrety: Miss A.E.K. Warwick: F.C. Reed.

Honours Awards
O.B.E.
Colin Campbell, Town Clerk and A.R.P. Controller
J.F. Knape, Deputy A.R.P. Controller
Major F.G. Fleury, Home Guard Anti-Aircraft Rocket Battery.

M.B.E.
Major John Bedford, Home Guard Anti-Aircraft Rocket Battery
John Ainsworth, City Treasurer and Food Control Officer
P.H. Cole, Entertainments Manager
Mrs. M.A. Wordley, Women's Voluntary Service Organizer
A.S. Hicks, Wardens' Service
Mrs. P.A. Mill, Y.M.C.A. Women's Auxiliary
B.M. Edyvean, Managing Director, Messrs. Willoughby, Ship Repairers
H.M. Pattinson, Fire Guard Organizer.

B.E.M.
Inspector W. Dustow, City Police: Senior Company Officer F.C. Cobbledick, National Fire Service: L. N Tope, Casualty Services: G. Seyd: F.R. Jordan: J. Simcock: G.H. Foster: W.P. Finch: L. Martin: N.J. Attrill.

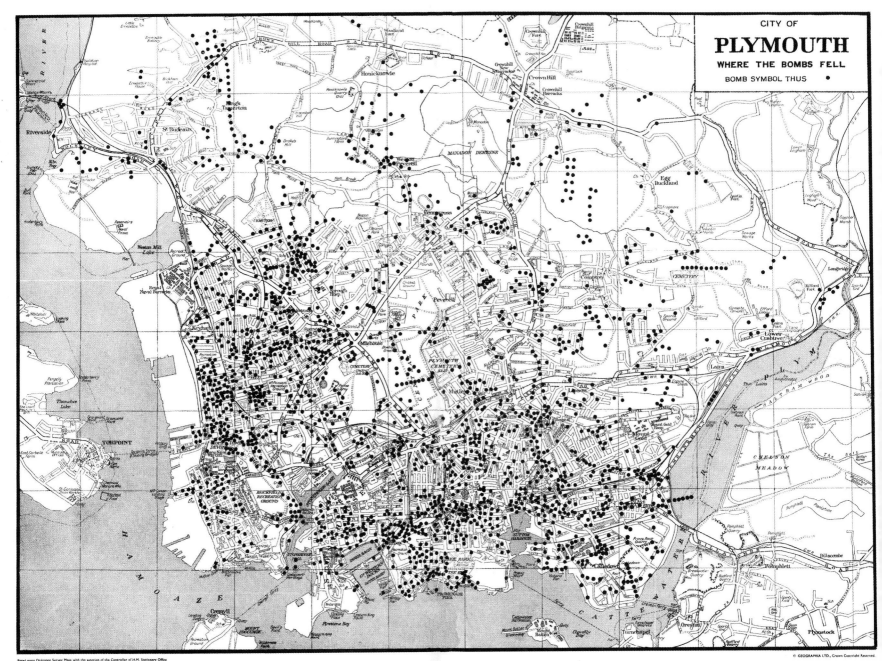

CITY OF
PLYMOUTH
WHERE THE BOMBS FELL

BOMB SYMBOL THUS •

Based upon Ordnance Survey Maps with the sanction of the Controller of H.M. Stationery Office

© GEOGRAPHIA LTD., Crown Copyright Reserved.

Above "where the bombs fell". Right, George Street, the morning after.